Bernard of Clairvaux
On the Life of the Mind

THE NEWMAN PRESS
SIGNIFICANT SCHOLARLY STUDIES

The Newman Press imprint offers scholarly studies in historical theology. It provides a forum for professional academics to address significant issues in the areas of biblical interpretation, patristics, and medieval and modern theology. This imprint also includes commentaries on major classical works in these fields, such as the acclaimed Ancient Christian Writers series, in order to contribute to a better understanding of critical questions raised in writings of enduring importance.

Bernard of Clairvaux On the Life of the Mind

by
John R. Sommerfeldt

THE NEWMAN PRESS
New York/Mahwah, N.J.

Cover design by Cynthia Dunne

Book design by Celine M. Allen

The typeface used for chapter titles in this book is Clairvaux.

Library of Congress Cataloging-in-Publication Data

Sommerfeldt, John R.
    Bernard of Clairvaux on the life of the mind / by John R. Sommerfeldt.
      p.   cm.
    Includes bibliographical references and index.
    ISBN 0-8091-4203-1 (alk. paper)
  1. Bernard of Clairvaux, Saint, 1090 or 91–1153. I. Title.

B765.B54 S66 2004
230'.2'092—dc22

                                  2003023805

Published by
THE NEWMAN PRESS
An imprint of Paulist Press
997 Macarthur Boulevard
Mahwah, New Jersey 07430

www.paulistpress.com

Printed and bound in the United States of America

Contents

*With profound gratitude, I dedicate
this volume to the memory of my mentor
and spiritual guide*

JEAN LECLERCQ

Table of Abbreviations

General Abbreviations

ASOC
Analecta Sacri Ordinis Cisterciensis; Analecta Cisterciensis. 1945–.

Bernard de Clairvaux
Bernard de Clairvaux. Commission d'histoire de l'Ordre de Cîteaux, 3. Paris: Editions Alsatia, 1953.

Bernardus Magister
John R. Sommerfeldt (ed.). *Bernardus Magister: Papers Presented at the Nonacentenary Celebration of the Birth of Saint Bernard of Clairvaux, Kalamazoo, Michigan, Sponsored by the Institute of Cistercian Studies, Western Michigan University, 10–13 May 1990.* Cistercian Studies 135. Kalamazoo, Michigan: Cistercian Publications; Saint-Nicolas-lès-Cîteaux: Cîteaux: Commentarii Cistercienses, 1992.

Bernhard von Clairvaux
Joseph Lortz (ed.). *Bernhard von Clairvaux, Mönch und Mystiker: Internationaler Bernhardkongress, Mainz 1953.* Veröffentlichungen des Instituts für europäische Geschichte Mainz, 6. Wiesbaden: Franz Steiner Verlag GmbH, 1955.

BGPTM
Beiträge zur Geschichte der Philosophie und Theologie des Mittelalters, 1891–.

CCCM
Corpus Christianorum, Continuatio Medievalis. Turnhouti, Belgium, 1971–.

CF
Cistercian Fathers [series]. Spencer, Massachusetts; Washington, D.C.; Kalamazoo, Michigan: Cistercian Publications, 1970–.

Cîteaux
Cîteaux in de Nederlanden; Cîteaux: Commentarii cistercienses, 1950–.

ix

Coll   *Collectania o.c.r.; Collectania Cisterciensia,* 1934–.

CS   Cistercian Studies [series]. Spencer, Massachusetts; Washington, D.C.; Kalamazoo, Michigan: Cistercian Publications, 1969–.

CSQ   *Cistercian Studies* [periodical]; *Cistercian Studies Quarterly,* 1961–.

Feiss   Hugh Feiss. Translation of *On Baptism* appended to the article "*Bernardus Scholasticus:* The Correspondence of Bernard of Clairvaux and Hugh of Saint Victor on Baptism." In *Bernardus Magister,* pp. 349–78.

James   Bruno Scott James (trans.). *The Letters of St. Bernard of Clairvaux.* London: Burns Oates, 1953. Reprinted Kalamazoo, Michigan: Cistercian Publications, 1998.

Luddy   *St. Bernard's Sermons for the Seasons & Principal Festivals of the Year.* Trans. A Priest of Mount Melleray [Ailbe J. Luddy]. Reprint, Westminster, Maryland: The Carroll Press, 3 vols., 1950.

PL   J.-P. Migne (ed.). Patrologia latina. Paris: apud J.-P. Migne editorem, 221 vols., 1841.

RB   *Regula monachorum sancti Benedicti.*

Sint Bernardus *Sint Bernardus van Clairvaux: Gedenkboek door monniken*
van Clairvaux   *van de noord- en zuidnederlandse cisterciënser abdijen samengesteld bij het achtste eeuwfeest van Sint Bernardus' dood, 20 Augustus 1153–1953.* Rotterdam: N.V. Uitgeverij De Forel, 1953.

Spiritual   John R. Sommerfeldt. *The Spiritual Teachings of Bernard*
Teachings   *of Clairvaux.* An Intellectual History of the Early Cistercian Order, [1]. Cistercian Studies 125. Kalamazoo, Michigan: Cistercian Publications, 1991.

The Works of Bernard of Clairvaux

SBOp	Jean Leclercq et al. (eds.). *Sancti Bernardi opera*. Roma: Editiones Cisterciensis, 8 vols. in 9, 1957–1977.
Abael	*Epistola in erroribus Abaelardi*
Abb	*Sermo ad abbates*
Adv	*Sermo in adventu Domini*
And	*Sermo in natali sancti Andreae*
Apo	*Apologia ad Guillelmum abbatem*
Asc	*Sermo in ascensione Domini*
Bapt	*Epistola de baptismo*
Conv	*Sermo ad clericos de conversione*
Csi	*De consideratione*
Ded	*Sermo in dedicatione ecclesiae*
Dil	*De diligendo Deo*
Div	*Sermo de diversis*
Ep	*Epistola*
Gra	*De gratia et libero arbitrio*
Hum	*De gradibus humilitatis et superbiae*
JB	*Sermo in nativitate sancti Ioannis Baptistae*
Mart	*Sermo in festivitate sancti Martini episcopi*
Mich	*Sermo in festo sancti Michaëlis*
Miss	*Homelia super "Missus est" in laudibus Virginis Matris*
Mor	*Epistola de moribus et officio episcoporum*
Nat	*Sermo in nativitate Domini*
I Nov	*Sermo in dominica I novembris*
O Asspt	*Sermo in dominica infra octavam assumptionis*
OS	*Sermo in festivitate omnium sanctorum*

Par	*Parabola*
Pasc	*Sermo in die paschae*
Pent	*Sermo in die pentecostes*
IV p P	*Sermo in dominica quarta post pentecosten*
PP	*Sermo in festo ss. apostolorum Petri et Pauli*
Pre	*De precepto et dispensatione*
QH	*Sermo super psalmum "Qui habitat"*
SC	*Sermo super Cantica Canticorum*
I, II, or III Sent	*Sententia* (series prima, series secunda, series tertia)
Sept	*Sermo in septuagesima*
Tpl	*Ad milites Templi de laude novae militiae*
V Mal	*Vita sancti Malachiae*
V Nat	*Sermo in vigilia nativitatis Domini*

Biblical Abbreviations

Ac	Acts
Bar	Baruch
2 Chr	2 Chronicles
Col	Colossians
1 Cor	1 Corinthians
2 Cor	2 Corinthians
Dn	Daniel
Dt	Deuteronomy
Eph	Ephesians
Est	Esther
Ex	Exodus

Ez	Ezekiel
Gal	Galatians
Gn	Genesis
Heb	Hebrews
Hg	Haggai
Hos	Hosea
Is	Isaiah
Jas	James
Jb	Job
Jer	Jeremiah
Jl	Joel
Jn	John
1 Jn	1 John
Jos	Joshua
1 K	1 Kings
2 K	2 Kings
Lam	Lamentations
Lk	Luke
Lv	Leviticus
2 M	2 Maccabees
Mal	Malachi
Mk	Mark
Mt	Matthew
Nm	Numbers
Phil	Philippians
Prv	Proverbs
Ps	Psalm

1 Pt	1 Peter
2 Pt	2 Peter
Qo	Ecclesiastes; Qoheleth
Rom	Romans
Rv	Revelation
Sg	Song of Songs
Si	Ecclesiasticus; Sirach
1 Sm	1 Samuel
2 Sm	2 Samuel
Tb	Tobit
1 Thes	1 Thessalonians
1 Tm	1 Timothy
2 Tm	2 Timothy
Ws	Wisdom

Preface

The last section of this book is a discussion of the epistemological implications of the controversy between Bernard and Abelard. The very first paper I wrote on Bernard, back in the mid-1950s, was entitled "The Attitude of Bernard of Clairvaux Toward Reason: The Conflict with Abelard." In fifty years, I have come full circle.

The paper eventually saw the light of day in 1961, published in an abbreviated form in the *Papers of the Michigan Academy,* with the likewise abbreviated title "Abelard and Bernard of Clarivaux."[1] Because that journal did not have a wide circulation, I sent offprints to the giants of medieval scholarship, boldly and brashly offering a correction to their opinions on the question. The answer I received from Jean Leclercq was amazingly generous and encouraging. It included this sentence: "I hope you will be able to go on in your studies on Bernard and Abelard." Little did he—or I—know!

To his death on 27 October 1993, Jean Leclercq continued his own overwhelmingly important contributions to bernardine scholarship, to which the bibliography in this book gives massive—but only partial—recognition. He also continued to encourage beginning students and continuing studies by more advanced scholars with his characteristic humility and generosity.

As an example of that encouragement, I offer this passage from a paper delivered by him in 1973 before the Stubbs Society at Oxford:

> There is still a great deal to be said on all these points, for Bernard's genius defies categorization. The most original contribution to work in this field has been made by John Sommerfeldt, director of the Institute of Cistercian Studies at West[ern] Michigan University. He is concentrating his

research on Bernard's epistemology, for he thinks that Bernard's concept of knowledge should give us the key to his apparent inconsistencies. According to this theory Bernard has a specific and unique logic arising from his personal spiritual inspiration, difficult to define and impossible to classify in the categories with which we are familiar.[2]

"The most original contribution in this field has been made by" should have read "the only one foolish enough to work in this field is," but one can imagine how such a passage encouraged me to continue my virtually solitary task. I have done much less well at it than Jean Leclercq's description would indicate, but the praise mistakenly given has inspired me to collect my thoughts on the subject in this book. And so it is only just and fitting that I should dedicate this volume to the man who so kindly and consistently encouraged my work—Jean Leclercq.

He did still more than inspire my work and make it possible through his critical edition of Bernard's works and the vast number of his books and articles on Bernard. Not only was he my patient mentor, he was also a source of spiritual inspiration to me.

Before Jean's death the story long circulated that, if one had a long enough layover in any airport in the world, one would surely meet Jean Leclercq. I know the story to be true, for once, when waiting for a connection at Logan Airport in Boston, surely enough I spied my mentor. I apologized at that meeting for something I had written in my last letter to him—something I thought (correctly) was unbelievably pretentious. He looked at me wisely and, like a Desert Father, gave me this word: "John, be free! Like me!" Although I have rarely followed his advice, his insight has given me a goal to which I constantly aspire. For Jean Leclercq was a living example of the sanctity that comes from freedom, and of the freedom that comes from sanctity.

If Father Jean's constant peregrinations gave rise to well-intentioned humor, it was a humor in which he shared. He saw himself as a clown, and for many years wore ties decorated with clowns given him in appreciation of this wonderful clown of God. He once told me that, when his abbot asked him to make his monastic vows of obedience, stability of place, and conversion of life, he understood the abbot to say "conversion of place and stability of life"—and readily agreed. But Jean Leclercq was no gyrovague; his many travels to remote corners of Africa, Asia, and Latin America were always meant to encourage the local folk—most often nuns—in their spiritual quest. His stability was always assured, for he brought his monastery with him—an interior monastery of dedicated quiet.

There are others whose contributions to this work I must in justice acknowledge. Foremost among these is Cathy Carol, whose great talent I have taxed in the preparation of the typescript for this book. She has exhibited great patience with my mangled manuscript and often erratic orthography. Sometimes, she has helped straighten out my crooked thought patterns as well. I am also deeply indebted to Alice Puro, the head of the Interlibrary Loan Department at the University of Dallas Library. She has found and provided a vast amount of material—and always done so with cheerful willingness and thorough efficiency.

The translations in this volume are mine, though I was sometimes saved from error by Professor Elizabeth Giedeman of Western Michigan University and Professor Francis Swietek of the University of Dallas. For those who might wish to examine the context of the passages quoted, I have indicated for each their location in the readily available translations.[3] This volume would have presented a much less effective understanding of Bernard's wisdom had it not been for the wisdom and guidance of Dr. Christopher Bellitto, the academic editor of Paulist Press.

As always, this work would have been impossible without the support of my wife Patricia. To her I dedicated my first published volume on Bernard, *The Spiritual Teachings of Bernard of Clairvaux*. In the introduction to that volume I wrote: "To him [Jean Leclercq] this volume would have been dedicated were there not one still more important to this work, one whom I hold still dearer: my wife Patricia."[4] Father Jean's reply was: "Tell Pat I am not jealous." She is not jealous at the dedication of this work.

John R. Sommerfeldt
University of Dallas

1
Bernard and the Life of the Mind

The nine-century chasm that separates us from Bernard of Clair-vaux and his time seems unbridgeable. And, indeed, for many any effort to span these centuries seems silly as well as fruitless. Why should one study the past at all? Surely race, peace, and pollution problems are more deserving of our efforts. Why should we disturb the dust of the centuries when our own time demands so much work?

There is a great deal of truth in this position. Unless we have something in common with the people of the past—and thus can learn from them—I see no reason for studying that past. Without some bond between ourselves and the folk of past ages, the past is merely a useless curiosity that should be left to antiquarians and eccentric professors.

As an eccentric history professor, I try to tackle this problem with my students by asking them: What is it that you want more than anything else? The response is both impressive and revealing. The resultant list often includes comfort and money, security or opportunity, peace or justice, peace of mind or sexual gratification—and a host of other goals. The students seem to be more divided than united by this discussion. But then I ask them: *Why* do you want what you want most? After some further discussion, most of them are united. They agree that they want whatever they want because they will be better off somehow for having it—they think that it, whatever it is, will contribute to their self-fulfillment, to their happiness. And they do want to be happy, or at least avoid unhappiness. This is my opportunity. I tell them what they really already know: that the people of the past wanted to be happy too.

Just as all humans desire happiness or self-fulfillment, they are all faced with the necessity of choice. We must all choose whether or not to get out of bed in the morning; we must even choose whether to run or stand when an automobile bears down on us. Even though in this latter case the choice is more or less automatic in adults, it must be learned; we do not allow small children to cross the street alone.

The necessity of choice prompts the universal question: What should I choose in order to attain the happiness I desire? All people are surely not aware that they ask or answer this question; for many, if not most, the question is implicit in their behavior and only occasionally rises to the level of consciousness. Some people do consciously ask the question and many of these conclude that one's choices are predetermined—in Marx's terms by one's economic environment, in Freud's terms by one's infant sex life, for example. But they are still faced with the day-by-day, hour-by-hour, minute-by-minute necessity of choosing: whether to get out of bed or cross the street or whatever. Again, all people wish to do that which they think will benefit them; even masochists inflict pain on themselves because they think they benefit thereby.

What will benefit me? What is it that will make me happy, give me self-fulfillment? To answer, I must know something of my own nature and the nature of the universe about me. Even in crossing the street, my decision whether to run or stand when an auto approaches will depend on what that object really is. If it is a solid and I am a solid and two solids are not interpenetrable, I had better run. If the auto is made of sponge rubber, it might be fun to stay and bounce a bit.

A. The Centrality of Epistemology

But how can one, how can I, know what is (the metaphysical question) and what to do about it (the ethical question)? To answer these questions, one must have a method or methods of answering questions, of ascertaining the nature of reality, of finding the truth. Just as ethics is the discipline that asks the fundamental question "What should I do?" and in metaphysics one attempts to answer the question "What is?" so epistemology is the search for the answer to the question "How do I know?" Clearly, one must begin one's search for happiness or self-fulfillment with the epistemological question, for, unless one has a method of answering questions, one cannot determine the nature of reality and begin to cope with it.

I do not mean to suggest by all this that the study of the past will provide us with answers to all our problems. But we do share a common quest with the people of the past, and, perhaps, we can learn something from their efforts to solve their problems and even learn from their mistakes.

If I have made my point, we can see the utility of studying the past. But why the Middle Ages? It is true that the Middle Ages are still with us in many ways. Our law is medieval, our representative institutions are largely medieval, much in our literature is medieval, our religion—sometimes even our reason for rejecting it—owes more to the Middle Ages than many care to admit. Our philosophies are often unknowingly medieval, and our scientific method was born in the Middle Ages. Even the concept of a university is medieval.

Despite all this, we surely tend to identify ourselves with the culture of classical antiquity rather than with that of the "dark ages." We think ourselves more akin to the supposed rationalism of Greece and the much vaunted hedonism of Rome than to the "Gothic" barbarism and religiosity of the Middle Ages. Legend has it that each time that Voltaire, the eighteenth-century *philosophe,* was in Paris, he would go down to the Ile de la Cité, walk around Notre Dame cathedral, and remark on the incredible waste of time and talent involved in the building of such a barbarous, such a "Gothic" monument to ignorance and superstition. If this story is true—and it ought to be if it is not—it is a remarkable illustration of how deeply Voltaire felt about Christianity. He did not merely reject it; he hated it. It is surely true that Voltaire spent a great part of his life satirizing Christianity; this was because Christianity—above all in its "medieval" form—was all-important to him, so important that Voltaire must be described as "anti-Christian," not merely as "a-Christian." We modern folk who owe so much to the eighteenth-century Enlightenment are much like its intellectual leader Voltaire. Words like "Christianity," "religious," and "medieval" are important to us. We feel deeply about them. This is because we are Western men and women.

And the fact is that Western culture was born in the Middle Ages. In studying the Middle Ages, in studying the twelfth century—an age somehow quintessentially medieval[1]—we study the genesis, the coming to be, of our own culture. And thus we can learn much about our culture and about ourselves. Because the leader, the extra-ordinarily powerful leader, of Europe in the first half of the twelfth century was Bernard of Clairvaux,[2] we shall turn to him for insights into our culture. Because Bernard had elaborate and sophisticated solutions to the epistemological question that we all face, we shall investigate and explicate his thought on the ways one can pursue truth.

Epistemology is basic to the quest of all individuals, societies, and cultures for happiness or self-fulfillment. Conversely, one learns much about an individual, society, or culture by examining his, her, or its epistemological presuppositions. The way a person or group comes to know reality largely determines how that person or group sees reality and attempts to deal with it. And so an examination of Bernard of Clairvaux's world of ideas and values must surely take into account his epistemology.

B. Mysticism, Humanism, Scholasticism, and Common Sense

The first, tentative title of this volume included the phrase "a Cister-cian epistemology." At that time, some ten years ago, I deeply desired to avoid what I thought were ill-defined and misleading words like "mysticism," "humanism," and "scholasticism."

Two men, both colleagues and friends, contributed to my con-version. One was Father Luke Anderson, prior of the Cistercian Monastery of Saint Mary in Pennsylvania and a deeply insightful master of Cistercian intellectual history. He pointed out that my use of "epistemology" in this book was "broader than the conventional meaning," including, for example, Bernard's attitude toward canon law. Father Luke was right; canon law stayed and "epistemology" was dropped from my title.

But that hardly explains my inclusion in this book of words that I had earlier rejected for a title—words like "mysticism," "humanism," and "scholasticism." Including "mysticism" was especially painful. I have long railed against the use of this word in describing the thought of twelfth-century Cistercians. I have long insisted—with, perhaps, excessive zeal—that the writers of that century, surely the Cistercians among them, used the Latin equivalents of "mystical" and "mysticism" simply to describe an allegorical meaning assigned to a scriptural passage.[3] On one occasion, at the International Medieval Congress in Kalamazoo, I rehearsed this message once more. Father Chrysogonus Waddell, that most saintly of Cistercian scholars, completed my conversion. The learned monk of Gethsemani Abbey humbly admonished me with words something like this: "If Bernard did not misuse the word mysticism, he did not use the word epistemology at all."

In this book I shall use "mysticism" to indicate non-rational—perhaps better, super-rational—means of ascertaining the truth, of discovering the nature of things. Bernard speaks of three such methods: faith, charismatic knowledge, and contemplation—the last sometimes, and improperly I think, identified as mysticism.

"Humanism" is an equally slippery word. I shall not employ this word in the way it is often used to describe—incorrectly, I think—the Italian Renaissance.[4] Here "humanism" will not mean a rebirth of classical culture in a secular context.[5] Classical literature and law, ancient science and medicine, Greek and Roman philosophy and theology—both pagan and Christian—were eagerly studied in the twelfth-century Renaissance for the truths they were thought to contain about God and his universe. Classical culture had been thoroughly baptized by Bernard's time, and, conversely, he and his contemporaries had been deeply immersed in the classics as boys and young men. I shall use "humanism" here to indicate those classical literary approaches to describing reality which aim at achieving wisdom through an appreciation of beauty, especially beauty in literary expression.[6]

"Scholasticism," as used here, will not mean any particular philosophical or theological school or teaching—this was the meaning ascribed to the word by scholars of the nineteenth and early twentieth centuries.[7] Scholasticism is properly understood, I think, to indicate whatever was taught in medieval schools. The difficulty with using "scholasticism," even in this restricted sense, is that the literary approaches to reality described above under the rubric "humanism" were a prominent part of the twelfth-century curriculum. The tension between humanism and scholasticism came later—in the thirteenth through sixteenth centuries.[8] In the twelfth century, the arts emphasizing beauty of expression were studied in the schools as grammar and rhetoric. These were the first two of the disciplines called collectively the *trivium*, the three ways to truth. Under the rubric "scholasticism," then, I shall confine myself to discussing the third of the "trivial" arts, dialectics. We shall see how Bernard applied the tools of this discipline to philosophical and theological questions. We shall also see his view on the application of logic to the rationalization and systemization of a discipline only just emerging in his day, canon law. It is in this limited sense only that my earlier association of canon law with epistemology can be seen as valid.

Mystical, humanist, and scholastic sources of knowledge are not—except in the case of faith—the normal, everyday way people learn. Bernard knew this and recognized alternative, common-sense sources in his writing. What received the least of his literary attention was the sort of vocational training necessary to each group in society. Apparently this source of knowledge was so obvious that Bernard and his audience assumed it without much overt attention.

But there were at least two ways of gaining information that were widespread and, Bernard thought, necessary to the life of his society and the welfare of those living within it. Counsel, good counsel, was a source of practical knowledge available to, and needed by, monks and clerics, rulers and merchants, artisans and farmers. Those same groups were also urged by Bernard to take time for meditation. Putting aside one's everyday duties for a time each day would, Bernard thought, enhance one's ability to cope with those duties and, also, to place them in their proper context, the presence of God. Hence we shall, under the rubric of common sense, examine Bernard's advice to folk of all sorts about their practical, everyday means of solving problems and answering questions.

In the process of explicating Bernard's epistemology, in this broad sense, recurring eccesiological and soteriological themes will emerge. The results of Bernard's ruminations on epistemology and, indeed, on every other subject are heavily conditioned by his understanding of society and Church and by his experience of the saving power of God.

C. The Social and Ecclesial Context

Bernard's answers to epistemological questions are meant for real people in the real world. The world of which he was a part was divided into a number of classes or callings, but was unified by one overarching construct, the Church. Bernard believed that some means to the truth were needed by all classes, some could be used by members of every group, and some were appropriate to a specific calling. Hence, Bernard's view of society and Church provides the context within which we can best understand his epistemology.

Bernard's view of society cannot be separated from his view of the Church, since he views each and every person and social group in the light of their role in the spiritual process aiming at individual and corporate perfection.[9] Bernard is sure the Church is called to union with God, and thus all within the Church are so called.[10] Bernard insists that "all the elect are what the Church is."[11] And he sees God's net cast widely in search of those elect; even those who now live recklessly, ignoring their goal of perfection, must be considered part of the Church.[12] The Church, then, is for Bernard not merely an institution or a corporation. She is the sum total of all those pursuing, however feebly, the path to perfection and consequent happiness.

The many images of Church that Bernard employs speak to the interrelationship of communal and individual realities. Perhaps the most enduring image of Church in Bernard's works is that of bride espoused to her Savior: "... The Bridegroom of the Church [is] Jesus Christ, our Lord...."[13] It is love that unites the Bridegroom to the bride. "I have only one desire," Bernard writes, "... to show the hidden delights [of the love] between Christ and the Church."[14] And because it is the people of God who are the Church, "the Bridegroom is our God [see Ps 47:15], and we, I say in all humility, are the bride—we and the whole multitude . . . whom he acknowledges."[15]

The same relationship of individual and community is evident in Bernard's images of Church as a mother,[16] as a vineyard,[17] as Jerusalem,[18] and as a sheepfold.[19] It is in the image of the Church as the body of Christ[20] that one discovers Bernard's vision of his own role in the Church. Writing to the people of Rome standing in rebellion against their bishop, Bernard compares the pope to the head of the body and himself to the tongue which speaks for that body:

> This great trouble affects even me, although I am the least of all, because what affects the head cannot but affect the body of which I am a member. When the head is suffering, does not the tongue cry out for all members of the body that the head is in pain? And do not all the parts of the body confess by means of the tongue that the head is theirs and the pain too?[21]

I think this image contains an accurate description of Bernard's role in early twelfth-century Church and society. Bernard could be the tongue of his time because his penetrating analysis of the anatomy of the contemporary social body enabled him to express so well the values and ideals of that society—and its epistemological needs as well.

Although Bernard's Church is body, bride, city, vineyard, and sheepfold, he requires a more dynamic image to describe the life of the Church, for that life is a process that leads to perfection and is, at the same time, that perfection.[22] The image that Bernard employs is the sea; life is the crossing of a sea. But that sea is crossed by more than one means and by more than one sort of person:

> My brothers, this extensive sea [see Ps 103:25] . . . is traversed by three classes of persons, each crossing safely in its own way—so that they may pass over in deliverance [see Is 51:10]. The three are [typified by] Noah, Daniel, and Job [see Ez 14:14], of whom the first crossed by ship, the second by a

bridge, the third by a ford. Those three men signify the three orders of the Church.[23]

Bernard identifies these three orders. The first is that of prelates (bishops and abbots), represented by the steersman and navigator Noah. The second order is of monks, represented by Daniel, the man of deep desires. And the third order is composed of lay folk, symbolized by Job, who dispensed well, as Bernard puts it, the goods of this world. These last, he says, "may justly be called the people of God [see Ps 84:9] and the sheep of his pasture [see Ps 94:7]."[24] These three orders, though distinct, have much in common. They are all in need of God's mercy,[25] and they are all capable of producing heroes of the faith.[26]

Whatever order in society to which one belongs, Bernard is confident that balance and integration between individuals and orders are found in the community that is the Church:

> Although none of us would dare arrogate to his or her own soul the title of the Lord's bride, nevertheless we are members of the Church who rightly boasts of this title and of the reality that it signifies. And hence we may justifiably assume a share in this honor. For what all of us together possess in a full and perfect manner, that each single one of us undoubtedly possesses by participation.[27]

Bernard responds to this participation in perfection with gratitude, a gratitude well deserved by God. For the riches of perfection God gives not merely to a select few—as Bernard understands is the teaching of contemporary heretics—but are available to all people.[28] God's redemptive gift of perfection must, therefore, take many forms, each form appropriate to the individual needs of the recipient.[29]

Unity in diversity is the fundamental motif of Bernard's teaching on Church and society. The differing lifestyles of celibates and married folk, of monks and clerics, contain no condemnation of the other. Noah, Daniel, and Job all have a share in the same kingdom, though their ways of life differ. Mary and Martha, whose efforts to

please their Lord were so very unlike, live together in the peace and
harmony of the Church—a Church, Bernard insists, "arrayed like a
queen in variety, with many dissimilar orders."[30]

Bernard sees the different orders of the Church united in one
robe, many-colored like Joseph's but now belonging to Jesus:

> To his bride, the Church, he [Jesus] left his own robe as a
> pledge of her inheritance [see Eph 1:14], a many-colored
> robe [see Gn 37:23], woven from top to bottom [see Jn
> 19:23]. It is many-colored because of the many orders, dis-
> tinct in many ways, which are in it. It is seamless because of
> the undivided unity of indissoluble love.[31]

Within the Church, "all contribute to the consummation of the
saints; all run toward human perfection according to the measure of
Christ's fullness [see Eph 4:12–13]."[32] Therefore, Bernard urges,

> let there be no division within the Church. Let her remain
> whole and complete according to her inherited right. For
> about her it has been written: "At your right hand stands the
> queen in a golden robe, surrounded with variety [Ps 44:10]."
> This is why different people receive different gifts [see 1 Cor
> 7:7].... This applies to every order, to every language, to
> both sexes, to every age, to every condition, in all places,
> through all time from the first person down to the last....
> Let us work together to form a single robe, and let this one
> robe include us all.[33]

However important the unity of Church and society is, it must
never be gained at the cost of healthy diversity. Both on earth and in
heaven unity is achieved in one love, but "just as there are many
rooms [see Jn 14:2] in one house there [in heaven], so here [on
earth] there are many orders in one Church."[34] So there is—and
should be—within the Church "at once a concordant discord and a
discordant concord...."[35] Bernard is confident that, in the unity of
love, each and every person will be led to his or her goal of happiness, no matter what social order to which he or she belongs, no

matter what path he or she follows. And so Bernard is careful to provide each and every social order with a wide range of epistemological
support on its journey. For "there is not just one path to follow, just
as there is not only one [heavenly] room toward which we journey.... For whatever path one follows to whatever room, one will
not be left outside the Father's house."[36]

11

Mysticism:
The Truth as Gift

A. The Certainty of Faith

For Bernard, by far the most important of the "mystical"—that is, super-rational—paths to truth is faith, for faith is the means to truth preeminently available to all persons, all classes, and all callings in the Church in which he lives.[1]

What does Bernard mean by "faith"? He relies on Paul for one definition: "The apostle quite rightly defines faith as the substance of things hoped for [Heb 11:1], for clearly no one can hope without confidence, any more than one can paint on empty space."[2] More helpful is Bernard's definition in *On Consideration:* "...Faith is a sort of voluntary and certain foretaste of truth not yet apparent...."[3] This sentence is indeed pregnant with meaning: faith is the result of choice; the knowledge that results is both certain and not clearly comprehended.

Bernard repeatedly asserts the certainty of the knowledge received in faith. For example, in his *Fifty-ninth Sermon on the Song of Songs,* he writes:

> What is heard [in faith] confirms what is seen, so that the witness of the two [see Mt 18:16]—I speak of the ear and the eye—is validated. That is why the Lord said: "Go and tell John"—for he was speaking to John's disciples—"what you

have heard and seen [Lk 7:22]." He could not have expressed
to them more briefly or more clearly the certainty of faith.[4]

One "sees through faith"[5] as well as hears, and what one sees and
hears is the truth: "What wonder is there if the ears catch the truth,
since faith comes from hearing and hearing by the word of God [see
Rom 10:17], and the Word of God is Truth [see Jn 17:17]?"[6] The
source of the knowledge conveyed in faith is God, Truth himself.
Bernard defends his teaching on baptism, for example, by an appeal
to John the Baptist: "... But if we deny to the herald of Truth what
we give to another, contrary to proclamation of Truth, this is not only
an injury, it is blasphemy. Clearly it contradicts not only John, but
the Truth."[7] One should believe the testimony of the Truth, as
David did: "'I have believed [Ps 115:10],' he says, the words of the
Truth: 'Whoever follows me does not walk in darkness [Jn 8:12].'
What is he confessing? That in believing I have known the Truth."[8]

If the Truth is the source of the knowledge given in faith, one
can, through faith, gain that "knowledge of God [see 2 Cor 10:5]
which is the Christian faith."[9] This knowledge fills Bernard with confidence in the accessibility of Truth. He urges his hearers:

Seek [Christ] with longing; follow [him] in action; find [him]
in faith. What does faith not find? It attains the inaccessible; it
discerns the unknown; it comprehends the boundless; it
apprehends that which is least experienced; it somehow encom-
passes even eternity itself in its vast embrace. I speak in faith: I
believe in—though I do not understand—the eternal and
blessed Trinity. I hold fast by faith what I cannot grasp with my
mind.[10]

Although faith, which is based on God's authority, and reason, which
leads to understanding, are parallel means to the truth,[11] faith is,
at least in some cases, a surer guide to reality than either reason or
the senses: "Faith is ignorant of ignorance; faith, in comprehend-
ing the invisible, does not feel the poverty of the senses. It even
crosses the limits of human reason, the capacity of nature, the bounds

of experience."[12] Faced with questions too deep to be solved by any other method, Bernard urges his readers to "defer your decision; suspend your judgment. In matters reserved for faith, do not trust in the determination of your senses. Faith will determine more worthily and more surely what it comprehends more fully. In faith's mystical and profound embrace, it grasps what is the length, width, height, and depth [see Eph 3:18]. What eye does not see, what ear does not hear, what surpasses the human heart [see 1 Cor 2:9], faith carries within herself as if wrapped in a covering, as if kept under a seal."[13] Faith, then, leads one surely to truths not ascertainable by other means.

But, in this life, the truths ascertained by faith are often still cloudy and unclear. Bernard acknowledges this in his *On Consideration:*

> These two [faith and understanding] possess certain truth. But faith possesses truth hidden and obscure.... Faith possesses no uncertainty, or, if it does, it is not faith but opinion. How, then, does it differ from understanding? Even though faith is no more uncertain than understanding, still it is obscure, as understanding is not.[14]

Farther on in the same book, Bernard gives the example of the Christian's knowledge of the existence of the Trinity:

> Does anyone ask how this [unity in Trinity] can be? Let it suffice for such a one to hold that it is indeed so, and this not as evident from reason or as an uncertain opinion, but as convinced by faith. This is a great mystery, worthy of veneration not of investigation. How can plurality exist in unity— and such a unity—and unity exist in plurality? To scrutinize this is temerity; to believe it is piety; to know it is life—and life eternal [see Jn 17:3].[15]

Faith, then, allows one to know with certainty the otherwise unknowable, with a knowledge that transcends but does not match the penetration and clarity of reason's understanding.

The knowledge gained from faith is not only certain and cloudy, it is also the result of choice. Faith is a gift from God, but that gift can be rejected. Bernard's model of acceptance is Mary's response to the angel's annunciation. He counsels her, knowing she needs no such counsel:

> Blessed Virgin, open your heart to faith, your lips to consent, your womb to the Creator. Behold, the one desired by all the nations [see Hg 2:8] stands at the gate and knocks [see Rv 3:20]. Oh if, at your delay, he should pass by, and you should have to seek in sorrow him whom your soul loves [see Sg 3:1–4]! Rise up! Run! Open! Rise up by faith; run by devotion; open by consent![16]

Freedom of choice, without which it is impossible to be truly human,[17] requires a voluntary response to the gift of faith.

Bernard also believes faith is necessary to the human being—at least to live human life fully as a Christian—because much of the knowledge imparted in faith is otherwise inaccessible. God's trinitarian nature is such an otherwise unknown object of faith, as Bernard writes in his *First Sermon for the Feast of Pentecost:*

> Today the Holy Spirit reveals to us something about himself, just as before this we came to know something about the Father and the Son. For a complete knowledge of the Trinity is life eternal [see Jn 17:3]. Now, however, we know in part [see 1 Cor 13:9]; we believe the rest which we are not at all capable of understanding.[18]

Through faith, Bernard affirms, the eternity and immutability of the Father, otherwise inaccessible, are known. "About the Son too, I know by his grace," Bernard says, "something great: his incarnation" —a truth impossible to apprehend or comprehend rationally. Of the Spirit, Bernard knows by faith "his procession, that he proceeds from the Father and the Son." This knowledge, Bernard exclaims with the psalmist "is made wonderful to me; it is powerful, and I cannot master it [Ps 138:6]."[19] If God's eternity and immutability, the Incarnation of the Son, and the procession of the Holy Spirit are beyond the human mind to discover for itself, that information—some of which, Bernard thinks, is necessary to human fulfillment[20]—must be revealed by God's inspiration and known through faith.

Baptism is a case in point for Bernard. He writes Hugh of Saint Victor that the need for baptism is not "a natural precept" open to discovery by reason. It is, rather, "a positive prescription" which "arises from faith."[21] That faith is necessary to the pilgrim setting out on the path to truth and happiness. Faith's limitations will be resolved in the blessed state awaiting the pilgrim at the end of his or her path.[22]

It is God's mercy that leads to that faith and state of blessedness.[23] Conversely, the faith of the believer leads to mercy,[24] and that mercy is made manifest by faith. Thus, "if we wish to have Christ as our frequent guest, it is necessary for us to keep our hearts always fortified with the testimonies of our faith [see Eph 3:17], our faith in the mercy of him who died and in the power of him who rose."[25] God's merciful and loving purpose in giving that faith to humans is to promote their spiritual welfare by making known to them those things that will promote their well-being, both immediate and ultimate, both in this life and the next.[26]

Faith, we have seen, involves a certain, though unclear, intellection of truth; it also involves a voluntary response.[27] Faith thus requires the activity of both intellect and will.[28] The soul's volitional response to the gift of faith should be love: "Faith surely enjoins on me the need for loving him all the more whom I perceive as so much greater than I, for [in faith] I receive from him not only the gift of myself but of himself."[29] Moreover, faith also requires the loving action of the body: "While in the flesh the soul walks by faith [see 2 Cor 5:7], which clearly is necessary to acting in love [see Gal 5:6]. If it does not act, it is dead [see Jas 2:20]."[30]

To be sure, faith must precede the loving response that is necessary to good works; Bernard is no pelagian or semi-pelagian.[31] He tells his brothers in his *Fifty-first Sermon on the Song of Songs*: "...Faith must come before good works. Without faith, moreover, it is impossible to please God, as Paul attests [in Heb 11:6]. Still more, he teaches: 'All that does not proceed from faith is sin [Rom 14:23].'

Hence, there is no fruit without flower or good work without faith."[32] But faith must be lived to be genuine: ". . . Clearly not everyone who has faith lives by faith. For 'faith without works is dead [Jas 2:20]' and cannot give the life which it lacks."[33]

By his gift of faith, God also provides a guide to good works: "True and full faith complies with all [God's] precepts. . . ."[34] To those who do have faith and comply with its precepts Bernard promises an appealing reward. He has the Father tell them: "Be beautiful and touch me; be faithful, and you are beautiful."[35] To the faithful is promised the beauty of complete fulfillment: "Possess faith, possess dutiful love, possess wisdom—but the wisdom of the saints, which is fear of the Lord [see Ps 110:10; Si 1:16]—and you have what is yours."[36]

Faith, then, has both profound soteriological as well as epistemological consequences. The very lack of clarity of the knowledge conferred in faith is a blessing to pilgrims on their path to truth and happiness. Bernard is sure that "it is good that faith is shadowy. It tempers the light to the dim-sighted eye and prepares that eye for the light. . . . We who walk by faith [see 2 Cor 5:7] live in the shadow of Christ."[37] But that shadow of faith, Bernard believes, brings no uncertainty and will lead, in due time, to the understanding that will inform the life of the blessed.[38]

B. CHARISMATIC KNOWLEDGE

Besides faith, there is, Bernard believes, still another means to truth accessible to all folk—if not directly, then through the agency of others. That means is charismatic knowledge, knowledge imparted directly to the mind as a gift of the Holy Spirit. Bernard is sure that his contemporary, Hildegard of Bingen, possesses such a gift, and he writes her: "I am filled with joy at the grace of God which is in you [see 1 Tm 4:14]. . . . Since you have the inner knowledge and the anointing which teaches all things [see 1 Jn 2:21], what can I teach or counsel you?"[39] It is none other than the Holy Spirit who has anointed Hildegard and infused her with a profound knowledge of reality.

This knowledge is certain, Bernard believes, for it comes from an unimpeachable source:

> Ignorance, the most evil of mothers, has borne two daughters as evil as she; they are falsehood and doubt. The first is more wretched, the second more pitiable; the first is more destructive, the second more troublesome. When the Spirit speaks, both of them yield; for he speaks not only the truth, but the certain truth. Surely he is the Spirit of truth [see Jn 15:26], the very opposite of falsehood. He is the Spirit of wisdom, which, since it is the splendor of eternal life [see Ws 7:26] and reaches everywhere because of its purity, does not allow obscurity or ambiguity.[40]

Thus, truth, the knowledge of reality, and wisdom, the source of right attitudes and actions, are accessible through a direct gift of the Holy Spirit.

It is the duty of preachers to proclaim to their hearers the knowledge that the Spirit imparts. Bernard the preacher often urges his monastic hearers to join in prayer that the Spirit may enlighten him and, thus, them.[41] Prayer for the enlightenment of this inspiration is especially appropriate in attempting to understand the meaning of difficult scriptural passages, in which the meaning of Scripture "is obscure and altogether beyond the reach of those already wearied."[42] Bernard is confident in the efficacy of his monks' prayers, for "'the Spirit of wisdom is kind [Ws 1:6]' and easy of access to those who call on him. Often, even before they call on him [see Is 65:24], he says: 'Behold; here I am [Is 58:9].'"[43]

Preachers must not only solicit the inspiration of the Spirit, they must convey it to their hearers and thus ensure that those not similarly inspired will reap the fruits of the preachers' inspiration. One of Bernard's models for the preacher is John the Baptist: "He shone ... by his example, by pointing the way with his words, by showing us himself by his actions, by showing us ourselves through his preaching."[44] But, unlike John, who "was taught by inspiration," other folk must be "taught by preaching."[45] And so those whose office includes the duty of preaching, abbots and secular clergy alike,[46] must share their inspired experience with those to whom they are bound so to minister[47]—those who "have been given wisdom by God"[48] must share that gift.

Preaching is a great burden for Bernard, for it is a distraction from the meditation in which he finds great joy. But, since the Spirit offers his gifts of knowledge through the agency of the preacher, Bernard must bear that burden:

> How I wish that all had the gift of teaching! I should be rid of the need to preach these sermons! It is a burden I should like to transfer to another. Or, rather, I should prefer that none of you would need to exercise it and that all would be taught [directly] by God [see Jn 6:45]. Then I should have leisure to contemplate God's beauty [see Ps 45:11].[49]

But Bernard concludes his *Seventh Sermon on the Song of Songs* with the promise that he will continue to respond dutifully to the Spirit's gift:

> I do not wish to prolong speaking to you now of the kiss [of the mouth; see Sg 1:1]. But tomorrow you will hear whatever words, through your prayers, the anointing which teaches all things [see 1 Jn 2:27] may see fit to suggest to me. For flesh and blood do not reveal [see Mt 16:17] such a secret, but only he who searches the depths of God [see 1 Cor 2:10], the Holy Spirit, who, proceeding from the Father [see Jn 15:26] and the Son, lives and reigns equally with them for ever.[50]

The necessity of preaching raises a problem inherent in charismatic knowledge. If the Spirit enlightens his people through the agency of preachers whom he inspires, how is the hearer to know whether the preacher is truly inspired? If God communicates his counsel to his friends, as Bernard believes,[51] how can the hearer know that the preacher is indeed God's friend? Bernard is well aware of the problem; he acknowledges that heretics too have their charismatic preachers. The source of their teaching is diabolical, he believes:

"...The devil's power can be exercised not only over people's bodies, but even in their hearts...."⁵² How is one to know whether one's preacher is inspired by divine or diabolical forces?

Bernard is indeed aware of the problem and offers one possible resolution. Writing to Pope Eugenius III of the failure of the Second Crusade, Bernard addresses the question:

> But perhaps they [the crusaders] are saying: "How do we know that this [Bernard's] message has come from the Lord? What sign do you give, so we may believe you [see Jn 6:30]?" I am not the one to respond to this; my shame should be spared. You should respond for me and for yourself, according to what you have seen and heard [see Mt 11:4], or certainly according to that with which God has inspired you.⁵³

This answer responds well to the needs of rhetorical argument; Bernard is here attempting to convince Eugenius that the crusade has failed because of the crusaders' ineptitude and sinfulness. But what is rhetorically effective is not philosophically satisfactory. If Bernard were here writing a treatise on epistemology, he might well have explicated the difficulty. But the difficulty remains: if the test of charismatic knowledge in one person is the inspiration of another, how can one know if the second person is truly inspired?

There is still another problem with charismatic knowledge, as Bernard sees it. How is one to distinguish in oneself between the inspiration of the Spirit and self-generated impulse? Bernard sees this as a problem not only for the acquisition of knowledge but for the right order of society and Church:

> If all are carried away by their own impulses, in accord with the spirit they receive, and apply themselves willy-nilly to everything they feel suggested—rather than as they judge by reason—until no one is content with his assigned duty, but all simultaneously undertake to take charge of everything indiscriminately, clearly there will be no unity but confusion instead.⁵⁴

There is a social and ecclesiological dimension to, as well as an episte-mological difficulty in, the ambiguities inherent in charismatic knowledge.

Bernard knows the traditional test of the truth of statements sup-ported by the claim of inspiration: miracles.[55] According to this test, the testimony to God's support of spiritual leaders is the miraculous deeds he performs in and through them.[56] Bernard is confident that the Spirit, the source of miracle and charismatic knowledge, contin-ues to work in his own day: "The Spirit operates, through the hands of all sorts of folk, in miracles—in signs, in prodigies, in various works of power. These rekindle his wonderful deeds of old, so that the faith of the past may be built on in the present."[57]

In the end, Bernard is confident that God, in his goodness, will cut through the difficulties attendant on charismatic knowledge—or any other means to the truth—and lead the soul who seeks to the truth which is God himself:

> I tell you, Father Eugenius, God alone can never be sought in vain [see Is 45:19], even when he cannot be found [see Is 55:6]. Your experience may teach you this. But, if not, believe an expert, not me but the Spirit, who says: "You are good, Lord, to those who hope in you, to the soul who seeks you [Lam 3:25]."[58]

Bernard's confidence in the Spirit's direction is, perhaps, best shown in his *Seventeenth Sermon on the Song of Songs,* which also shows Bernard's sensitivity to the problems inherent in charismatic knowledge:

> The Spirit searches not only human hearts and affections [see Ps 7:10] but even the depths of God [see 1 Cor 2:10]. So, whether it be a matter of ourselves or of the depths, I follow him securely wherever he goes [see Rv 14:4]. He guards well our hearts and minds [see Phil 4:7], lest we think he is pre-sent when he is not and erratically follow our own feelings instead of him. He comes and goes as he wills, and no one can easily know whence he comes and whither he goes [see Jn 3:8]. Ignorance of this will not lessen our hopes for salvation,

but to be ignorant of when he comes and when he goes would clearly bring the greatest risk. For, when we do not attend with the utmost vigilance to this alternation in the Spirit's gifts to us, we neither desire him in his absence nor glory in his presence.[59]

Without the gifts of the Spirit, humankind is doomed to ignorance of the truth; when the Spirit does not teach by his gift, humans should peacefully and confidently accept incertitude: "Even if he should leave us suspended in ambiguity, he does not abandon us to what is false."[60] This teaching expresses well Bernard's sensitivity to the difficulties of charismatic knowledge—especially the danger of self-deception. It also demonstrates his confidence that God's goodness will overcome human weakness and lead humankind to knowledge of the truth.

C. CONTEMPLATION: THE MONK'S MEANS TO THE TRUTH

As faith leads one by a sure path to the truth, so contemplation has profound epistemological consequences. But, whereas Bernard sees faith and charismatic knowledge as appropriate to all the people of God, he seems to reserve contemplation to those who have embraced monastic life. Nowhere does Bernard deny the possibility of contemplation to those who are not monks—indeed, the proper preparation for contemplation, growth in humility and love, is precisely the path which must be taken by all Christians.[61] But he seems to regard monastic life as specially designed to promote contemplation, and, when speaking on the subject, he seems to address specifically only monks.[62]

Bernard assumes, I think, that contemplation is the "business" of monks—as he assumes (and sometimes asserts) that other paths to the truth are the special "business" of those called to other vocations.[63] Bernard gives some indication of this at the very beginning of his long series of sermons on the Song of Songs:

The teaching I shall give you, my brothers, will differ from that I should give to those living in the world—certainly the manner of teaching will be different. He who follows the apostle Paul's teaching will give those folk milk to drink and not meat [see 1 Cor 3:2; Heb 5:12–14]. Following Paul's example, he will serve more solid fare to those more spiritually oriented. For he says: "We speak, not with the learned words of human wisdom, but in the Spirit's teaching, comparing spiritual things with the spiritual [1 Cor 2:13]."[64]

Bernard is confident that his monks are among those "perfect" people to whom Paul promised to speak of wisdom in 1 Corinthians 2:6. For they have "long and steadfastly studied heavenly matters, overseen [their] senses, and meditated day and night on God's law [see Ps 1:2]." The bread that Bernard will break for them is "the bread of Solomon," contained in "the book called the *Song of Songs.*"[65] It is precisely in the breaking of Solomon's bread that Bernard gives much of his teaching on contemplation.

What is this contemplation of which Bernard speaks, and what are its epistemological implications?[66] Bernard defines both in writing to his monastic son and ecclesiastical superior, Pope Eugenius III: "...Contemplation can be defined as the true and certain sight of the soul about something, or the apprehension beyond doubt of reality...."[67] Contemplation attains the same certainty as faith, Bernard asserts, but contemplation has a clarity of vision that faith does not. Contemplation is not meditation or consideration, for "consideration can be defined as thought searching intensely for the truth or the stretching out of the soul in the search for the truth."[68] Then, too, contemplation is a communication of a vastly different sort than that made by God in visions or dreams,[69] for contemplation is an internal experience of the soul.[70]

Indeed, "experience" is the key to Bernard's understanding of contemplation. Contemplation is, above all, the experience of a lover:

Happy is the one who has merited to attain the fourth [degree of love]—loving to the degree that one loves even oneself only because of God. "O God, your justice is like the mountains of God [Ps 35:7]." Love is this mountain, God's towering peak. In truth, it is "a fruitful mountain, a fertile mountain [Ps 67:16]." "Who will climb the mountain of the Lord [Ps 23:3]?" "Who will give me wings like a dove's, that I may take flight and seek my rest [Ps 54:7]?"[71]

This "rest" in contemplation is hardly restful. Still Bernard desires it mightily:

When will this feeling be experienced, that, drunk with divine love, my mind may forget itself, become in its own eyes a broken dish [see Ps 30:13], enter totally into God, and, clinging to God, become one with him in spirit . . . .[72]

The experience Bernard seeks totally transcends normal human existence and awareness:

I would say that person is blessed and holy to whom such an experience, so rare in this mortal life, has been given either occasionally or only once—and this suddenly and for only the space of scarcely one moment. To utterly lose yourself somehow, as if you no longer existed, to cease completely to be aware of yourself, to be emptied of everything, and to be reduced to almost nothing, this is a matter of heavenly intercourse, not of human feeling [see Phil 2:7].[73]

This is an experience affecting the whole human being. All the faculties of the soul are affected: the intellect, will, and feelings.[74] Our primary concern here is with the effect of contemplation on the intellect, with the epistemological implications of this rapturous experience.

The knowledge received in the contemplative experience is wide-ranging indeed. Bernard writes in his *Twenty-third Sermon on the Song of Songs:*

The Bridegroom has a place from which he discerns and disposes his plans as ruler of the universe, ordering his laws for all creatures—their weight, measure, and number [see Ws

11:21]. This is a lofty and secret place—but one far from quiet.... And he does not allow the contemplative, who might boldly reach this place, to rest.[75]

The contemplative experience thus brings a knowledge of the nature of reality and the reality of nature. Contemplation is the kiss of the Bridegroom—Christ—bestowed on the bride—the soul. And that kiss is the Spirit "in whom both Father and Son are revealed to her,"[76] thus bestowing on the bride transcendent knowledge of her Lover.

The contemplative's experience also brings a knowledge of the right ordering of things, justice. In knowing justice, the contemplative thus knows much about God, for God is Justice itself.[77] The contemplative kiss thus conveys knowledge of the moral order of things, the possession of which brings the contemplative wisdom:

> There is another place, from which God, the just judge [see Ps 7:12], watches secretly and strictly over his rational creatures, whether reprobate or unmoved.... Do not be surprised that I have assigned the beginning of wisdom [see Ps 110:10] precisely to this place and not to the first. For there [in that first place] we hear our mistress, Wisdom, teaching all things [see 1 Jn 2:27] as if in a lecture-hall; here we receive her within us. There we are indeed instructed, but here we are affected. The instruction makes us learned; affective experience makes us wise.[78]

Knowledge of reality makes the contemplative "learned";[79] the effect on the soul of affective experience adds wisdom to knowledge—a wisdom that perfects the will in love,[80] just as knowledge perfects the intellect.

The effects of contemplation are thus far-reaching and extend beyond the intellect and its search for a means to the truth. In the ecstatic embrace of the Bridegroom, the bride's intellect is filled with knowledge and her will fulfilled in love:

> The favor of the kiss brings with it a freely given and two-fold gift: knowledge of the light and increase of devotion.

Truly, the Spirit of wisdom and understanding [see Is 11:2], like a bee bearing wax and honey, is fully equipped both to kindle the light of knowledge and to infuse the savor of the gift. . . . So let the bride, about to receive the twin gifts of this most holy kiss, make ready her two lips, her reason for the gift of knowledge and her will for that of wisdom.[81]

The soul, her intellect perfected in humility and her will perfected in love, is united to God in contemplative marriage,[82] and these perfections of the intellect and will are themselves inextricably linked in the happy bride: "Happy is the kiss, through which not only is God known but the Father loved—the Father who is never fully known unless perfectly loved."[83] Indeed, Bernard insists, on the level of the infinite, in the embrace of God, knowledge and love are one.[84]

The kiss of the Bridegroom brings the bride a fullness of that knowledge and love. In their ecstatic embrace, the bride is intoxicated with him:

> . . . Holy contemplation has two forms of ecstasy: one in the intellect, the other in affection, one in light, the other in fervor; one in knowledge, the other in ardor. Tender affection, a heart glowing with love, the infusion of holy ardor, and even the impetuousness of a spirit filled with zeal are obviously not carried away from any other place than the wine cellar [see Sg 2:4] . . . .[85]

This intoxicating experience brings with it a profound knowledge not acquired by any other means. Contemplation has enormous epistemological ramifications.

Those epistemological effects are the result of a gift. The soul may desire her Lover and prepare her couch for his embrace,[86] but his coming into her bed is a free gift of love. Bernard gives the example of Paul's rapture:

> . . . Paul tells us that he was rapt up into the third heaven [see 2 Cor 12:2]. But why does he say "rapt" instead of "led"? If the great apostle says that he had been rapt to that place

which the learned did not know or [to which] those [merely] guided could not go, then I, who am undoubtedly a lesser man than Paul, must not presume to attain it by my own effort.... One who is rapt, carried up somehow to a place unknown, not by one's own powers but borne by another, has nothing of which to boast, either in whole or in part. Such a one has accomplished nothing, either singlehandedly or with another. The apostle could ascend to the first or second heaven with the guidance and help given him, but, to attain to the third, he had to be rapt.[87]

Contemplation is thus not the fruit of human effort but of a generous gift of God.[88]

Bernard is bold enough to believe his monastic audience may indeed share in the gift of contemplation. This is surely the reason why he so extensively instructs that audience about the possibility of the contemplative experience:

I wish to tell you of my experience—as I have promised. Not that it is of any importance [see 2 Cor 12:1]. But I do so soundly, in order to help you. If you derive any profit from it, I shall be consoled for my foolishness. If not, my foolishness will be revealed. I acknowledge both that the Word has come to me—I speak in my foolishness [see 2 Cor 11:17]—and that he has come to me many times.[89]

Bernard does indeed expect the revelation of his experiences to be of use to his audience, a monastic audience that has traveled long and well the difficult road of virtue. For the outwardly unheard song that the bride hears and sings in contemplative union with the Bridegroom[90] requires a highly trained voice and ear:

Surely this song is not sung or heard by immature or neophyte souls, or by those recently converted from worldliness. But only minds already advanced and accomplished, only these will be already so mature in their great progress—pushed on by God—that they will have reached the perfect age and years—years measured by virtues, not time—for any sort of marriage. These will be capable of nuptial union with the heavenly Bridegroom . . . .[91]

Those who have reached this maturity Bernard encourages to anticipate the nuptial kiss of contemplation—"a kiss of greatest intimacy and wondrous sweetness."[92] To invite the contemplative kiss, Bernard urges his monks to practice the art of seduction:

So now, when the bride thinks the opportunity is ripe, she declares the bed-chamber is decorated. And, pointing with her finger to the little bed, she invites the Beloved to rest there. . . . She entices him to be the guest of her soul and impels him to spend the night with her.[93]

The monk whose soul is filled with overwhelming love for her Bridegroom[94] has in that love a sign of readiness for the nuptial union of contemplation. And Bernard encourages both that love and the expectation of union that derives from it:

The soul which has attained this degree [of perfection] now dares to think of marriage. Why should she not so dare, when she perceives herself ready for marriage to him whom she so resembles? His loftiness has no terrors for her, for she shares his likeness, she is united to him in love, and she is coupled to him by promise. . . . When you see a soul who has left all to cling in everything to the Word by solemn vows, to live in the Word, to rule herself by the Word, to conceive by the Word what she will give birth to by the Word, . . . know her a bride married to the Word.[95]

Bernard expects that his monks will be open to the gift of contemplation, receive it, and share in its fruits. Bernard expects this gift to be sought again and again: "Anyone who has received this spiritual kiss from the mouth of Christ even once surely solicits this intimate experience and joyfully seeks its return."[96] The bride's anticipation can be confident, for she knows that the Bridegroom loves her.[97]

The fulfillment of this expectation brings a knowledge otherwise unknown. The ecstatic union of the soul in spiritual marriage with God brings a rebirth that transcends ordinary human experience:

> In this highest kind of birth, the soul sometime exceeds and even secedes from her bodily senses, so that she who discerns the Word is not aware of herself. This happens when her mind is so seduced by the sweetness of the ineffable Word that it withdraws from itself—or, rather, it is seized and freed from itself, withdrawn from itself by the Word.[98]

But, Bernard is confident, such an experience of the truth of the Word—so like the beatific vision of the blessed—is indeed possible in this life.[99] Bernard's contemplative monk thus experiences on this earth a foretaste of the unity with God he will one day experience in the beatific vision.[100] Even now, his contemplative experience will bring a vision of Truth of great significance to himself and the society of which he is a part.[101]

III
Ḫumanism:
Beauty and the Pursuit of Truth

To be learned in Bernard's day, one would have studied and mastered the curriculum offered in contemporary schools. The disciplines studied in this curriculum were called collectively the *artes litterarum,* the seven liberal arts. The first two steps in this education involved study of the Latin literature of antiquity, under the traditional rubrics "grammar" and "rhetoric." The student was then to master the techniques of rational investigation, under the heading "dialectic." Together these were the trivial arts, those disciplines that comprised the *trivium.*[1]

The prevailing scholarly measure of Bernard's attitude toward the *trivium* concentrates almost exclusively on the stance he took toward the third of the trivial arts—dialectic, most often viewed in light of his much misunderstood controversy with Peter Abelard.[2] When Bernard's position on the other two trivial arts, grammar and rhetoric, is considered, it is most commonly examined through studies of Bernard's own literary genius and command of the Latin language.[3] I should like to suggest that an additional insight into Bernard's thought on the question can be gained through viewing his comments, direct or implicit, on the cultivation of literature and rational investigation in the light of his ecclesiology—more particularly his position on the ecclesial role of bishops and others dedicated to pastoral ministry in the world.[4]

For Bernard, as we have seen, the Church is the sum total of all those pursuing the path to perfection.[5] Bernard's images of the clergy who minister to that people and Church are rich and diverse: they are the Noahs who steer the ark,[6] physicians who care for ailing souls,[7] mothers who suckle their children,[8] friends of the Bridegroom,[9] public fountains and reservoirs from which all may drink,[10] bridges over which their folk walk to God,[11] shepherds who feed their flocks,[12] and gardeners who cultivate and water God's garden.[13] They are sweating farmers hoeing the Lord's fields,[14] the beams and panels that hold together God's house,[15] and watchmen guarding the city of God.[16]

A. THE LEARNED CLERGY

To fulfill the obligations implicit in the use of these images, Bernard believes that the clergy must be both virtuous and learned. He tells his monks:

> If I am not mistaken, to guard the city [which is the Church] is the work of a strong, spiritual, and loyal man. He must be strong in order to repulse all violence to it; he must be spiritual in order to detect any ambush which threatens it; he must be loyal so as not to be seeking his own interest [see 1 Cor 13:5]. . . . How can an uneducated shepherd lead the Lord's flock into the pasture of divine eloquence? But, if he were learned but not good, I fear he would not suckle his people with the breasts of his teaching but harm them by the barrenness of his life.[17]

Bernard cites the book of Malachi to refute anyone who might question his joining of learning to virtue as a qualification for pastoral leadership: "If you should say: 'What is this to me? [Mt 27:4],' then this sentence would censure you: 'The lips of the priest shall guard knowledge, and they shall seek the law from his mouth; for he is the messenger of the Lord [Mal 2:7].'"[18] Underscoring his insistence on the coupling of clerical virtue and learning, Bernard complains, not without hyperbole: "Who would give me learned and holy men as pastors presiding in God's churches—if not in all, certainly in many, at least in some?"[19] Bernard's insistence on clerical virtue is easily understood, but why should the clergy be learned?

Bernard's answer is that learning is necessary if clerics are to fulfill their function in society and Church. The clergy must serve the Church, be she seen through the image of city, bride, or sheepfold.[20] Clerics are to nourish their people with the milk of doctrine,[21] instruction in both faith and holiness.[22] Bernard's clergy must labor to bring about Christian justice in the world—in *this* world.[23] This task requires the clergy's continuing efforts to preserve the Church's freedom, the freedom to promote justice.[24] Justice requires peace as well as freedom, and Bernard sees the clergy as preeminent peacemakers.[25] The peace and justice which Bernard would have the clergy foster are internal as well as external; they must correct the evil intents and actions of individuals as well as reform society and Church.[26] Pastors must likewise be paternal in their care for the poor, those suffering from want of physical necessities[27] or from want of the true faith.[28] Clerics must do battle with heresy by their preaching;[29] but, Bernard insists, those found in heresy should be taught, not fought with force.[30]

This manifold ministry demands heroic virtue and devotion to duty. But, as Bernard sees it, it also requires considerable sophistication—a sophistication provided, in large part, by the cleric's learning. To fulfill their function, then, the clergy must possess "the ornaments of knowledge and erudition."[31]

Sometimes Bernard can seem to disparage clerical learning in defending clerical virtue. But he is well aware of his own hyperbole in so doing, as he reports in his *Thirty-sixth Sermon on the Song of Songs:*

> Perhaps you think I have gone too far in scorning knowledge, as if to censure the learned and condemn the study of letters. God forbid! I am not ignorant of how much the Church's learned have benefited her, whether by refuting her opponents or by instructing the ignorant. For I have read: "Because you have rejected knowledge, I have rejected you, that you may not function as priest for me [Hos 4:6]." I

have read: "Those who are learned shall shine as the vault of heaven, and those who have instructed many in justice shall shine as stars for all eternity [Dn 12:3]."[32]

Bernard's clergy must be learned to fulfill their function of preaching sound doctrine, instructing their folk in the truths they must know to pursue the path to the happiness of perfection.

To carry out successfully his ministry of teaching and preaching, the cleric must know that which he would impart to others.[33] Love for the flock is not enough; the knowledge that comes from a thorough course of study must fill the clergy as well. For errant, ignorant, or unwise sheep must be "persuaded by pleas and convinced by reason."[34] Zealous love for those who have strayed from the faith is necessary but insufficient. Learning is the buttress of the preaching which may win heretics back to true belief. Bernard declares: "... Heretics are to be caught rather than driven away. They are to be caught, I repeat, not by force of arms but by arguments by which their errors may be refuted...."[35] Bernard insists: "Faith must be a matter of persuasion, not of imposition";[36] hence heretics "must be convinced by invincible reasoning."[37]

Bernard's insistence on the necessity of clerical learning extends even to liturgical matters. Writing to the canons of Lyons, in reaction to their institution of a liturgical celebration of Mary's conception, Bernard declares:

> ... I am amazed that some of you might wish to change your finest color [see Lam 4:1] by introducing at this time a new celebration. This is a rite which the Church does not know, which reason does not demonstrate, and which the ancient traditions do not commend. Are we more learned or more devout than the Fathers? We presume at our peril something which they in such prudence passed over.[38]

All this presupposes a knowledge of the Church's tradition, a thorough acquaintance with the Church Fathers, and an ability to employ reason correctly—in short, learning.[39]

B. Friend of the Learned and Patron of Scholars

The need for learning in the clerical ministry leads Bernard to befriend many of the learned clergy of his time.[40] William of Champeaux, Abelard's former master at Paris; Alberich, the noted master of the cathedral school at Reims; and Hugh of Saint Victor, master at his Paris house's famed school, are all friends of Bernard's. To Master Geoffry of Loreto, Bernard writes: "You have the favor of God and the people alike [see Lk 2:52]; you have knowledge [see 1 Cor 8:1]; you have the spirit of liberty; you have the living and effective word [see Heb 4:12], a speech seasoned with salt [see Col 4:6]...."[41] In another cordial letter Bernard praises the virtue and learning of Master Gilbert, who has become bishop of London:

> Such progress [in virtue] gives witness to the clarity of your own philosophy; this great clarity is the fulfillment of your study.... He is wise who, taking his pleasure in all the letters and studies of the wise of this world, has also studied all the Scriptures....[42]

Erudition is praiseworthy in Bernard's eyes when coupled with virtue—especially praiseworthy in one who has undertaken the ministry of bishop.

And Bernard goes beyond recognizing the utility of learning in those who possess it to encourage the education of young men destined for the clerical life. Among Bernard's famous protégés are Peter Lombard and John of Salisbury, both of whom would fulfill Bernard's educational program for the clergy by being elected bishops, Peter of Paris and John of Chartres. For Peter, arguably the founder of scholastic theology, Bernard obtains lodging at the Abbey of Saint Victor, to aid him in his studies at Paris.[43] On behalf of John of Salisbury, the great humanist and historian, Bernard writes a letter full of praise of John's erudition, in the hope that the recipient, Archbishop Theobald of Canterbury, would support the already successful scholar.[44]

In supporting the academic pursuits of another scholar, Robert Pullan, Bernard praises the program of studies at Paris by writing to Robert's bishop at Rochester:

> If I have advised Master Robert Pullan to spend some time at
> Paris, for the sake of the sound teaching which is known to
> be imparted there, [it was because] I thought it necessary—
> and I still do. If I have asked you to allow this, I would ask
> the same even now—except that I have sensed your indigna-
> tion at my prior request.... By the witness of my conscience,
> I dare still to present my request as well as my counsel, that,
> with your full support, Master Robert might stay for some
> time at Paris.[45]

It has been argued that Bernard's support for Robert and many
other scholars is given in spite of Bernard's distance from their intellectual culture. This support has been seen merely as a sign of
Bernard's great liberality and broadmindedness.[46] The letter that
Bernard writes to Robert Pullan—by this time a cardinal—on the
occasion of Eugenius III's election as pope, reveals an entirely different sentiment:

> Blessed be God, who, according to his mercy [see 1 Pt 1:3]
> to our—or, rather, his—Eugenius, has gone before him with
> blessings of sweetness [see Ps 20:4], to prepare a lamp for his
> anointed [see Ps 131:17], sending in advance a faithful man
> [see Prv 28:20] for his help and my great consolation as
> well.... Be concerned, dear friend, for him for whom God
> has appointed you consoler and counselor. Watch over him
> carefully, according to the wisdom given you [see 2 Pt
> 3:15], so that, amid the tumult of manifold affairs, he will
> not be beset by the deceit of the wicked and snatched away
> by their words—all of which would be unworthy of Euge-
> nius's apostolate.[47]

Eugenius is a Cistercian and was, at one time, a monk at Clairvaux;[48]
he is thus Bernard's spiritual son. Yet Bernard entrusts the care of
one schooled in the monastery to a man whose education was in the
schools. The reason seems to me quite clear: Eugenius has embarked
on a ministry to the folk of the world, a ministry that requires the
counsel of one whose education suits the task.

C. Education in the Literary Arts

The educational program that properly prepares prospective clergy for their ministry, Bernard believes, is the curriculum offered in the contemporary schools.[49] This was Bernard's own educational experience. Bernard began his education at the age of seven[50] with the study of grammar. William of Saint Thierry reports that Bernard's mother, "as soon as she could, handed him over to the teachers of letters at the church of Châtillon for his education."[51] Under the tutelage of the canons of Saint Vorles at Châtillon, Bernard studied at least the first three of the liberal arts, grammar, rhetoric, and dialectic—the *trivium* which we call the "humanities."[52] William tells us that "in his pursuit of letters, he [Bernard] progressed beyond his equals [see Gal 1:14] and out of all proportion to his age."[53]

Bernard did not later reject his literary education. Throughout his writings one discovers citations from classical authors: Cicero, Horace, Juvenal, Ovid, Perseius, Seneca, Statius, Tacitus, Terence, and Virgil.[54] Bernard's frequent redactions of his own works[55] seem to indicate that his citations were not accidental or unconscious references to authors for whom he had little regard or merely passing interest. Quite to the contrary, Bernard sometimes identifies the source of his classical quotations. Now and again his reference is not specific: "the wise man once said,"[56] or "according to the gentiles,"[57] or "as that gentile poet puts it,"[58] or "what a gentile asked his fellow gentiles,"[59] or "according to a certain wise man."[60] At least once, Bernard cites his source by name: "according to your Ovid."[61] That Bernard expects considerable literary sophistication in his audience is indicated by his references to Terence by that classical author's genre only: "according to that comic dramatist"[62] and "according to the comic author."[63] On one occasion at least, Bernard refers to Ovid simply as "a certain poet."[64]

Much more frequent and obvious than Bernard's citations of classical authors is his use of the vast array of rhetorical techniques and devices learned from the ancients studied in his youth. For Bernard, beauty of expression is both "a means and an expression of the love of truth."[65] He writes: "... The knowledge of letters, which adorn and refine the soul, makes it possible to instruct others."[66]

And Jean Leclercq comments: "...Literature helps,...makes others less rough and rude [*erudit* = instruct], so that they become more refined, more sensitive to beauty and to truth."[67] Instructing others in the truth is, of course, one of the primary functions of the clergy.

William of Saint Thierry tells us that, as a boy, Bernard "so submitted himself to the pursuit of letters that he soon learned to discover God in the Scriptures."[68] To preach the truth, one must discover it—primarily by searching through that vast body of literature which is the Bible, a search immeasurably assisted by a sophisticated understanding of the many literary forms found there. Communicating the truths thus discovered is also immeasurably aided by a knowledge of those rhetorical techniques learned through a classical education. The effort and literary sophistication necessary to communicate these truths Bernard underscores in writing to Oger, a canon regular whose vocation requires facility in teaching:

> How much tumult is there in the mind which is composing, where a multitude of words resound, a variety of phrases and a diversity of meanings join in battle. Where often the word that occurs must be rejected, the word which is needed escapes one's grasp. Where what gives a more beautiful literary effect, what conveys the meaning more suitably, what is more accurately understood, what is more useful to the conscience, what then should be placed after or before what, must all be strictly scrutinized. And many other things must be assiduously observed by those learned in such matters.[69]

To those clerics whose style reflects this effort and erudition Bernard offers high praise, as to Hildebert, the archbishop of Tours: "...In your writings, others can be exceedingly pleased with the learning shown, the sweet and pure language, the rich eloquence, the welcome and praiseworthy brevity...."[70] All this requires learning—learning in the classical literary arts, a learning to be had only in the schools.

Beauty of expression is also essential, Bernard believes, in the liturgy, which is for him a powerful means of conveying divine wisdom. Asked by Abbot Guy and the brethren of Montiéramey to

compose a liturgical office in honor of Saint Victor, Bernard writes of
the goal of his efforts:

> The unmistakable sense [of the words] should shine with
> truth, resound with justice, incite humility, teach modera-
> tion. The words should offer light to the mind, shape to
> behavior, the cross to vices, devotion to the affections, disci-
> pline to the senses.[71]

To accomplish all this the author must be both virtuous and learned:

> Clearly, in such an important matter it is not a friend you
> desire, but one who is learned, one who is worthy. Look for
> one whose authority is greater than mine, whose life is holier,
> whose style is more mature, and whose work illuminates and
> harmonizes with holiness.[72]

Those whose office requires instructing others must be learned in the
literary and rhetorical skills.

Of course, the study prerequisite for such learning is not independent, Bernard thinks, of moral considerations. Proper motivation
must inform literary—and any other—study. He writes:

> If, for example, someone decides he or she must pursue the
> truth—and this solely out of love for the truth—is this not
> obviously honorable both in matter and in motive? But if
> that person's desire is less for the truth than for empty
> glory [see Gal 5:26; Phil 2:3], or if that person intends to
> obtain, through the truth, another end or any sort of tem-
> poral favor, . . . you would not hesitate, I think, to consider
> that person partially deformed, . . . disfigured by a shameful
> motive.[73]

Study must be motivated by an unadulterated and unswerving desire
for truth.

Learning should be sought for its own sake—but also for the
sake of others who will benefit from it:

Paul says: "If any one thinks he or she knows something,
that person does not yet know as he or she ought to know [1
Cor 8:2]." ... What ... does he say this manner of knowing
is? What, except that you know what order, what effort, and
what end are necessary when investigating anything? As for
the order: you should prefer that which is more useful for
salvation. As for effort: you should pursue more eagerly that
which is more powerful in promoting love. As for the end:
your purpose should not be empty glory or [mere] curiosity
or anything like that, but wholly directed toward your welfare or the welfare of your neighbors.[74]

Knowledge of classical letters is indeed useful in promoting one's
own welfare and that of others, but literary study must be preceded
by an awareness of God and of one's true self to attain meaning and
utility.[75]

The student must always recognize that, in the end, knowledge
of the liberal arts, while useful, is not necessary to humankind's ultimate goal:

Even lacking knowledge of all those arts called liberal—as
much as those studies may be quite honorably and usefully
taught and practiced—how many more people have been
saved by their lives and deeds? How many does the apostle
enumerate in his letter to the Hebrews [11], those made
dear [to God] not by their knowledge of letters but by their
pure conscience and by their genuine faith [see 1 Tm 1:5]?
All pleased God by their lives, lives of merit, not of knowledge. Peter and Andrew and the sons of Zebedee and all the
other disciples were not chosen from the schools of rhetoric
or philosophy; yet through them the Savior made his salvation effective throughout the world [see Ps 73:12].[76]

IV

Scholasticism: The Roles of Reason

ernard writes that the apostles "Peter and Andrew and the sons of Zebedee and all the other disciples were not chosen from the schools of rhetoric or philosophy...."[1] But, as we have seen, Bernard believes their successors, the bishops and other clergy, must have an education in classical literature to fulfill their function of preaching and teaching. What of the third of the trivial arts: dialectic? What is the role of reason, what is the role of philosophy in Bernard's educational program for the clergy?[2]

A. BASIC ASSUMPTIONS

Bernard's response is an enthusiastic endorsement of philosophic studies. That enthusiasm is based on three fundamental assumptions: the rational order of the universe, the accessibility of that ordered universe to the human mind through the senses, and the ability of that mind, structured according to the same rational pattern as the universe, to analyze and synthesize sense data properly.

1. A Universe Ordered by Reason

Bernard is sure that God has created an ordered universe, a universe ordered by his wisdom and power. Bernard writes, in one of his sermons for Pentecost:

40

> We must ponder three things about the great work which this world is, namely, what it is, how it exists, and for what purpose it is established. Inestimable power is shown even in the existence of things, for they are created so many, so marvelous, so diverse, and so splendid. Clearly, a unique wisdom is apparent in the manner [of creation], for some things are placed higher, some lower, and some in between—all in a most orderly fashion.... All things were created with perfect power; they were created beautiful with perfect wisdom; they were created beneficial with perfect beneficence.[3]

The universe Bernard inhabits is beautiful in its order and friendly to those who live in that order.

This beautiful order is the product of a Creator "in whom there is no inconsistency,... in whose decisions there is likewise no inconsistency."[4] Thus it is possible for all rational beings to attain knowledge of the author of creation by studying that creation:

> ... This immense variety of forms and multitude of kinds in the created universe, what are they but rays of the divine nature, showing that he from whom they come truly is, but not defining precisely what he is? Hence, what you see is from him but is not he himself. Still, when you see all that is from him—though not him himself—you know beyond doubt that he exists whom you ought to seek, so that means are not denied the seeker and ignorance not excused those who ignore the means.[5]

As the order of creation is a source of knowledge about the Creator, Bernard is also sure that that order is a means of knowing those actions that will promote one's own well-being. For there is, he believes, an order in the universe, a natural law that both drives the behavior of things and can inform humans about their proper behavior. Even without a revelation of God's benevolent mandates, human beings can know fundamental ethical principles. Bernard is sure that natural law makes available to all people principles such as the "golden rule." "Natural precepts" such as these can be "discovered by reason," for they are implicit "in nature."[6]

2. *The Essential Service of the Senses*

Access to the rationally ordered universe, Bernard is certain, comes
only through the agency of the human body. He writes in his *Fifth
Sermon on the Song of Songs:*

> That which God has made—that is, all beings corporeal and
> thus visible—comes to our attention only through the instru-
> mentality of our bodily senses. Therefore, the spiritual crea-
> tures which we are must have a body. Without it we can
> by no means attain to that knowledge which we perceive
> is the only basis for knowing those things essential to our
> happiness.[7]

Thus, "that spirit which is clothed in flesh and dwells on earth strives
to acquire knowledge—in a step-by-step, gradual way—by progress-
ing in the consideration of sensible things . . . ."[8]

Sensation is, for Bernard, "a vital activity of the body, alert to
that which is external."[9] The data provided by the senses are essential in knowing the created world, for knowledge does not come
directly to the mind through the agency of angels or any other spiritual entities:

> Know this: no created spirit can of itself act directly on our
> minds. It is evident that, without the mediation of our or its
> bodily equipment, it cannot interact with us or infuse our
> minds so that, by its [merely spiritual] activity, we may be
> made learned or more learned, made good or still better.[10]

Human knowledge, and thus human life, is both constrained by and
immeasurably assisted by the corporeal nature of humans. The spiritual component of the human being requires the invaluable support
of the senses in the search for truth:

> . . . In this life, the bodily senses exert themselves freely and
> powerfully, but the spiritual eye is shrouded in a perplexing

darkness. What wonder, then, if the stranger [the soul] stands in need of the natives [the senses]? Happy is the traveler in this time who can turn to his or her service the kindness of these citizens—without whom he or she cannot continue the journey.... Great is the traveler who is content to consider the use of the senses as the treasure of these citizens, dispensing that wealth for his or her own benefit and that of many others.[11]

Bernard calls this quest for knowledge based on sense data "dispensative consideration": "Consideration is dispensative when it uses the senses and sensible things in an ordering and synthetic way...."[12] Thus, the senses are the firm bases of the naturally acquired knowledge needed by all in their quest for happiness.

3. The Function and Limits of Logic

Though sense data are the bases of the knowing process, they require "an ordering and synthetic" method to attain true knowledge. That method is reason or logic,[13] mastered by the study of the principles of dialectics.

Bernard defines the human being as a "rational animal" and considers this a "dignity."[14] As evidence of this dignity, Bernard gives the example of the incarnate Second Person of the Trinity: "Surely the Son of God, manifestly the Word and wisdom of the Father, actually assumed the first of our soul's powers, which is called reason...."[15] Likewise, humans "share with angels the best natural gift, and it is reason."[16]

The ability to reason is a gift of God. Bernard writes: "...The light of reason, as a little spark, has been given to us by [God's] insuperable mercy."[17] Just as God has bestowed on the human body the power of sensation, so he has given the human soul a rational power; these two gifts enable humans to "discern between what is proper and what improper, between good and bad, between truth and falsity."[18] Logic applied to sense data can thus lead humans to knowledge of what is, the truth, and what to do, the good. Even "wood and stone,"

Bernard says, could attain such knowledge if likewise endowed with the powers of sensation and reason.[19] This sort of knowledge is the result of what Bernard calls "scientific consideration."[20]

Thus, for Bernard, philosophy attains "understanding" of reality.[21] Like faith, understanding achieves certainty,[22] but understanding possesses an epistemological efficacy that faith does not. While faith's knowledge is "hidden and obscure," that of understanding is "naked and manifest."[23] Consequently, Bernard is sure that rational investigation, analysis, and synthesis of sense data result in true knowledge, knowledge of the truth. Clearly, philosophical conclusions and all other knowledge obtained and transmitted by "rational disputation"[24] are of immense importance to the clergy whom Bernard would have master the art of dialectics in the schools of the time.

Logic has its limits, to be sure, as do the philosophy and theology that employ it. This is especially true, Bernard believes, in pursuing knowledge of God's nature.[25] God's love, too, is only inadequately understood by the human mind.[26] Even God's actions in space and time are sometimes only incompletely comprehended. Bernard writes, for example, of the Incarnation: "Who can grasp with understanding and discern with reason how the inaccessible splendor could pour itself out into a virginal womb or how?"[27] But, clearly, to see the limits of logic is not to deny its efficacy.

Rational investigation has still other limitations, as Bernard sees them: "reason can ignore truth . . .";[28] the method can be inappropriately used[29] or used not at all. In addition, prudence must be used in its application. Bernard writes that

> Paul said: "By the grace of God given to me, I say to all among you not to be wiser than you ought to be, but be wise soberly [Rom 12:3]." He does not forbid being wise but being wiser than one ought. But what does it mean to be wise soberly? It means to observe most vigilantly what one ought to know more and first. For the time is short [see 1 Cor 7:29]. To be sure, all knowledge is good in itself—provided it be founded on truth. But you, who hasten to work out your salvation with fear and trembling [see Phil 2:12] because of

the brevity of time, should take care to know more and first what you feel is more bound up with your happiness.[30]

To prioritize the objects of rational inquiry is not, of course, to deny validity to that inquiry. Rather, Bernard's admonition clearly carries the conviction that logic properly and prudently applied to sense data results in truths of fundamental importance to the happiness of the cleric whom he would have study philosophy—and to the flock to which that cleric would one day minister.

B. THE RANGE OF REASON

Reason or logic can be applied, Bernard believes, not only to data derived from the senses but also to data provided by revelation. Reason is a tool of the theologian as well as of the philosopher. In this sense Bernard is both, although he does not explicitly distinguish philosophy and theology or define them.[31] Granted, Bernard does offer at least one statement, in his *Forty-eighth Sermon on the Song of Songs*,[32] that seems to echo, at least faintly, Anselm of Canterbury's view of theology as faith seeking understanding.[33] But far more useful than a search for Bernard's definition of theology—or philosophy, for that matter—is a description of how he applies logic to the questions he considers fundamental to human happiness.[34]

1. God: The Ultimate Reality

Bernard does not hesitate to apply the dialectical method to God himself. In his *On Consideration*, Bernard asks: "What is God?" In response he presents an argument for what sounds suspiciously like an Uncaused Cause. "That from which everything began," he asserts, "clearly did not itself begin, for, if it began, it clearly had its beginning from something else." Bernard continues: "It is clear that nothing exists as its own beginning. Moreover, what had its beginning from another was not first." He concludes by saying: "Therefore, the true beginning in no way had a beginning, but began totally from itself."[35] My condensation of Bernard's argument hardly does justice to it. But it is clear, I trust, that the argument depends for its force on the logic employed.

Bernard is not done with his question, however. "What is God?" he asks again. And he answers: "That than which nothing better can be thought."[36] This response is surely reminiscent of Anselm of Canterbury's *Prologion* definition.[37] However, Bernard does not use it as a basis for a demonstration of God's existence, as did Anselm,[38] but as a stepping stone toward an affirmation of God's unity and the relationship of that unity to divinity. Bernard argues: "If you accept this"— that God is that than which nothing better can be thought—"it is not appropriate for you to assert that there is anything from which God has his existence and which is not God. Such a thing would be better [than God]. How could it not be better than God, if it were not a God which gives God existence?" "But," Bernard concludes, "it would be better for us to acknowledge that the divinity, by which God is said to be, is nothing other than God." Those who argue for a distinction between God and divinity affirm that God is not a Trinity but a quaternity. "Many things are said to be in God...," Bernard replies, "but these many are one. Otherwise,...we should have not [merely] a quaternity but a cententity."[39]

Bernard's God is not multiple; he is one. Furthermore, Bernard argues, God is simple:

> ...God does not have this or that, as he does not have these or those. He is who is [see Ex 3:14], not what he is. Pure, simple, entire, perfect, unchanging in himself, he is no way temporal, in no way local.... He does not consist of parts ...; he is not subject to forms.... He is his own form; he is his own essence.[40]

This is the heart of the matter for Bernard. Although he insists that God, as eternal and thus beyond time, is uncreated, interminable, and immutable[41]—although he affirms God's incorporeality and omnipotence,[42] as well as his omnipresence[43]—all this leads Bernard to what is for him an inescapable conclusion: God's essence is his existence. In his *On Consideration* Bernard writes:

> If you were to say of God that he is good or great or blessed or wise or any such thing, in one word the response would be made that he is: he is Is. For this is being for him, what all these attributes are. If you were to add a hundred such attributes, you would not have diminished his [pure] being. ... If you have already seen how singular, how supreme his being is, do you not judge that, in comparison, whatever is not this sort of being is really not, is rather not-being than being?[44]

Once more Bernard asks: "What, again, is God?" And he answers: "That without which nothing exists [see Jn 1:3]." God "who is his own being," is indeed the being "of everything else,"[45] for he created them.[46] God creates, Bernard is sure, out of his unsurpassable goodness. And Bernard is equally certain that knowledge of God's goodness is accessible to all, Christians and others alike, who are capable of rational reflection. In his treatise *On the Need for Loving God*, Bernard asserts: "Truly, an innate sense of justice, not unknown by reason, cries out within [all humans, believers and non-believers alike] that they should love with their entire being him to whom they know they owe everything."[47] God's goodness—and much else—can be known by all those who apply reason to the fundamental questions of human existence. They can do so with confidence, Bernard is sure, because the ability to reason is itself a gift of God.[48]

2. The Human Condition

That gift of reason can and should be employed in the search for truth about God's noblest creation: the human being. Rational reflection, Bernard believes, will demonstrate that human nature is intrinsically noble. In the fourteenth of his quadragesimal sermons on Psalm 90, Bernard urges his reader to "think of how he [God] made you. For in your body he made you an illustrious creature, and still more so in your soul, seeing that you are the extraordinary image of the Creator [see Gn 1:26], participating in his reason...."[49] Human rationality, the human capacity to discover truth through reason, is, for Bernard, a participation in the very nature of God—and this truth is itself discovered by reason.

But, Bernard thinks, if rational analysis demonstrates the grandeur of human nature, the application of reason to the everyday experience of want and pain forces humans to face the reality of their condition, of their predicament.[50] The source of that predicament is in the human will, the faculty of choice. Bernard concludes that human suffering is the result of a freely chosen self-negation, a rejection of the rule of reason.[51]

Bernard's exposition of the story of human restoration is, of course, based primarily on scriptural exegesis, but it is remarkable how often and to what an extent that story is couched in a form and vocabulary dependent on rational analysis and employing philosophical terminology. By way of illustration, I offer the following passage from Bernard's *Sermon on the Feast of Saint Martin the Bishop:*

> ... Although one may say that the human being is, in a way, heaven and has, without doubt, a relationship of similitude to celestial spirits, both in substance and in form—in substance because spiritual, in form because rational—nevertheless these two [properties] do not now suffice to raise him or her [high enough] that he or she may deserve to hear: "Because you are heaven, to heaven shall you go."

In the course of Bernard's exposition, in this sermon, of the solution to the human dilemma—which solution is, of course, the unmerited bestowal of God's grace—Bernard quotes both Isaiah and Romans. But he does so in language derived as much, if not more, from philosophical than from scriptural sources. For example, he writes: "For grace comes between us and God"—a phrase clearly evocative of Isaiah 59:2. Then Bernard adds: "not by separation but by reparation and conjunction."[52]

Much of Bernard's writing on human nature and its perfection, on the human condition and its restoration, takes the form of meditations on Scripture, usually expressed through the literary form of sermons. But many of Bernard's descriptions of the process of human perfection are rational investigations and expositions of specific questions expressed through the medium of a treatise. In one such, titled *On Consideration,* Bernard informs his reader, Pope Eugenius III, of the method employed in the treatise and Bernard's goal in selecting that method:

> Although the investigation of the first [question, who you are,] is more philosophic than apostolic, nevertheless there is in the definition of the human being, whom the philosophers call a rational animal, the notion that humans are mortal. And this, if you wish, you may look into more carefully. For there is nothing inherent in such an investigation which might stand in the way of your calling or oppose your dignity. It can, [rather,] truly contribute to salvation.[53]

Bernard's subject is an aspect of human nature, his method is rational analysis, his goal is the perfection and happiness of Eugenius and others, and his audience is a bishop. Although Eugenius is also a Cistercian, his ministry has become that of a secular cleric: serving the salvation of his flock. Clearly, Bernard thinks that knowledge of human nature, gained through the philosopher's method, is eminently useful in the pursuit of that salvation. Thus, Bernard responds to the needs of one who ministers to the people of God by using a method, dialectic, which he assigns especially to the clergy and which he would have them master in the schools.

3. Knowledge of Moral Principles

But Bernard is also convinced that knowledge gained through rational investigation—knowledge of God, of the human condition, of the possibility of perfection—is useless without concomitant knowledge of basic moral principles. One must know how to deal with the reality that one knows. For Bernard, reason is efficacious in determining ethical standards because the moral order is determined by a Creator who is Reason itself. "He," Bernard says, "is the certain principle of reason and equity...."[54] Because the moral order is a rational order, reason should govern one's assessment and choice of the good.[55] Thus, rational deliberation is the prudent predecessor of any action. Bernard writes:

> Spiritual persons . . . precede every undertaking with a three-fold consideration: first, whether it is lawful; second, whether it is suitable; last, whether it is advantageous [see 1 Cor 6:12, 10:22]. Even though it can be established beyond question in Christian philosophy that nothing is suitable unless it is lawful and that nothing is advantageous if it is not suitable and lawful, nevertheless it does not follow that everything that is lawful will result in that which is suitable or advantageous.[56]

Rational investigation and reflection are as necessary to the pursuit of moral norms as to the discovery of the nature of things. Thus, for Bernard, the existence of objective ethical standards is complemented by an epistemological method that makes those norms accessible to all—whether believers or not. In his *On the Need for Loving God,* Bernard writes: "Reason and natural justice urge [even] unbelievers to surrender their whole being to God, from whom they received it; [reason and justice] urge them to love God with all their might." Immediately, Bernard adds an admonition directed at himself as a believer: "Faith surely commands that I love him [God] much more [than they], inasmuch as [by faith] I understand how much more God must be valued, since I possess as his gift not only myself but himself as well."[57] For Bernard, faith complements and completes reason,[58] but it does not supersede or supplant it.

C. REASON AND THE LAW

Bernard sees the clergy able to fulfill their teaching function through their mastery of the literary and logical skills taught in the schools of his time. But, as we have seen,[59] Bernard would also have the clergy minister to their flocks by striving to provide them with justice. Again reason provides the method: as logic applied to sense data leads to knowledge of reality, so, too, does rational analysis provide insights into the right ordering of things that is justice.

Bernard's clergy must be judges[60] as well as teachers. They must offer their flocks the institutional structures that will provide them justice; they must labor constantly to reform those structures so that justice will continue to prevail.[61] The law of the Church, canon law, which aims at this justice, is based, for Bernard, on three sources: tradition, authority, and reason. For example, in criticizing excessive claims to power by Pope Eugenius III's curia, Bernard writes:

> I say one thing [on this topic] which is no secret: it is ridiculous for your ministers to try to place themselves over your fellow-priests. Reason does not support this; it does not have the force of ancient tradition; no authority agrees with it.[62]

Reason is a source of law because of its "kinship" to justice. Bernard states this in the form of an allegory in his second *Parable:* "Prudence said: 'Reason, my armor-bearer, will precede us. He is an expert navigator and is well-known to Justice, since he is his blood-brother.' And so Reason led the way, and the rest followed . . . ."[63] More philosophically, Bernard affirms that justice is based on "the unchanging order of divine equity"[64] and, thus, is accessible to reason.

The clergy, who must know justice so that they may provide it, must be trained in the principles and practices of law and justice. Bernard's *Forty-sixth Sermon on the Song of Songs* speaks of the need for this training; there he compares church communities to the "houses of cedar" of the Song of Songs:

> By "houses" [Sg 1:16] understand the ordinary communities of Christians. Those who hold high office [see 1 Tm 2:2] . . . strongly bind them together with laws justly imposed, as beams bind walls, lest, living by their own law and will, they should fall apart like tilting walls and tottering fences [see Ps 61:4] and the whole building fall to the ground and be destroyed. The panels firmly attached to the beams add impressively to the beauty of the house. And this seems to

designate the courteous and disciplined behavior of a well-educated clergy who carry out their duties correctly.[65]

Clerics, both high and low, must be trained in the law that binds them together and all to their flocks.

Bernard's *Life of Malachy* provides a number of references to canon law and, implicitly, to the need for training in it. Bernard praises Malachy for introducing the order of law into the Church of Ireland:

> His eye did not spare [see Dt 7:16; Ez 5:11] whatever he found disordered, shameful, or deformed. . . . So he labored with all his might to thrust such practices from his presence and wipe them out among his people [see Gn 17:14]. The best of legislators, he substituted heavenly laws for all these practices. He laid down laws filled with justice, full of moderation, and deserving of honor. In all the churches, he established the apostolic sanctions and decrees of the holy fathers, and especially the customs of the holy Roman Church.[66]

On the basis of this ecclesiastical law, Malachy "went here and there to sow his seed [see Lk 8:15], arranging and judging church matters with complete authority, like one of the apostles."[67] To support his canonical authority, Malachy resolved to seek the mark of metropolitan power, the *pallium,* from the pope, since "it seemed to him unsatisfactory to engage in such activities without the authority of the apostolic see . . . ."[68] In all this, Bernard praises Malachy's "holiness of life and zeal for justice."[69] In Bernard's mind, zeal for justice and knowledge of the provisions of canon law are clearly correlative.

The *Life of Malachy* clearly reflects Bernard's own knowledge of canon law. Commenting on Malachy's ordination, Bernard exposes that knowledge and, more importantly, his conviction that the canons should be observed in all but the most exceptional cases. Bernard writes:

> Malachy was, however, only about twenty-five years old when he was ordained. If it should seem that canonical form

was violated in both his ordinations, that would be true; he was ordained to the levitical ministry [as priest] when less than twenty-five years old, and to the sacerdotal dignity [of bishop] when less than thirty. This should be attributed to the zeal of the ordaining prelate and to the merits of the ordinand himself. I think this ought not to be condemned when dealing with a saint, but I consider that it must not be the practice when the person is not [so clearly] a saint.[70]

For Bernard, proper procedure is essential to the promotion of justice. He writes Pope Eugenius:

...We cannot abandon the oppressed; we cannot refuse judgment to those who suffer injustice [see Ps 102:6; Ps 145:7]. If cases are not tried and litigants heard, how can judgment be given? Let cases be tried, but in a suitable manner. The way frequently followed now is completely detestable. It would scarcely suit the marketplace, let alone the Church.[71]

The purpose of correct legal procedure is clear in Bernard's protest to Eugenius against the abuse of appeals to the papal curia:

...Bishops are appealed against so that they do not dare dissolve or prohibit illicit marriages. They are appealed against so that they do not dare in any way to punish or restrain pillage, robbery, sacrilege, or any such crime. They are appealed against so that they cannot reject or remove unworthy and disreputable persons from sacred offices or benefices.[72]

Bishops must be free to promote justice according to canonical norms. Bernard writes Bishop Ricuin of Toul:

Mindful of my humble status and the limits of my office, I take the greatest care not to overreach either by assigning punishment to anyone, especially in criminal cases, saving only those persons I recognize as under my jurisdiction. It would be rash of me to undertake what is the business of bishops, since I recognize myself as a sinner and quite unskilled in such matters. When any serious question arises which I do not know how to settle, or cannot settle, or do not dare to settle, I, like everyone else, reserve it for the determination of bishops, as is proper. How could I be secure [in my judgment] without first being fortified by the judgment or counsel of the high priest? Let the sick sheep be looked after by his or her own shepherd, and by a shepherd who knows the canons and the medicine of suitable penance . . . .[73]

If popes, prelates, and—despite his rhetorical humility—even Bernard himself must know proper legal procedure, surely all clerics must study canon law to discover the rational methods by which they can one day provide justice to their flocks.[74]

Bernard would have bishops serve as Noahs in steering the ark of the Church across the sea of life;[75] he would have all clerics assist their steersmen in this ministry. The burdens of that ministry are heavy indeed: they must shepherd their flocks and teach their people; they must provide the Church peace, freedom, and justice.[76] To bear their burdens well, to exercise their ministry successfully, the clergy must be both virtuous and learned. The means Bernard offers are many. The clergy have at their disposal the faith common to all believers. They should be agents in disseminating the charismatic knowledge that comes to them, directly or indirectly, from the Holy Spirit. Through their schooling the clergy have, or should have, not only the literary sophistication needed to mine the Bible for the truths contained, often obscurely, therein, but also the rhetorical skills necessary to disseminate the wisdom they have gained. Bernard would have the clergy master, too, the dialectical skills that enable them to know much of God, themselves, and the moral and legal principles by which they and their flocks can live a life oriented toward the happiness of perfection. Lastly, Bernard offers the clergy a share in some down-to-earth, "non-scientific" sources of wisdom in consideration and counsel. To the last we shall turn next.

V

Common-sense
Consideration and Counsel

aith is, for Bernard, a source of knowledge open to all who would believe. As for charismatic knowledge, the Holy Spirit inspires whom he wills, and those inspired are responsible for disseminating to all the knowledge thus gained. Bernard speaks of "mystical" contemplation only in connection with monks, but, as we shall see, the fruits of contemplation must also be shared through counseling others. The insights discovered through the mastery of the literary arts, the wisdom gained through sensitivity to beauty, are specific to Bernard's program for clerical education. But it is quite clear that these insights, this wisdom, are to be shared by shepherds with their sheep. The same is true of the knowledge acquired through "scientific consideration," the application of logic to data provided by the senses or by Scripture—data appropriated to the search for truth in philosophy, theology, and canon law. Some means to truth are common to all classes; some are specific to a special sort of calling. But all produce knowledge of some part of reality, as well as information useful in dealing with that reality. And all members of the Church, all those wending their pilgrim way toward the goal of happiness, are served by that knowledge.

Although we have seen Bernard casting his epistemological nets widely, he has still other practical, down-to-earth ways to offer his fellow humans as a service to their quest for knowledge and happiness. Bernard urges all members of society and Church to practice meditation, which he most often calls "consideration." Bernard also believes that all those in authority in Church and state, clerics and lay rulers alike, need the aid of counsel in determining how to provide justice to their people. Of the common-sense skills and know-how necessary to the activities of various lay occupations, Bernard speaks little but effectively.

A. PRACTICAL CONSIDERATION

Bernard uses the word consideration in three ways. What he calls "scientific consideration" is the rational investigation of reality employing the tool of logic or dialectics. "Speculative consideration" is the recollection that frees the mind of worldly distractions as a preparation for contemplation of God. What Bernard urges on all manner of folk—monks, clergy, and laity—is "practical consideration."[1] This sort of consideration is not "mystical" contemplation that leads to "the mind's true and sure intuition, the apprehension of truth without doubt." Consideration, or meditation,[2] "can be defined as thought searching for truth, the mind's searching to discern truth."[3] True meditation requires not only this rational activity of the human mind but also the Spirit's gift of intuition, which fructifies that activity. Bernard writes that "the word of God, winged with the Spirit's fire, can cook the raw reflections of the sense-bound human, giving those reflections a spiritual meaning that feeds the mind, inspiring him or her to say: 'My heart became hot within me, and as I mediated a fire burst forth [Ps 38:4].'"[4]

The first object of meditation should be, Bernard believes, oneself. But to know oneself truly, one must know oneself in relationship to other human beings, to the natural world, and to God.[5] This sort of meditation is necessary, Bernard is sure, to the search for humility, for the self-knowledge that is the virtue fundamental to each and every person's pursuit of perfection. The effects of this meditation are indeed many and salutary: "... Consideration purifies its source, the mind. ... It controls the emotions, guides actions, corrects excesses, improves behavior, confers dignity and order on life, and even imparts knowledge of divine and human affairs."[6]

Bernard's approach to monastic meditation is one of great antiquity. As I have written elsewhere, "the meditative, prayerful reading of Scripture was particularly appealing to one who listened day-by-day, year-by-year to the reading of Benedict's *Rule*—a rule which makes *lectio* a cornerstone of the spiritual life."[7] *Lectio*, monastic reading, is a slow chewing, not a rapid devouring, of the scriptural text before one.[8] Like other forms of meditation, it demands human effort, but it also requires an openness to the Spirit, who will, the monk trusts, inform the text with rich meaning.[9] Prayerful reflection on Scripture and scriptural commentaries by the Church Fathers allows the monk to taste "the sweet savor of Christ which is now everywhere [see 2 Cor 2:15]."[10] But it is also part of a program of meditation on, of consideration of, oneself and one's relationship with God, fellow humans, and the whole of creation.

Bernard is sure that meditation is essential to the effective ministry of clerics. Bernard describes the model cleric in his friend Malachy of Armagh, newly consecrated bishop of Down, a man filled with "the humility of holy poverty, the rigor of conventual discipline, the leisure of meditation, constant attendance to prayer...."[11] Leisure, taking time from other activities,[12] is indeed requisite to both the mental effort and the openness to the Spirit necessary for meditation.[13] Taking time from action for mediation also has the effect of making that action more efficacious, and, conversely, "action itself suffers if not preceded by consideration."[14] The leisure of meditation is not sloth; it is the responsible preparation for apostolic labor. Bernard urges Pope Eugenius III to the tasks of his ministry thus: "You should have meditated already; the time for action is at hand.... So act! Consider that this is the time for pruning, but only if meditation has led the way."[15]

Clerical meditation has a threefold effect, Bernard believes; it can be "a source of knowledge, sought for practical application, or used to set your ministry in order and employed on its behalf."[16] The practical application of which Bernard speaks is, I believe, a fostering of personal virtue. Thus, in his third Easter sermon, he offers the image of the leprosy of vice and proposes meditation on the life of Christ as the healing agent. This leprosy, Bernard says, "takes possession of us in seven forms: in possessiveness toward earthly goods, in vaunting rich clothing, in bodily gratification, in two oral forms, and similarly, in two ways of the heart."[17] Although Bernard offers meditation as the cure for all seven, an account of the healing of the first three will, perhaps, illustrate his point adequately:

> The first is the leprosy of the house [see Lv 14:36], which is our desire for the riches of this world. From this we may be cleansed if we immerse ourself in the Jordan, in [reflection on] Christ's descent. For we shall thus realize that he who was rich was made poor for our sake [see 2 Cor 8:9]. . . . Then there is the leprosy of clothing [see Lv 13:47]; by this I mean all the pomp and vanity of this world. From this too you will be washed by immersion in the Jordan when you discover the Christ of the Lord [see Lk 2:26], wrapped in common swaddling clothes [see Lk 2:12], made the reproach of humans and the outcast of the people [see Ps 21:7]. We shall also be cleansed of the flesh in that same Jordan when we, pondering thoroughly the passion of the master, are ashamed at our indulgence in bodily gratification.[18]

Practical consideration, or meditation, thus promotes clerical virtue as well as knowledge essential to clerical ministry.

Although lay folk have received the gift of faith—a method of knowing common to all Christians—they also share with monks and clergy a means of knowing in meditation or consideration. Bernard writes to the newly widowed Queen Melisande of Jerusalem:

> Before God you are a widow, before your people a queen. Consider the queen whose worthy or unworthy deeds cannot be hidden under a bushel basket, but are set up high on a candelabrum, that they may be apparent to all [see Mt 5:15]. Consider the widow whose concern is not now to please her husband [see 1 Cor 7:34] but solely to able to please God.[19]

Through meditation Melisande will not only see herself as God sees her. She will also learn from Christ himself how to fulfill her obligation to provide justice—especially to the poor:

> "The Queen of the South came to hear the wisdom of Solomon [Mt 12:42]," that she might learn how to rule and thus know how to rule herself. "And behold, there is one greater than Solomon here [Mt 12:42]." I speak of Jesus, and him crucified [see 1 Cor 2:2]. Unite yourself to him in ruling yourself; taught by him, you will know how to rule. Learn from him, as a widow, that you might be gentle and humble in heart [see Mt 11:29]; learn from him, as a queen, for he "judges the poor with justice and reproves with equity on behalf of the meek of the earth [Is 11:4]."[20]

Meditation thus enables lay persons, too, in making the moral judgments that will enable them to fulfill their functions in Church and society.[21]

B. THE NEED FOR GOOD COUNSEL

There is still another practical, "non-scientific" means by which monks, clerics, and lay folk alike can attain the virtue and knowledge necessary to their ministry: counsel. Ignoring the good counsel of others is sign of the leprosy of pride of which Bernard speaks in his third Easter sermon:

> Surely, the leprosy of self-counsel is still more dangerous than this [leprosy of self-will], because it is more hidden. The more it increases, the healthier the victim sees himself.... Those so infected are dividers of unity, enemies of peace, destitute of love, swollen with vanity. They please only themselves [see 2 Pt 2:10] and are great only in their own eyes.... What greater pride is there than when one person prefers his or her own judgment to that of the entire community, as if

that person alone possessed the spirit of God [see 1 Cor
7:40]?[22]

The remedy for this form of leprous pride is to follow the Christ who
heard and obeyed the counsel of others. To make this point, Bernard
constructs a homely scene in which the lad Jesus, rebuked by Mary
and Joseph for teaching in the Temple, resolves to leave off his
"Father's business":

> He was not taken with himself; he went down—to the extent
> that he was even subject to them [see Lk 2:51]. Who would
> not be ashamed to be obstinate in his own counsel when
> Wisdom himself abandoned his? Thus he altered his counsel
> so that the work, which he had then begun, he abandoned at
> once, from then until his thirtieth year. For you will find
> nothing concerning his teaching or works from that, his
> twelfth year, until the age of thirty.[23]

Christ himself followed the counsel of others; so, too, must the wise
monk, cleric, or lay person.
    Good counsel requires good counselors, and so Bernard is
demanding in the qualifications necessary to that service. He writes
Ardutius, bishop of Geneva:

> "Take counsel in all things [Si 32:24]," not from everyone
> or anyone, but only from the good. Have good people in
> your council, people good in accommodating themselves to
> you, people with whom you can live comfortably. These will
> be guardians of your life and integrity—and witnesses to it.
> You will be proven good if you have the witness of good
> people.[24]

Bernard is sometimes more specific when describing the qualities
counselors should not have; he tells Archbishop Henry of Mainz that
he, and all bishops, should reject counsel from "mere youths or
worldlings."[25] Bernard writes Pope Eugenius that counselors should

represent a cross section of those to whom the bishop ministers.[26] Bernard also bids Eugenius beware of those who seek the role of counselor:

> Surely such an office should not be had for the asking; appointment must be made through deliberation, not at request. . . . Some ask for others; others ask boldly for themselves. He for whom you are petitioned should be suspect; he who asks for himself is already judged [see Jn 3:18]. . . . A cleric who frequents the curia but is not a member of it belongs, you know, to the same class of self-seekers. Put in the same class with petitioners the person who flatters and speaks so as to please everyone, even if he asks for nothing. It is not the face of the scorpion you should fear; he stings with his tail![27]

But Bernard also couples his grim warnings, based sometimes on his own experience of papal counselors,[28] with assertions that there are indeed advisors available who will fit the bishop's bill: those who are "farsighted in counsel."[29]

To aid clerics in their choice of counselors, Bernard sometimes offers specific recommendations. To Archbishop Bruno of Cologne, Bernard suggests the counsel of Norbert of Xanten: "You have Norbert closer to you [than I], one of whom you can expeditiously inquire about such things. Such a man as he can open the divine mysteries more quickly, since he is known to be closer to God."[30] To Pope Eugenius, Bernard writes that the bishop of Beauvais "should do nothing independently, but arrange everything according to your counsel, on which he totally depends."[31] On behalf of Eugenius, then newly chosen pope, Bernard writes to the cardinals and curial bishops who had seen to his election:

> If you have any power of consolation in you, any virtue of love in the Lord, any pious pity, any compassion in your hearts [see Phil 2:1], assist and work together with him in the ministry to which the Lord has lifted him through you. "Whatever things

are true, whatever seemly, whatever just, whatever holy, whatever worthy of love, and whatever of good report [Phil 4:8]," these suggest to him, of these persuade him, these do, "and the God of peace will be with you [Phil 4:9]."[32]

Bernard is not only helpful in recommending the good counsel of others, he also assumes the role of counselor himself. He writes many letters of counsel to bishops and other clergy; some of them are so lengthy we count them as treatises. Thus, Bernard's letter (42) to Henry, archbishop of Sens, is usually referred to as *De moribus et officio episcoporum (On the Virtues and Office of Bishops)*.[33] Surely the most significant of Bernard's works in this genre is his *On Consideration,* a veritable mirror for popes.[34]

Bernard's counsel was so prized that, on one occasion, the election to the see of Langres in 1138, the chapter of Langres and the metropolitan, the archbishop of Lyon, put the matter in Bernard's hands. Bernard tells the story:

> When I was still in Rome, the archbishop of Lyon arrived. With him came Robert, the dean of Langres, and Canon Olricus. They were seeking permission for the archbishop, and the chapter of Langres, to conduct an election of a bishop. They received a mandate from the pope not to presume to do this without the counsel of religious men. When they sought me out and asked me for this counsel, I replied: "I shall not give it unless I know with certitude that you intend to elect a good and suitable person." They replied that it was their intention to make the matter dependent on my choice and that they would do nothing without my counsel. This they solemnly promised.[35]

In Bernard's eyes, his counsel, and that of others, was crucial, not only in the choice of ministers, but also in the daily exercise of the clerical ministry.

Bernard also offers his counsel to assist lay folk in their ministry. In writing to King Louis VII of France, for instance, Bernard boldly corrects what he perceives as that monarch's errors, strengthening his case by an appeal to the authority of the Holy Spirit:

> I have believed that, touched and enlightened by God, you would see clearly all the evil of your actions and would acknowledge your error. I have believed that, following the advice of all your wiser counselors, you would wish to withdraw your foot from this snare....Although I have been deeply disturbed, I have not utterly despaired of the Spirit's help, whom I perceived had soundly smitten your soul for your past sins....[36]

The Spirit is the hitherto unattended source of Louis's enlightenment, and one of the ways the Spirit speaks is through Louis's counselors—including the self-appointed Bernard.

Bernard would think Suger, abbot of Saint Denis and the now-crusading Louis's regent, is the wisest of counselors because he has attended to the voice of "the Spirit of counsel [see Is 11:2] and consolation [see Ac 9:31]."[37] For another of Louis's counselors, Bishop Jocelin of Soissons, Bernard lists the most important qualifications for that role:

> It pleases me—and pleases many—that the king trusts and confides in you. For I know that you have zealously and assiduously striven for the good of the king and the kingdom's honor, and I know no less that the spirit of counsel [see Is 11:2] is with you. It is only fitting that this ordering and rational principle, this sort of foresight, be in the man of counsel, that he might love, that he might be wise. In the mouth of these two, love and wisdom, shall stand every word of counsel [see 2 Cor 13:1]. If these two come together in one, he [the man of counsel] will be able to utter a good word [see Ps 44:2] and to direct the king's work.[38]

If counsel is not based on love and wisdom, then Bernard fears for the welfare of the kingdom:

. . . If, in the ministry of counsel, either love should abandon
prudence, or prudence its only love, then "woe to the land
where the king is a child [Qo 10:16]!" "May my soul not
come under the counsel of those [Gn 49:6]" who, though
loving me, are not prudent, or of those who, though prudent,
do not love me. Thus fell poor Adam from the steps of eternity, when he walked in the counsel of the impious [see Ps
1:1], of the loving though imprudent Eve, of the prudent
though least loving serpent.[39]

To prudent and loving counselors, King Louis, and all those in
power, must listen. But Louis sometimes scorns their advice, and in so
doing he scorns the Spirit speaking through them, bringing Bernard's
reproof:

It is evident that you are very quickly and capriciously recoil-
ing from the good, sound advice which you had accepted. As
I have heard, you are hastening back to your former evil ways,
to those fresh wounds, which only recently and with good
reason you regretted—by what diabolical counsel, I do not
know.[40]

Louis should, rather, "promise to obtain the counsel of myself and
other good folk."[41] Not only does Bernard offer counsel to Louis,
but when asked he counsels Louis's counselors. Writing to Suger of
Saint Denis, Bernard says: "You have promised that, without my
counsel, you would not act in this matter for any reason, and, if I
were to hide my opinion, in that I should sin."[42]

The more important the matter at hand, the more is counsel
necessary and the more counselors should be sought. The prospect
of a crusading venture to the Holy Land leads Bernard to write Peter
the Venerable, abbot of Cluny:

Our fathers, the bishops of France, together with the lord
king and the princes, are to meet at Chartres, on the third
Sunday after Easter [7 May 1150], to consider this question.
I sincerely hope that we may be favored with your presence.

To carry on this great council correctly requires the counsel
of all the eminent persons [of the kingdom] . . . .[43]

Great causes demand the counsel of the great.

Bernard offers counsel to many of the great lay folk of his time. In
addition to the king of France, Bernard writes letters of advice to the
emperor Lothar, the emperor-elect Conrad III, the kings of Bohemia,
England, Jerusalem, Portugal, Scotland, and Sicily. Bernard also offers
his advice to the dukes of Aquitaine, Burgundy, Brittany, Lotharingia,
and Normandy, and the counts of Anjou, Angoulême, Auvergne, Burgundy, Champagne, Flanders, Nevers, Savoy, and Vermandois.[44] By
and large, the recipients of Bernard's counsel accepted his advice; the
reason is clear, at least so it seems to Bernard. He writes to Count
Theobald of Champagne: "Who am I that such a prince as you should
have cared for one so insignificant, unless you have all along believed
that God was with me?"[45] In Bernard's world, the counsel of contemplatives is viewed as valuable.

That counsel is available to lay women as well as to their male
counterparts.[46] Bernard writes to Mathilda, the duchess of Burgundy:
". . . When I was recently in Dijon, Hugh of Bese pleaded with me that
I might placate your justifiable anger toward him, so that you might
approve his son's marriage. . . . I see no gain for you, rather great danger, if you should prevent the union of those whom God has perhaps
determined to join."[47] And Bernard adds immediately what sounds
more like a command than advice: "Distribute your grain to Christ's
poor, that you may reap your reward with interest in eternity."[48]

Bernard expands the latter part of this counsel in writing to a
friend apparently still more dear, Queen Melisande of Jerusalem:

Take care of pilgrims, the needy, and, especially, prisoners,
"for by such sacrifices God's favor is obtained [Heb 13:16]."
Write to me often; writing will not hurt you, and it will help
both of us if I know more fully and surely your state and
good intentions.[49]

Bernard's affection for Melisande urges him to congratulate her for
seeking the advice of others as well: ". . . My dear uncle Andrew . . .

writes me . . . that you are peaceful and calm, that you are ruling yourself and your kingdom wisely, with the counsel of wise folk. . . ."[50]
However, Bernard believes his own counsel is more objective than
theirs, for he loves her with an unselfish love:

> Accept this brief but useful counsel coming from a far-off
> land [see Jos 9:6], from which, like a small seed, a great har-
> vest will in time spring up. Accept, I say, counsel from the
> hands of a friend who is not seeking his own advantage but
> your honor. No one can give you more dependable counsel
> than one who loves you and not your possessions.[51]

Bernard is thus able to appeal to love in urging his royal correspon-
dents to hear and heed his advice. With Queen Mathilda of England
he invokes sterner medicine: "If you fear God and wish to assent to
my counsel in anything, by all means see to it that that man [William
Fitzherbert] no longer occupies the see of York. . . ."[52] Bernard easily
equates heeding his counsel and fearing God.

But Bernard is fully aware of the limitations of counsel as a
means of securing knowledge of God's will, of discovering the standards by which clerics or lay folk should govern themselves or others.
Counsel may be false because counselors may be false to their function. Bernard writes to the king of the Romans and emperor-elect:

> "I become foolish [2 Cor 12:11]," when I, though a com-
> mon, ignoble person, intrude, as if I were great, into counsels
> of such weight and wisdom—and about such an important
> matter [as the rebellious Romans]. But the more ignoble and
> abject I am, the freer I am to speak what love suggests. And
> so, in my foolishness, I shall add this: if anyone should
> attempt to persuade you to anything different from what I
> have said to you—which I cannot believe—surely he either
> does not love the king or understands little what becomes the
> majesty of the realm. Or else he is convicted of caring more
> for his own interests [see Phil 2:21] than for those of either
> God or king.[53]

Counsel is so common and crucial to the business of rulers that Bernard finds it easy to attribute to evil counselors the wicked deeds of the powerful.[54]

Bernard does offer a partial solution to the problem by making his own counsel available to an astonishing number of people. His letters and the advice he gives in person provide counsel from a person many of his contemporaries thought to be close to the very Source of all truth and justice.[55] However, all twelfth-century lay folk could hardly have turned to him to solve all their problems.

But they could—and did—turn to those specifically charged with teaching them the ways of truth and justice: their clergy. Bernard urges the people of Toulouse:

> Obey your bishop! "Obey those set over you [Heb 13:17]," the teachers of the Church. . . . I remind you, my dear friends, of what I said when I was with you: do not receive any outside or unknown preacher, unless he be sent by your bishop or preaches with the permission of the pope. For "how shall they preach unless they are sent [Rom 10:15]?"[56]

In times of confusion, Bernard tells the Roman people, "gather together, you scattered sheep [Ez 34:5]; return to your pasture; return 'to the shepherd and bishop of your souls [1 Pt 2:25].'"[57] Through the clergy—even those who do not live up to their calling—God will direct his people: "Do what Jesus says, . . . what he commands through his ministers who are in the Church [see 1 Cor 6:4]. Be subject to his vicars, your leaders, not only to those who are gentle and kind, but even those who are overbearing [see 1 Pt 2:18]. . . ."[58]

Bernard sees the sources of knowledge available to the laity as many-faceted. Like monks and clerics, lay folk have faith as a font of truth and meditation as a means of making moral judgments. They can and must listen to the inspiration of the Spirit and the charismatic knowledge he offers. Counsel is a source of information of critical importance in a society in which law is so largely customary, making order and justice heavily dependent on the collective memo-

ries and wisdom of counselors. And lay folk can rely on God's direct-
ing love shining through their shepherds, his clerical vicars.

The great bulk of Bernard's teaching on the sources of knowledge available to the laity is directed toward the governing class
whose ministry he considers crucial to the happiness of all. But the
means to truth he offers to rulers are available to manufacturers and
merchants, to farmers and craftsmen. All lay folk—not only rulers—
are to avail themselves of the ordinary means of obtaining the skills
and guidelines necessary to the proper discharge of their office. The
means to truth of lay folk is not so much a formal epistemology as a
training for what they must know to fulfill their role in society.
Bernard spends much time and ink outlining the means of obtaining
necessary moral guidelines and almost none on the manner of acquir-
ing the basic skills necessary to the lay person's ministry of service. I
think this is because they were so obvious to him and to his audience. Thus Bernard assumes, for example, that those charged with
the defense of society must be "superbly trained in warfare [see Sg
3:8]."[59] A passage from Bernard's moving lamentation over the
death of his brother Gerard also shows this—as well as Bernard's
respect for the dignity of all sorts of lay occupations:

> Both in the greatest things and in the least Gerard was the
> greatest. For example, in the buildings, in the fields, in the
> vegetable gardens, in the water systems—indeed, in all the var-
> ious arts and trades of country folk—who, I say, could fail to
> see his skill in all this sort of work? He could easily function as
> master to the masons, the carpenters and smiths, the farm
> workers, the gardeners, the shoemakers, and the weavers.[60]

VI
The Relationship Between the Paths to Truth

In Bernard's eyes, all the folk who form the flock of Christ have at least two means of discovering the knowledge needed to pursue happiness. These common means are faith[1] and charismatic knowledge.[2] The necessity of counsel Bernard urges on both clerics[3] and lay folk.[4] But the response to the guidance of counsel that Bernard calls obedience is, for him, a necessary part of the path to perfection for all[5]—and surely for monks as well as for lay folk and clerics, for Bernard puts much of his teaching on counsel and the virtue of obedience in a context that is indisputably monastic. For example, in his third Advent sermon, Bernard says: "We [monks] owe our brothers, in the midst of whom we live, counsel and aid, by the law of fraternity and human fellowship. This counsel and aid we wish they would lavish on us as well: counsel which instructs our ignorance, aid which supports us in our infirmity."[6] Counsel is thus available to all, though Bernard alters his emphasis to suit the needs of each social and ecclesial group.

The same is true of Bernard's counsel to seek out the truth through consideration. Those lay folk charged with the administration of justice must seek in meditation the principles on which they can build their lives and ministries.[7] Clerics charged with pastoral care can also learn much about themselves and their ministries through meditation.[8] Monks must also seek, through consideration, the self-knowledge that is necessary to their contemplative calling.

The practice of the meditative, prayerful reading of Scripture is enjoined on monks by the *Rule* of Saint Benedict,[9] and in this Bernard follows with enthusiasm the lead of his monastic father.[10] The specific meditative practices that Bernard enjoins may differ according to the calling of his audience, but his message to all is the same: meditation is a proper means to the exercise of one's ministry.

Bernard believes that all people, including those who do not possess the Christian faith, have at their disposal the ability to reason to the basic truths of existence and to the elementary rules of human conduct.[11] But his call for education in the scientific application of logic is directed only to the clergy, for their pastoral calling requires mastery of the dialectical method.[12] Just as dialectical reasoning is proper to clerics, so is contemplation the means by which monks may learn of fundamental reality.[13]

The knowledge obtained by each calling within society and Church is essential to its ministry to the others. Conversely, each social and ecclesial group requires the ministry of the others and thus depends, albeit indirectly, on the means to knowledge proper to the other groups, or on their special application of methods common to all. Thus, monks, nourished by their contemplative experience of ultimate Reality, follow Saint Paul in sharing the fruits of contemplation with the world.[14] Those fruits include profound insights into the nature of reality, the ordering principle of justice that informs it, and the moral order that reflects both.[15] These insights monks share through their counsel of lay folk and clerics. Those clerics, educated in the literary and dialectical skills necessary to understanding Scripture—and fortified by their mastery of canon law, the meditation necessary to their ministry, and good counsel—preach and teach the truths thus discovered to their fellow pilgrims on the path to perfection. Lay folk, who are charged with governing society, with producing, manufacturing, and distributing the physical necessities and amenities of human life, share the results of their insights—gained through mediation, inspiration, counsel, and practical experience—with monks and clerics. And all profit from the gift of faith and share their special insights into that faith with the others.

A. AN EPISTEMOLOGICAL HIERARCHY?

But are some insights superior to others? At one time I was convinced that Bernard's social and epistemological theories were arranged hierarchically. I thought that, just as Bernard viewed society hierarchically—with the monastic life superior to the clerical vocation, and this in turn superior to the life of lay folk—so Bernard's epistemology was hierarchical: contemplation being superior to reason, which was in turn superior to the various means of ascertaining reality available to lay folk. Thus I could write:

> ... Although [for Bernard] the states of life were all good, there was an ethical factor which established them in a hierarchical relationship. I would argue that Bernard applied the same value hierarchy to the epistemological methods appropriate to the various states of life. ... Bernard had no doubt that the contemplative epistemology he associated with the monastic way of life was at the summit of the hierarchy of means to truth. ... Praise of active life, patronage of scholars, and high regard for the method and goals of the schools were not inconsistent with Bernard's mysticism. The layman, the cleric, and the monk, with their attendant means to the truth, were also prized by Bernard. But the contemplative life of the monk was best, because most efficacious.[16]

A deeper study of Bernard's social theory, of his ecclesiology, as well as a reassessment of his epistemology in the light of that better understood ecclesiology, have convinced me that I was dead wrong.

Bernard's anthropology will not support a hierarchical view of society and Church. If Bernard were hostile to the human body and, consequently, to things of the "flesh," then a hierarchical social structure would inevitably emerge. If one reads Bernard as if he were an neo-platonist—albeit a Christian neo-platonist—then the anthropology that results sees the human body—as all things physical—as one step above non-being and immeasurably inferior to the human soul and spiritual substance. The social theory that results from such a reading is then equally neo-platonic: the greater a social group's involvement in things of this world, in material things, the lower is that group's status in such a social hierarchy. Monks, being spiritual, are at the summit of such a hierarchy; clergy, active in the world, are less "spiritual" and hence assume a lower position; laity, heavily involved in the cares of the world and permitted the physical act of procreation, occupy the lowest rank. The life of people in the world then becomes "worldly life."

It was just such an unconsciously neo-platonic reading that led me to conclude that Bernard's social theory was hierarchical. My assessment was wrong because I had misinterpreted Bernard's anthropology. But Bernard's teaching on the body is not so simple as I had thought, and what emerges from a study of his many texts on the matter[17] is an overwhelmingly positive attitude toward human beings and their bodies. Bernard's anthropology is not neo-platonic, and so his social theory is likewise not susceptible to a neo-platonic interpretation. There is indeed a hierarchical evaluation within Bernard's teaching on vocations, but it is a hierarchy based not on the worthiness of the social class but on the response of the individual to his or her calling—whatever that calling may be. And what is true of Bernard's social theory is equally true of his epistemology.

Bernard uses the adjective *doctus* to describe those who are learned, skilled, versed, or experienced in whatever means to truth pertains to the person's calling, to his or her role in society and Church. Thus, the contemplative experience of monks makes them learned: "The instruction [gained through contemplation] makes us [monks] learned; affective experience makes us wise."[18] By the same token, Bernard writes of clerics: "I am not ignorant of how much the Church's learned men have benefited her, whether by refuting her opponents or by instructing the ignorant."[19] And lay folk, too, can be learned; those knights who are "superbly trained" for warfare Bernard describes as "most learned" *(doctissimi)*.[20] Learned lay folk, learned clerics, and learned monks all make their unique contribution to the knowledge necessary for the welfare of all.

There are indeed passages in Bernard's works that speak—or that seem to speak—of a gradation in the means to truth, in the modes of knowing. One such occurs in his letter/treatise *On Consideration:*

Great is the traveler who is content to consider the use of the senses as the treasure of these citizens [of earth], dispersing that wealth for his or her own benefit and that of many others. The traveler is no less great who uses philosophy to establish the senses as a step toward invisible things, except that the latter method is evidently more pleasant, the former more useful—the latter more fruitful, the former more courageous. But that person is greatest of all who, rejecting this use of things and senses—as much indeed, as permitted to human frailty—has accustomed herself or himself to soar aloft occasionally in contemplation, not by ascending steps but by unexpected ecstasies.[21]

One could interpret this as an assertion that contemplation is superior to the use of reason, which is, in turn, superior to sensation. But Bernard is here speaking of the components of consideration, or meditation, a method he counsels all to use. The senses—properly restrained—are the source of information on which one should reflect; that consideration is made through the exercise of the rational faculties; and, occasionally and for some, the human effort expended in meditation is transcended in contemplation. Bernard presents as the ideal situation the combination of all three. Without the use of the senses and the rational faculties, that use cannot be transcended. Contemplation may indeed be a mode of knowing superior to meditation, but God grants the contemplative experience only rarely[22]—and those to whom it is given bear the responsibility of sharing its fruits with others.[23] There is indeed a sort of "hierarchical" principle here, but only in that God's gifts of knowledge do indeed transcend human efforts to attain it.[24]

The penultimate sentence of *On Consideration* offers an observation that has been taken by some[25] to indicate an epistemological hierarchy in Bernard's thought. Bernard writes Pope Eugenius: "He [God] must yet be sought who has not yet been sufficiently found and who cannot be sought too much, but he is more worthily sought and more easily found by prayer than by discussion."[26] "Discussion" is *disputando* in Bernard's Latin, and, if one were to take it to mean "disputation," it could lead one to the conclusion that Bernard ranked prayer above rational investigation in the search for the truth. There are at least two difficulties with this interpretation. First, "discussion" is clearly Bernard's meaning, as the context of the quotation indicates. Bernard is speaking of his own discursive efforts in the treatise he is now concluding, his own final attempts to help Eugenius to answer the question "What is God?"[27] Second, it seems clear, at least to me, that prayer is scarcely an epistemological method; nowhere, I am convinced, does Bernard speak of prayer as fulfilling an epistemological function. In this quotation Bernard is surely speaking of the efficacy of prayer in seeking to establish a personal relationship with God. In that sense, Bernard is asserting that Eugenius's relationship with God is better served by Eugenius's prayer to God than by Bernard's discussion of God. There is a "hierarchy" here, but it is not an epistemological one.

B. Faith, Reason, and Opinion

The relationship between faith and reason *is* surely an epistemological question. Bernard certainly holds that faith is, in some cases, a better means to truth than reason: "Faith even exceeds the limits of human reason, the capacity of nature, the bounds of experience."[28] For Bernard, faith is certainly efficacious in some matters that are beyond rational inquiry. One such matter is the Christian teaching on the Trinity: "I speak in faith: I believe in—though I do not understand—the eternal and blessed Trinity. I hold fast by faith what I cannot grasp with my mind."[29] Another matter beyond reason, but accessible to faith, is the reality of Jesus' presence in the Eucharist; Bernard affirms that, "in this matter, faith is the source of my riches; my intellect is a pauper."[30] The mystery of the Incarnation is likewise beyond human understanding; it is known only "when we believe more in the oracular than in the ocular, when we hold most firmly to those things which were said and done, doubting not at all."[31] Thus, "if understanding [based on reason] should attempt to break the seal of faith, it is reckoned a burglar, a scrutinizer of majesty [Prv 25:27]."[32]

But if faith holds the seal that reason cannot break, faith has limitations that are transcended, Bernard believes, by reason: "Even though faith is no more uncertain than understanding [based on reason], still it is obscure, as understanding is not."[33] Both faith and reason "possess certain truth, but that of faith is hidden and obscure, that of understanding is naked and manifest...."[34] Within its sphere of competence, reason is superior to faith; beyond that sphere, faith must take precedence.[35]

The fifth book of the treatise *On Consideration* is an excellent source for Bernard's view of the relationship between faith and the understanding that is based on reason. But Bernard casts his epistemological net still wider in that book; opinion joins faith and understanding in his analysis: "Of these [means to truth], understanding relies on reason, and faith on authority, while opinion is supported only by similitude to truth."[36] Unlike faith and understanding "opinion can err...."[37] Faith and reason result in certain truth; "opinion, on the other hand, possesses no certainty but seeks truth through what appears true rather than by grasping hold of it."[38] And this leads to Bernard's definition: "...Opinion is holding something as true which you do not know to be false."[39]

The uncertainty of opinion does not disturb Bernard. There are for him few things that everyone must know, and they are those matters on which everyone's happiness depends. In his *Thirty-sixth Sermon on the Song of Songs*, Bernard summarizes these as self-knowledge and knowledge of God: "But see now how each kind of knowledge is necessary for your well-being; lacking neither you will be capable of salvation."[40] Bernard continues in the next sermon: "Other matters are indifferent: if known they do not bring salvation; ignorance of them does not bring damnation."[41]

If few things need to be known by everyone, some things need to be known only by some. Bernard cites all sorts of skills, arts, crafts, and learning which some must master for the good of society, but which are not necessary for all:

> First, I think, we must discover whether all ignorance is worthy of condemnation. It seems to me that this is not true; all ignorance does not condemn. There are many matters—innumerable matters—of which one may know nothing without detriment to salvation. For example, if you are ignorant

of the craftsmen's arts, whether of the carpenter or the mason or any other of those various skills which are practiced by people for the purposes of this present life, does this impede your salvation? Even lacking knowledge of all those arts which are called liberal—as much as those studies may be more honorably and usefully taught and practiced—how many people have been saved . . . ?[42]

As worthy—indeed, indispensable—as this knowledge is, ignorance of these matters does not disturb the well-being of those whose ministry to society and Church does not require their mastery.

There are some matters that need not be known at all, and so certitude about them is not necessary to anyone. And these matters include many theological questions. For example, Bernard asserts that the existence of angels—and many things about them—

we hold by faith. But, as for their bodies, some are doubtful not only about their source but whether they exist at all. Because of this, if anyone should judge this more a matter of opinion, I do not dispute his or her judgment. . . . Likewise, certain [angelic] names are known to us by hearing, through which we can, to some extent, detect and discern the offices of these blessed ones, their merits, dignities, grades, and orders—even though the hearing of mortals does not perceive them clearly. But what does not come by hearing does not come from faith, for "faith comes from hearing [Rom 10:17]." Therefore, we speak of these as matters of opinion.[43]

Opinion is legitimate, though certainty must not be claimed for it. Opinions may thus differ legitimately, as have the Fathers' opinions on angels. "But," says Bernard, "I think that knowledge of these things will not contribute greatly to your perfection."[44] The utility of knowledge thus seems to be the criterion for seeking it.

Is, then, opinion to be avoided? No, not even on questions the answers to which seem beyond obvious utility. Bernard writes:

> What if there were living things about which we might
> [someday] discover how unfit they were for their own utility
> and not at all fit to serve human needs? ... Even if those crea-
> tures did not provide food or perform a service, they would
> certainly challenge the natural capacity of those who surely
> attend, through the use of reason, to everything which pro-
> motes the general understanding by which the invisible
> things of God are clearly seen, being understood by the
> things which are made [see Rom 1:20].[45]

The rational process, on which many opinions are based, serves to
enlighten humans about their God-given world, and thus to apprehend something of him who is their author. No object is unworthy
of this search, even though the knowledge that results is not certain.

Thus Bernard feels free to form opinions on a variety of subjects,
free to present opinions, and free to change his mind when the occasion warrants. For example, Bernard is capable of teaching, in his *On
Grace and Free Choice,* that humans, created in the image and likeness of God, lose, in the Fall, the likeness but not the image.[46] Yet, in
his eightieth through eighty-second sermons on the Song of Songs,
and in his second sermon on the Nativity, Bernard teaches that the
image is lost, but not the likeness.[47] He is well aware of his apparent
inconsistency; he concludes his *Eighty-first Sermon on the Song of
Songs* with this acknowledgment:

> In the book I wrote on grace and free choice, one can read
> discussions of the image and likeness which are, perhaps, dif-
> ferent from these, but not, I think, opposite. You have read
> that book; you have heard these words. Which should be
> accepted I leave to your judgment; if you think one of them
> better, in that I rejoice and shall rejoice [see Phil 1:18].[48]

Various opinions, even on such important questions, are legitimately
held and cheerfully changed.

But, Bernard holds, opinions should not be arbitrary. Opinions
can be erroneous, and one must be cautious in affirming that of

which one is ignorant: "It is one thing to hold one or another position as an opinion when you are not certain; it quite another to affirm what you do not know."[49] In forming an opinion, Bernard declares, one must consult the tradition and authority of the Church, the opinions of the Fathers, and employ rigorous logical analysis.[50]

It is most important, Bernard cautions, to avoid confusing faith, understanding, and opinion. He writes in the treatise *On Consideration:*

> Above all, we must beware of confusion, so that faith does not fasten onto the uncertainty of opinion or opinion call into question what is firm and fixed in faith. Know this: opinion is foolhardy if it advances [unwarranted] assertions; faith is feeble if it hesitates; so too, if understanding should attempt to break the seal of faith, it is reckoned a burglar, a scrutinizer of majesty [see Prv 25:27].[51]

One must be sensitive to the method one employs in seeking the truth. One must be equally sensitive to the degree of certainty afforded by one's method.

One of the best examples of Bernard's own sensitivity to method and certainty is in his *Steps of Humility and Pride;* in sections 6 through 16, he considers the question whether the Second Person of the Trinity learned from his Incarnation. Bernard favors an affirmative answer:

> ... From the example of our Savior you will know how you must come to the aid of your neighbor. He willed to suffer that he might know compassion [see Heb 2:18]; to learn mercy he embraced misery. It is written: "And he learned obedience from the things he suffered [Heb 5:8]," and he learned mercy in the same way. Not that he did not know how to be merciful before; his mercy is from eternity to eternity [see Ps 102:17]. But what he knew from his nature from eternity he learned from experience in time.[52]

Bernard recognizes that his position is controversial, and that another opinion can be rationally derived from scriptural authority:

But perhaps you think it hard that I said that Christ, the wisdom of God [see 1 Cor 1:24], had learned mercy, as if he, through whom all things were made [see Jn 1:3], could ever have been ignorant about anything that exists. Especially so since the passage from the Letter to the Hebrews, which I cited as corroboration, can be understood in another sense—a sense not absurd—than that which I have advanced....[53]

After recounting the opposing interpretation, Bernard replies: "I do not deny this understanding, which may be correct. But there is another text in the same letter which seems to bear out the first interpretation...."[54] And Bernard proceeds to cite the text and reflect on it. In the course of his argument, Bernard cites a passage from Mark—misquoting it in the process. This causes Bernard to attach a retraction to his treatise, which reads in part:

In this little work, I cited rather improvidently the passage from the Gospel in which the Lord said that he did not know the day of the last judgment; this I did to bolster my argument and to strengthen its acceptance. Afterward I discovered that the passage was not written in the Gospel at all! The text reads: "Not even the son knows [Mk 13:32]." I wrote: "Not even the Son of Man knows"—thus, deceived rather than wishing to mislead, I quoted the words, but not the meaning, incorrectly from memory. So I based on this false citation the whole sequence of arguments I was trying to demonstrate. Since I discovered my error long after I had sent out the book and many copies had been made, and since I could not track down all the copies containing the error, I have thought it necessary to have recourse to the remedy of confession.[55]

The whole argument, and this retraction, demonstrates Bernard's method of theologizing: his dependence on Scripture, his closely reasoned analysis, his determination to distinguish theological opinion from dogmatic assertion, and his willingness to admit error. The retraction continues:

In another place I put forward an opinion on the Seraphim which I have never heard nor read. My reader will well note that I cautiously used the words "I think." By this, I wished to indicate nothing more than my opinion, for I was not able to support it with certainty from Scripture.[56]

VII
Inconsistency and Order

ernard's writings on the society and Church of his time are
filled with many apparent inconsistencies; there are as many
apparent contradictions in Bernard's words on epistemological
questions. From the beginning of my work on Bernard, I have been
concerned—some might say obsessed—with these seemingly contra-
dictory statements on the means to the truth.[1] My fascination with
this question is based on my continuing conviction that epistemology
is a crucial key to culture. In an article honoring the eighth centenary
of Bernard's canonization, I wrote:

> To "understand an age" would seem a hopeless task, even in
> the case of an age as relatively unified and consistent as the
> early twelfth century. Nevertheless, we historians persist in
> that task, and there is, I believe, an approach which is useful
> —perhaps the most useful—in our endeavor. I believe that
> most fundamental to the understanding of the *Weltanschauung*
> of an age is the study of the means to truth of that culture, for
> one's whole way of life is inextricably bound up with the way
> one seeks to solve the secrets of one's environment and attempts
> to obtain at least a measure of consistency.[2]

One possible solution to the many inconsistencies—or apparent
inconsistencies—in Bernard's epistemology is relatively simple: like
most great thinkers, his thought developed and changed as his penetrating mind matured in response to new situations and questions.

But this explanation will not work for Bernard, for we know, as a result of Jean Leclercq's labors,[3] that Bernard edited and reedited his works, so that any apparent contradictions are either real inconsistencies or deliberate attempts to approach a question from different though perhaps consistent standpoints.[4]

The sheer magnitude of Bernard's literary legacy makes it difficult to determine the degree of Bernard's inconsistency and the possible reasons for it. The complexity of Bernard's thought adds to the difficulty; as Goswinus Verschelden has said: "Whoever applies himself seriously to the reading and study of Bernard's majestic works inevitably gets the discouraging impression that he is standing before a complex and exceedingly rich life and teaching, to which he is missing the correct key."[5] Even without a claim to the right key, I shall attempt, in the pages that follow, to unlock Bernard's storehouse of apparent epistemological inconsistencies.

A. SHEPHERDS AND SCHOLARS

> To this day he [Bernard] confesses that what competence he has in understanding the Scriptures, whatever spiritual sensitivity he has for them, stems mostly from his meditation or prayer in woodland or field. Among his friends he jokes merrily of having had no other teachers for such lessons than oaks and beeches.[6]

William of Saint Thierry paints this bucolic picture in his biography of his friend. And there is some evidence that William's depiction is faithful to Bernard's thought, for Bernard writes in much the same vein to another friend, Aelred of Rievaulx, when describing the circumstances which led Aelred to write the *Mirror of Love*. Bernard first rehearses Aelred's objections to the task assigned:

> You pointed out the reasons for your inability, saying that you are little schooled in grammatical matters—quite to the contrary, almost illiterate—and that you have come to the desert not from the schools but from the kitchens. There,

living a rustic and rough life amid rocks and mountains, you sweat with ax and maul [see 1 K 6:7] for your daily bread. There one learns to be silent rather than to speak [see RB 6]; there the orator's elevator shoes are not allowed beneath the garb of poor fishermen.[7]

Bernard objects to Aelred's arguments with an apparent appeal to the superiority of sweat over scholarship:

I accept your excuses most gratefully, but I think they fan still more, rather than extinguish, the spark [see 2 Sm 14:7] of my desire. It would taste still sweeter to me if you produce something you have learned in the school of the Holy Spirit, rather than of some grammarian.... So I think that, with your maul, you will hammer out for yourself from those rocks something which you would not have gotten, by the keenness of your talented mind, from the bookshelves of the schoolmasters. I think that at times you will sense, in the midday's heat, in the shade of the trees, something you would never learn in the schools.[8]

The image of the rude rustic obtaining and sharing knowledge more profound than that of the professor seems to counter Bernard's support of scholarly study.

Even setting aside the clearly rhetorical character of the letter, one might explain away Bernard's apparently anti-intellectual stance by remembering that the recipient was a monk, not a cleric for whom learning was required by Bernard. Yet Bernard presents the same position in writing to a cleric and scholar, Henry Murdac: "...You will find more [wisdom] in forests than in books. Woods and stones will teach you what you cannot hear from professors. Do you suppose you cannot suck 'honey from rock and oil out of the hardest stone [Dt 32:13]'? Do you predict that mountains cannot rain sweetness, hills not flow forth milk and honey [see Jl 3:18], and valleys not abound with grain [see Ps 64:14]?"[9]

Though free of the rural references in, of the bucolic tone of, this letter to Henry, Bernard's message to Thomas of Saint Omar is basically the same: "You are deceived, my son, you are deceived if you think to find among the teachers of the world what is attained, through God's gift, only by Christ's disciples, by those who disregard the world. This knowledge is not taught by reading but by unction [see 1 Jn 2:27], not by the letter but by the spirit [see 2 Cor 3:6], not by instruction but by exercise in the Lord's mandates."[10] The same sentiment Bernard expresses to a certain T.:

> I believe it was he [the Spirit of Truth] who spoke with me through your mouth about your conversion. See, therefore, that you do not turn aside to the right or the left [see Nm 20:17], but come to Clairvaux "according to your word [Ps 118:25]."... Do not bring forward any excuses. If study is your reason, if you still wish to be taught and be under a schoolmaster, "the Master is present and calls you [Jn 11:28]," he, quite clearly, "in whom are hidden all the treasures of wisdom [Col 2:3]." He it is "who teaches humans knowledge [Ps 93:10]," who "makes the tongues of infants eloquent [Ws 10:21]," "who opens and no one closes, who closes and no one opens [Rv 3:7]."[11]

All this makes Bernard sound as if scholarship were a vain pursuit when compared with the insights into reality to be obtained in monastic meditation.

Indeed, Geoffrey of Auxerre, who left his studies at Paris to follow Bernard to Clairvaux after hearing the sermon called *On Conversion,* tells us of the motivation for his exodus: "A large number of clerics had gathered, since they always sought the word of God from him. Three of them in succession were filled with compunction and were converted from vain studies to the cultivation of true wisdom. They renounced the world and joined the family of God."[12] "Vain studies" is a phrase that Bernard also uses. He writes Master Walter of Chaumont, probably a professor at Paris: "As often as the sweetest memory of you enters my soul, 'I grieve for you [2 Sm 1:26],' my dear Walter, thinking much of... your noble character, which you waste in vain studies when you pursue transitory goals in such rewards, not in Christ, their author."[13] Studies may indeed be vain when the most important information about human happiness is made known not to scholars but to shepherds. Bernard writes of the nativity of Jesus in the second of his sermons on the Song of Songs: "Fortunate were those shepherds keeping their night watch [see Lk 2:8], for they had been worthy of the sight of this sign. Even then he was hiding himself from the wise and prudent and revealing himself to little ones [see Mt 11:25; Lk 10:21]."[14] All this seems a powerful indictment of learning, the very learning that Bernard praises in pastors, the learning that leads Bernard to befriend scholars and offer his support to students.[15]

What is one to make of all this? How can Bernard escape the charge of inconsistency? I think one must take all of Bernard's remarks seriously—even those betraying hyperbole or satire. I think, too, that one must always be aware of Bernard's audience and, thus, the purpose of his rhetoric.

Rhetorical overstatement is surely the basis of Aelred's claim to virtual illiteracy—and of Bernard's restatement of it. It is highly likely—indeed, virtually certain—that Bernard had read Aelred's *Mirror of Love* before sending the letter urging him to write it.[16] Bernard thus knew well Aelred's literary and theological competence—a knowledge Bernard could hardly have escaped in his capacity as "father immediate"[17] of Aelred's monastery of Rievaulx. But Bernard's rhetoric is not empty. Bernard is convinced that the "rustic and rough life" of the Cistercian monastery provides an ideal environment for the "silence" that senses, through meditation, the significance of much about oneself, about one's world, and about the God who created both. In his seventh *Parable*, Bernard has a monk, "a rough country man,"[18] say to his Lord: "Here [in the monastery] precious fabrics will be unrolled: readings, meditations, prayers, contemplations...."[19] Monastic mediation is a fruitful source of knowledge, and the rural setting of the Cistercian cloister promotes its acquisition. But this does not deny the clergy their source of knowledge in scholarship.

What then of Bernard's admonitions to Henry Murdac, to Thomas of Saint Omar, to T., and to the young scholars of Paris, the last of which led Geoffrey of Auxerre to forsake his studies for the quiet of Clairvaux? If the Henry the scholar "will find more in forests

than in books," if "woods and stones will teach . . . [him] what
he . . . cannot learn from professors," are there not then epistemological implications in Bernard's admonition to leave the academy for the
cloister, presumably a better location for learning? What of Thomas
of Omar? Must he turn his back on the "teachers of the world" to
embrace in the monastery the "knowledge which is hardly easy to
apprehend unless one is crucified to the world," and attained by only
"those who disregard the world"? Apparently, the proper schoolmas-
ter for T. is Christ, and to find him that student must leave his books
and "come to Clairvaux . . . ."

The crucial information that makes sense of Bernard's apparent
inconsistency is the context of his admonitions to his hearers to forsake scholarship and embrace the monastic life and means to knowledge. In two of these cases, the recipient of Bernard's admonitions
has already resolved to be a monk and then has found some excuse
to delay his entrance. Bernard writes that Thomas of Saint Omar
"had vowed with ardent desire to join our [Cistercian] order and our
house [at Clairvaux], had begun to be seduced [from his intent], and
so little by little to grow cold . . . ."[20] Bernard is clearly employing the
full force of his rhetoric to persuade Thomas to fulfill his vow.
Bernard likewise urges T. to "remember your promise, in which you
have given me hope [see Ps 118:49]."[21] Bernard clearly believes that,
in some cases, a failure to fulfill one's vow to enter the monastic life
is evidence of a failure to live up to one's potential.

His admonitions are part of a consistent, though complex, pattern of thought. Bernard also urges Romanus, a subdeacon in the
Roman curia, to leave the world and come to the cloister.[22] His letter
to Geoffrey of Liseaux is still more vehement in urging embrace of
the monastic life.[23] In both cases, it is clear that the recipient has
promised himself to the monastic life and then withdrawn or post-
poned the actual entry. But Bernard is quite capable of approving
such postponement when the needs of the individual—for example,
those of Count William of Nevers[24]—dictate. This is the point. In the
some fourteen of Bernard's monastic "recruitment letters," his basic
concern is for the welfare of the individual and the fulfillment of the
personal needs of the aspirant.[25] Sometimes Bernard will support
entry into a monastery but counsel against a Cistercian house. Some-

times he approves a Cistercian commitment; sometimes he suggests a Cistercian house other than his own. Nine of the letters indicate the recipients have promised to come to a Cistercian cloister or have clearly indicated their desire to do so.[26] Bernard's obvious concern in all of these cases is to assist the recipients of his letters to choose a life appropriate to their personal needs, to aid individuals in the pursuit of a life that will help them achieve their own perfection. Not all of these letters contain references to epistemological questions, but the same principle is applicable: if monastic meditation while hidden "bodily in cloisters and forests"[27] is more responsive to the individual's needs than study in the schools, then one should follow that monastic means to truth.

The case of Henry Murdoc is somewhat different. Bernard does not tell us that Henry had promised to become a monk—although, as a matter of fact, he would come to enter Clairvaux.[28] But the tone of Bernard's letter indicates that Henry was, at the time of writing, a young man filled with uncertainty about his future. "What wonder is it," Bernard says, "if, as you are tossed to and fro between prosperity and adversity, you have not yet gained a foothold on a rock [see Ps 39:3]."[29] Once more Bernard exhibits his conviction that individual needs take precedence over abstract principles; however worthy the life of learning, it is not for all.

The case of Geoffrey of Auxerre and his fellow students is still different. Bernard does indeed urge their conversion, and the sermon *On Conversion* which Geoffrey and his colleagues heard is filled with harsh criticism of the life of Parisian scholars. For example, Bernard tells those students:

> Little children, "who warned you to flee from the wrath to come [Mt 3:7]"? No one deserves greater wrath than the enemy simulating friendship. "Judas, you betray the Son of humankind with a kiss [Lk 22:48]," you, a familiar friend, who took sweet foods with him [see Ps 54:14–15], who have dipped your hand in the same small dish [see Mt 26:23]. You have no share in the prayer he prayed to his Father: "Father, forgive them, for they do not know what they do [Lk 23:34]."[30]

Bernard tells his hearers that they have betrayed their own, their clerical way of life,[31] and he contrasts their behavior with the virtues
demanded of the clerical vocation.[32] But he does not criticize that
vocation or its means to truth. Bernard's sermon is indeed an attempt
to convert the students of Paris, not to the monastic life but to a more
virtuous clerical life.

Why, then, do Geoffrey and his small band[33] leave their studies to
follow Bernard to Clairvaux? There is one passage in *On Conversion*
that could be considered an appeal to embrace the monastic life.
Bernard urges his hearers: "Flee from the midst of Babylon [see Jer
51:6]! Flee and save your souls [see Jer 48:6]! Flock to the cities of
refuge [see Jos 21:36] where you can do penance for the past, obtain
grace for the present, and confidently await future glory."[34] If Geoffrey
understood "cities of refuge" to mean "monasteries," then he might
well have seized on this passage to justify his coming to Clairvaux.

Bernard enunciates his own position on conversion to the monastic life in a letter to Thurstan, archbishop of York. Thurstan has
expressed his desire to become a monk; Bernard advises against it:
such an abandonment of Thurstan's pastoral change is permissible
only if he has sinned gravely or has the permission of the pope.[35] In
the sermon *On Conversion,* there is no mention of permission, but
Bernard clearly sees grave fault in his audience. Recognition by Geoffrey that he was "an exceedingly adverse and perverse man"[36] may
indeed have led him to embrace monasticism.

But what of the "vain studies" that Geoffrey left behind? If
Bernard urges the Parisian students to convert to a virtuous clerical
life—wishing only those whose needs demand it to follow him to
Clairvaux—what does *On Conversion* have to say of epistemological
questions? Another passage from the sermon might seem to bear an
anti-intellectual message:

> ...[Of] that hundredfold [reward; see Mt 19:29] presented
> in this world to those who disregard the world, do not hope
> to hear me singing the praises. It is the Spirit alone who
> reveals this [see 1 Cor 2:10]. You will consult books to no
> avail; you must, rather, seek experience of it.... Not erudi-

tion but unction teaches it [see 1 Jn 2:27]; not science but conscience comprehends it.[37]

One might see a rejection of learning in this passage, but Bernard nowhere claims that all things are susceptible to scholarly analysis. The passage has, I think, little or no epistemological significance. The scholars of Paris have not led virtuous lives, Bernard says; the experience of virtue's reward is thus denied them. It is possible that Bernard agrees with Geoffrey that *his* studies have been vainly pursued, but Bernard does not think scholarship a vain pursuit.[38]

What of the "vain studies" of Master Walter of Chaumont? Bernard speaks of the sense in which those studies are vain:

> ... Let us suppose, for the moment, that you may ascribe to yourself all this [your noble birth, fit body, fine appearance, quick mind, useful erudition, and honest habits], that you may glory in the praise [see Ps 105:47] they elicit, that you may "be called teacher by the people [Mt 23:7]," and that you may win for yourself a great name—at least on earth [see 2 Sm 7:9]. What will be left to you of all this after death, when, perhaps, only the memory of them will be left on earth—and this too only barely? It is truly written: "They have slept their sleep, and all the men of riches have found nothing in their hands [Ps 75:6]."[39]

Bernard likens Walter's life to that of a brute beast:

> If this [sleep] is the end of all your labors—forgive me for saying so—what more do you have than a beast of burden? The same is true of your steed; when it dies, all you will be able say of it is that it was a good animal. Ask yourself what will be the response when you stand before the terrifying tribunal, the response of him from whom you have received your life—and such a life—in vain [see Ps 23:4], if you were discover that you still have not prepared your immortal and rational spirit more than any one of your animals....[40]

Clearly, Bernard judges that Walter's problem is not intellectual but moral. Clearly, Walter's studies are vain, not in the sense that scholarship is unfruitful in the search for knowledge, but in the sense that his scholarly life is lived without adequate regard for the virtues that will bring him happiness. The conversion Bernard seeks with all his persuasive powers is not to a monastic life but to a suitable clerical life which will exhibit both virtue and learning.

Bernard would make the clergy shepherds of souls, not of ordinary sheep. The sheep pastures he would leave to the monk, and to those whose needs demand pasturing within the monastic fold.

B. The Dangers in Knowledge

Bernard surely holds that knowledge, however obtained, carries both burdens and dangers. Knowledge derived from reason and from experience—even from meditation—can be a source of pride and other vice. These dangers lead Bernard to a disturbing declaration in his *On Consideration*. After discussing the epistemological efficacy of faith, reason, and opinion, he asserts: "However, we prefer to know nothing more than that which we already know by faith."[41] Given Bernard's many positive comments on reason and opinion in the same treatise, how is one to understand this statement? It seems at least inconsistent, at worst evidence of obscurantism.

The principal danger of knowledge, Bernard believes, is that it can lead to pride. In his fourth sermon on the Ascension, Bernard compares the pursuit of knowledge to a mountain that the devil has successfully tempted humans to climb:

> Knowledge which puffs up [see 1 Cor 8:1] is a most evil mountain; yet even today you see many of the children of Adam crawling up it with eager craving, as if they did not know how far their father descended by his ascent of that mountain, or, rather, how heavily he fell, and how much his entire posterity was cast down and shattered by it.... The example of our father Adam does not call us back [from this ascent], nor does our own good sense and the experience of

harsh necessity to which we have been handed over by the
senseless appetite for knowledge.[42]

This senseless desire affects members of all callings in the Church, of
all classes of society. All sorts of people—monks, clerics, and lay
folk—seek knowledge by the means Bernard has described as appropriate to their calling—and which he now seems to condemn:

> You may see one eagerly striving for knowledge through
> learning, another for the knowledge which undergirds the
> management of the world's affairs. You may see this one
> ardently striving to maintain pleasing opinions which are dis-
> pleasing to God; you may see that one eagerly pursuing
> knowledge of the various arts and crafts. So intensely does
> each pursue knowledge that no one considers it work if only
> one can be considered more learned than the others. Thus
> they build up Babel [see Gn 11:4–9] and think they will
> attain likeness to God [see Gn 1:27]. Thus they crave what
> will do them no good and neglect what profits them.[43]

Clerics and those aspiring to clerical preference through their studies,
lay folk from rulers to merchants and manufacturers to craftsmen and
farmers, all share an inordinate desire for knowledge, for the knowledge that puffs them up with pride.

Monks are not exempt; their pride is fueled by remembering and
mentally reliving vices both physical and intellectual:

> From time to time we hear some who have taken the monastic
> habit and professed the religious life recalling and boasting
> shamelessly of their past misdeeds, for example, how they
> engaged manfully in tournaments or subtly in learned debates,
> or, indeed, in other vanities pleasing by worldly standards but
> destructive, indeed ruinous, to the soul's health . . . .[44]

Not only that, but the monk's very contemplative life and environment can also be an occasion for pride in knowing.[45] Thus, knowledge may puff up monks as well as clerics or lay folk.

However, for Bernard, it is not knowledge but pride that is the problem. Immediately following Bernard's generous praise of the learned and their scholarship in the *Thirty-sixth Sermon on the Song of Songs,*[46] he continues:

> But I recall reading: "Knowledge puffs up [1 Cor 8:1]," and also: "Whoever increases in knowledge, increases in trouble [Qo 1:8]." You see that there are different kinds of knowledge; one puffs up and the other saddens.... Without doubt you prefer that which troubles to that which inflates; for the inflation simulates health but stimulates trouble.[47]

For Bernard, humility, self-knowledge, is the basic virtue on which all else depends in the pursuit of perfection.[48] Humility is an intellectual virtue, effecting the perfection of the intellect, the human faculty designed for knowing. Knowledge that puffs one up with pride, knowledge that leads to the pride of self-deception, promotes vice, not virtue.[49] Knowledge is in itself good;[50] it is the use one makes of it that can be vicious.

Knowledge is potentially destructive to another virtue, love. And so Bernard can write: "... The wine of worldly knowledge can intoxicate, but with curiosity, not love; it fills but does not nourish; it puffs up [see 1 Cor 8:1] without building up; it makes one drunk without strengthening one very much."[51] Since, for Bernard, love, the perfection of the will, depends on the perfection of the intellect in humility[52]—since one must know in order to choose—the knowledge that puffs one up with pride is equally destructive to the volitional virtue of love.

But, for Bernard, this very relationship of love to knowledge is the means of overcoming the potential danger of the latter. Without love, even the most fundamental realities of the human condition and situation are not adequately known or properly understood. Bernard reports that "... the apostle says: 'The love of God has been poured into our hearts by the Holy Spirit who has been given us [Rom 5:5].' And perhaps that is the reason we do not read about those who, knowing God, did not glorify him as God [see Rom 1:21], that they knew by the Holy Spirit's revelation, since, although they knew, they did not love."[53] True wisdom thus depends on a loving response to whatever knowledge one may obtain by whatever means. Bernard writes: "One may know as much as one wishes, but I should not call one wise unless she or he were in awe of God, unless she or he loved God. How can I call a person perfect in wisdom whom I see is only a beginner? For 'the beginning of wisdom is awe before the Lord [Ps 110:10],' but its perfection is love...."[54] Knowledge without love leads one astray, but that is not an admonition to forsake the life of learning: "What would erudition do in the absence of love? It would puff up [see 1 Cor 8:1]. What would love do in the absence of erudition? It would go astray. Thus they went astray, of whom it is said: 'I give witness of them, that they have zeal for God, but not according to knowledge [Rom 10:2].'"[55] Learning of all sorts provides the knowledge without which one cannot properly choose. But, without well-ordered choice, which is precisely what Bernard means by "love,"[56] knowledge is indeed vain and learning a vain pursuit.[57]

Conversely, the dangers of knowledge can be overcome by living a virtuous life, a life of love in humility:

> What profit can any amount of knowledge bring us which is not less than the glory of being numbered among God's children? Small indeed! The earth itself and its fullness [see Ps 23:1] cannot be compared to it, even if one of us were given possession of all of it. On the other hand, if we remain ignorant of God, how can we hope in him whom we do not know? If we are ignorant of ourselves, how can we be humble, thinking ourselves to be something when we are nothing [see Gal 6:3]? We know that neither the proud nor the hopeless have part or fellowship in the lot of the saints [see Col 1:12].[58]

The acquisition of knowledge brings no dangers that the spiritually mature person cannot overcome. For Bernard, the virtues of humility and love are as necessary to the search for truth as they are for all other of life's activities—and for the realization of the truth that is God.

C. CURIOSITY

"The first step of pride is curiosity," Bernard tells his monks in his *On the Steps of Humility and Pride,*[59] and he continues:

> You discover it by these kinds of signs: if you should see a
> monk, whom you previously trusted confidently, beginning
> to roam with his eyes, hold his head erect, prick up his ears—
> whenever he stands, walks, or sits—you may recognize the
> changed inner man from the movements of the outer. For
> the perverse person "winks with the eye, nudges with the
> foot, speaks with the finger [Prv 6:12–13]." From this
> unusual motion of the body one detects a new disease in the
> soul, which grows slack in looking to herself, and whose
> neglect of herself makes her curious about other matters.
> Since she does not know herself, she is sent out to pasture
> her kids [see Sg 1:7]. I have rightly called the eyes and ears
> kids, which signify sin; for, just as death comes into the
> world through sin [see Rom 5:12], so by these windows it
> enters the mind [see Jer 9:21]. So the curious one occupies
> himself with pasturing these, since he no longer cares to
> know how he has left himself within.[60]

Curiosity is not only the first step on the path to pride, it is the final
obstacle to overcome in the life of virtue.[61] Curiosity is so fundamental to monastic vice that, in his treatise on humility and pride, Bernard
allots nearly as much space to curiosity, the first step of pride, as he
does to the all the other eleven steps together.[62]

 It would seem that the prerequisite to all scholarly activity is the
stimulation of the desire to know, and thus Bernard seems to exclude
intellectual endeavor in forbidding curiosity.[63] It might be argued that
the *Steps* are clearly addressed to monks—the work is, after all, a commentary on the *Rule* of Saint Benedict,[64] based on sermons on the
subject delivered to his monks[65]—and that it is therefore intended to
forbid curiosity only to monks. But Bernard offers the same harsh condemnation of curiosity in his sermon *On Conversion,* preached to the
scholars of Paris. In one section of his address turned treatise, Bernard

likens vices of the disordered human will to the sad antics and ailments of a crazy hag:

> Then the little old woman springs up madly and, totally oblivious to all her feebleness, storms out with her hair all disheveled, her clothes torn, her breast bare, scratching her sores, gnashing her teeth [see Ps 34:16; Mk 9:17], shriveling up, and infecting even the air with her poisonous breath.... [She exclaims]: "...If only you could have cut out the threefold malignity of the terrible disease from which I suffer; I cannot. I am voluptuous; I am curious; I am ambitious. Because of this triple ulcer, there is no health in me from the soles of my feet to the top of my head [see Is 1:6]."[66]

This pitiful soul, the pitiful will, is not only "given over to passionate pleasure..., her roving feet and undisciplined eyes are enslaved by curiosity."[67] Curiosity is thus as debilitating a vice for scholars as for monks.

Curiosity is a vice pursued in vain, Bernard tells the scholars of Paris, for it brings little consolation and much dissatisfaction:

> ...You will find that curiosity brings no happiness to humans. It brings only empty, useless, and futile consolation. I cannot imagine calling down a harsher curse than that one should always get what one asks for, when, fleeing sweet repose, one is seduced by such restlessness. It is clear, surely, that there is nothing in all these pleasures which brings benefits more than transitory.[68]

As with cupidity, "thus it is with curiosity, in which also 'the eye is not satisfied in seeing or the ear filled in hearing [Qo 1:8].'"[69] How clerics are to pursue scholarship without the stimulus of the desire to know, Bernard does not tell his Parisian audience.

He does offer to everyone devastating descriptions of curiosity. It is a perversion of the intellect: "...Led astray by curiosity, a person becomes like any other [animal], ignorant of having received more than they."[70] Curiosity ranks with vanity and voluptuousness as a "serious sacrilege."[71] Curiosity is a result of the Fall; before he sinned, Adam was not burdened with it.[72] It is a fetter from which humankind is freed only by the Incarnation.[73] William of Saint Thierry reports that Bernard, as a young monk, "had put to death all sense of curiosity. . . ."[74]

Yet Bernard himself longs to know the truth, to gain deeper insights into reality. In his *Thirty-second Sermon on the Song of Songs*, Bernard goes so far as to praise those "truly restless folk [who are] curious to penetrate deep secrets, to seize the more sublime, to test the more perfect. . . . [For] in all the treasure-houses of wisdom there is nothing which God, the Lord of all knowledge, would consent to hide from those desiring truth . . . ."[75] Intellectual restlessness and curiosity—even about the deepest, most sublime, and most perfect realities—are here virtues, virtues that will be rewarded by God with knowledge of the truth. Bernard recognizes and respects these qualities in his monks: "I know well your curiosity, which allows nothing to be passed over without scrutiny."[76] The avid, eager desire for knowledge seems here to be natural and praiseworthy. Curiosity can be commendable.

The key, for Bernard, is motivation. The natural desire for knowledge is good, but that desire becomes immoral when exercised for the wrong reasons: "There are indeed those who wish to know to the sole end that they may know. This is shameful curiosity. There are also those who wish to know that they may be known. This is shameful vanity."[77] The desire to know must be regulated by humility, which is self-knowledge; curiosity is a vice when "joined, in the human heart, with neglect of oneself."[78] In the absence of humility, curiosity can "be discovered as the beginning of all sin [see Si 10:15]."[79]

As humility is necessary to the regulation of the natural desire to know, so, too, is love. Bernard informs his monks of the "two reasons for your raising up your eyes without fault: to look for help or to give it."[80] Proper love of self is rooted in knowledge of self, which is humility. Love for others requires that one do whatever one can to promote their well-being.[81] Both require the search for knowledge about that which will enhance one's well-being. Without the motivation of love, the search for knowledge becomes self-defeating.[82]

Curiosity can thus be directed toward one's own or another's good, or it can be unregulated by love and humility and result in disaster to oneself and others.

Motivation is thus the key to Bernard's teaching on the desire to search out truth. Curiosity must have a purpose; seeking knowledge for knowledge's sake is misdirected curiosity.[83] But, given Bernard's conviction that the search to know even the most apparently useless matters is beneficial, at least in honing the mind's acuity,[84] utility is scarcely a burdensome limitation.

There is, of course, a limit to human curiosity, for, Bernard believes, all knowledge is not accessible to humans—at least not now: "Perfect knowledge is not possible in this life, and perhaps not desirable.... There [in heaven] all knowledge will be delightful where there will no longer be any blemish."[85]

D. PLATO, ARISTOTLE, AND THE "WORLDLY-WISE" PHILOSOPHERS

We have seen that Bernard's response to philosophical studies is enthusiastic endorsement. The universe is, for him, ordered by reason; that order is known through the senses, and the resulting data can be successfully apprehended by a human mind endowed with logic.[86] Thus, for Bernard, philosophy attains "understanding" of reality.[87] So much for the philosophical enterprise, but what does Bernard say about those who conduct that enterprise, the philosophers—above all the great teachers of all subsequent philosophers, Plato and Aristotle?

In Bernard's first sermon for the feast of saints Peter and Paul, he affirms that these apostles

> are our teachers, they who learned the paths of life [see Ps 15:11] and who teach us to the present day. What, then, have the holy apostles taught us or teach us? Not the art of fishing [see Mt 4:18] or of tent-making [see Ac 18:3] or any other art of this kind. Not to read Plato, not to be involved in Aristotle's subtleties, not to be always learning and never attaining the knowledge of the truth [see 2 Tm 3:7].[88]

Bernard certainly knows that Plato and Aristotle are taught in the schools of his time,[89] for he studied at one of them,[90] befriends the professors who teach in them,[91] and fosters the education and careers of their students.[92] Why, then, does he speak of the philosophical quest as "never attaining the truth" and, therefore, presumably unworthy of effort? In his *Thirty-sixth Sermon on the Song of Songs* he repeats his contrast between the efforts of philosophers and those of the apostles—and not to the advantage of the former: "Peter and Andrew and the sons of Zebedee and all the other disciples were not chosen from the schools of rhetoric or philosophy; yet through them the Savior made his salvation effective throughout the world [see Ps 73:12]."[93]

Bernard can sometimes be biting in his description of philosophers and their quest:

> We read . . . that at one time there were some whose greatest zeal and only concern was to investigate the mode and order of created things—with the result that many not only neglected to examine the utility of things, but also highmindedly scorned things themselves, content with the most meager and vilest food. These folk called themselves philosophers, but we rightly name them curious and vain.[94]

Bernard continues in the same sermon, his third for Pentecost, by contrasting the school of the Holy Spirit with that of the philosophers: "I rejoice that you are of this, the Spirit's, school . . . and affirm with the holy one: 'I have understood more than all my teachers [Ps 118:99].' . . . Is this because I have understood, or have labored to understand, the subtlety of Plato or the ingenuity of Aristotle? By no means . . . !"[95] The "subtlety of Plato" and "the ingenuity of Aristotle" are apparently of little or no utility and are not worth the effort one must expend to understand them. For the philosophers, Bernard says, are incapable of providing the knowledge necessary to carry on the good fight for the happiness of the virtuous life. "Worldly wisdom" and "the philosophical traditions" are incapable of providing the answers that, Bernard affirms, are found through "faith alone."[96] Here Bernard seems to appear in the obscurantist role that much of modern scholarship has assigned him. He surely seems to deserve the charge of inconsistency, as he both affirms and denies the efficacy of the philosophical method.

There is much in Bernard's writings to support either view. He writes that the "wordiness of the philosophers,"[97] their "windy chatterings, are not good rain showers; they have brought sterility rather than fertility."[98] Bernard declares that one should avoid philosophers, false shepherds who lead astray the flock of Christ:

> These [philosophers] are the folk who declare: "Look, here is Christ; look, there he is [Mk 13:21]," promising pastures [see 2 M 12:11] richer in wisdom and knowledge. People believe them, and many flock to them. . . . They are wanderers, they are not stable in truth's certainty—always learning but never coming to the knowledge of truth. This the bride [of the Song of Songs] states because of the varied and vain doctrines of the philosophers and heretics.[99]

This tirade contains new components. The context indicates that the "philosophers" to whom Bernard here refers are his contemporaries, not Plato and Aristotle or any of the ancients. And they are associated with heretics in teaching "various and vain doctrines." This not unusual for Bernard: he often links the "wordiness of the philosophers" to the "sophistry of heretics."[100] The reason is that

> the understanding of the philosophers and heretics does not have in it the splendor of purity and truth. Hence they make much effort to gloss it with coloring and to embellish it with verbal ornamentation and syllogistic cunning—lest, if it were to show itself naked, the deformity of its deceit would show itself as well.[101]

The minds of philosophers—or, at least, of some philosophers—are beclouded by error, and thus Bernard can associate them with the deceived and deceptive minds of heretics.

The minds of these present-day philosophers are given to error because they are subject to the greatest of vices, the pride that does

not know itself. Bernard contrasts their self-exaltation with the exul-
tation of the Lord: "You [Lord] exult like a giant in running your
course [see Ps 18:6], not only in running, but also in leaping on
mountains and skipping over hills [see Sg 2:8]. These giant philosophers have not exulted in running your course but in seeking vain-
glory, becoming vain in their thoughts [see Rom 1:21], not in the
humility of your virtues but their own."[102] The prideful self-exaltation of philosophers leads them away from the truth. Bernard contrasts their plight with the "philosophy" of Saint Paul:

> Consider how much Paul's philosophy is exalted above the
> philosophy of the wise [see 1 Cor 1:19] of this world, that
> philosophy which is folly before God [see 1 Cor 3:19]. For
> the philosophers look to nothing other than to delight in
> plaudits or, alternately, to seek glory....[103]

What is one to make of all this? One useful approach is to recognize that Bernard's vocabulary can lead to confusion. Bernard's philosophers can be ancients or moderns, and it is the moderns whom
Bernard associates with heretics in error. Sometimes Bernard simply
identifies those in error with the "wise of the world" or, perhaps
better, with the "worldly wise." Thus, in his *Twenty-second Sermon
on the Song of Songs,* Bernard remarks: "It must be said that in vain
have the worldly wise discussed [see 1 Cor 1:20] so much the four
virtues...."[104] Are these "worldly wise" to be identified with contemporary philosophers? They surely are in Bernard's comparison of Paul's
"philosophy" with "the philosophy of the wise of the world."[105] I
think it safe to say that Bernard rejects the "philosophy" of contemporaries whose "worldly wisdom" is in error because it is based on the
delusion of pride, on the philosophers' ignorance of themselves.
Bernard rejects these "philosophers" for their error—and also for the
moral turpitude that has led to their error. Both their motivation and
conclusions are erroneous, the latter because of the former.

Just as one must ask who Bernard's philosophers are, one must
also inquire about the meaning he assigns to the word "philosophy."
In his *Forty-third Sermon on the Song of Songs,* Bernard paraphrases
Paul's phrase in 1 Corinthians 2:2: "...This is my subtler, deeper

philosophy: to know Jesus, and him crucified."[106] Similarly, in *On Consideration*, Bernard speaks of "Christian philosophy," and the context is studded with allusions to 1 Corinthians (2:15, 6:12, and 10:22),[107] which seems to indicate that "Christian philosophy" is the "philosophy" of Saint Paul. This is scarcely a philosophical use of the word "philosophy."

The same treatise, *On Consideration*, provides additional insight into the meaning of "philosophy" in Bernard's thought. After discussing the virtues at length, Bernard urges Pope Eugenius to set aside time for meditating on them. Bernard then adds: "But what can you do? If you suddenly devote yourself completely to this philosophy, ... you will annoy many...."[108] If Paul's faith and Eugenius's meditation are both "philosophy," it seems clear that Bernard sometimes uses the term to mean all sorts of intellectual stances or rational investigations. Intellectual stances can be true or false, and so Bernard can criticize the erroneous "philosophy" of the "worldly wise."

However, "philosophy," in the sense of rational investigation, is a method that Bernard praises, not only in Eugenius's meditation, but in the more "philosophical" sense of the application of logic to sense data. It is in this sense that Bernard can say: "That person is ... great who uses philosophy to establish the senses as a step toward invisible things...."[109] Bernard's praise of the philosophical method is thus consistent with his condemnation of the "philosophy" of the "worldly wise."

So, Bernard's seeming derogation of "the subtlety of Plato or the ingenuity of Aristotle" can be recognized as hyperbole. Indeed, Bernard uses the ancient philosophers as sources or supports for some of his positions. In *On Consideration*, Bernard concludes his discussion of the virtue of temperance with a quotation from Aristotle: "... As the Philosopher says: 'Nothing to excess.'"[110] In the same treatise, and in his fifth sermon on the dedication of a church, Bernard bases his definition of a human being as a "rational animal" on the position of the philosophers.[111] In his fourth sermon on the feast of All Saints, Bernard praises the philosophers' method as well as their teaching: "As the apostle testifies [in Rom 1:20], the philosophers were able to see the invisible things of God through that which he made."[112] In that same sermon, Bernard goes on to praise the "wise of the world" for their teaching on human nature; he writes: "...The wise of the world have handed down this position on the human soul: that it is rational, irascible, and concupiscible."[113] Thus, even the "wise of the world" join philosophers in meriting Bernard's approval—when their method is correct and their teachings are true.

If Bernard's use of the words "philosophy" and "philosophers" and of the phrase "wise of the world" can lead to confusion, there is no doubt that his use of a philosophical vocabulary is frequent and sophisticated. Thus, in his third sermon on Pentecost, almost immediately after calling pseudo-philosophers "curious and vain," Bernard declares of created beings that "...[goodness] is their efficient cause, ...[benefit] their final cause."[114] Bernard also uses Aristotelian concepts and categories in his sermons on the Song of Songs. In the fourth he writes: "God is the being of all that he has made, but the causal, not the material, being."[115] In the eightieth he states: "His [God's] image is consubstantial with God, but, with everything to which he is seen to impart that same image, the duality is substantial, not accidental."[116] Again in the eightieth, he writes:

> ...No form is that of which it is formed. But greatness is the form of the soul. It must be its form, since it is inseparable from it. All substantial differences are of this kind, both in those special properties not of the lasting sort and in those special properties in the strict sense, those with innumerable other forms. The soul, therefore, is not its greatness, any more than the crow its blackness, the snow its whiteness, or the human being his or her risibility or rationality. But you will never find a crow without blackness, snow without whiteness, or a human being without risibility and rationality. So it is with the soul and the soul's greatness; even though inseparable, they are distinct from one another. How could they be other than distinct, since one is in the subject, the other is the subject and substance?[117]

No obscurantist wrote these words, however obscure their meaning.

Bernard employs similar arguments in *On Consideration*, in the midst of which he criticizes philosophers who seek the material cause of God.[118] Still, it is not the philosophic construct or category that he opposes but the conclusions of those philosophers. Indeed, Bernard applies categories of causation to God in his treatise *On the Need for Loving God,* where he asserts, for example, that ". . . God is the cause of our need to love God, . . . both the efficient and final cause."[119] In the same treatise, he uses the Aristotelian categories of quality, accident, and substance in speaking of the Trinity.[120] Likewise in Bernard's fifth sermon for the first Sunday in November, he can speak of the "indivisible simplicity of essence . . . and the unity of substance" in the Trinity, despite his admission that ". . . I do not know how to express these realities adequately in words . . . ."[121]

Despite Bernard's sometimes disparaging references to philosophy and philosophers, he is a friend of true philosophers—a friend of Plato and, especially, of Aristotle. The pursuit of philosophical insight is, for Bernard, always laudable when the motives for that pursuit are virtuous; the pursuit is reprehensible only when the pursuer is subject to vice. Moreover, Bernard is sure that, without the knowledge that results from virtuous philosophical endeavor, virtue's zeal would be misdirected. He tells the hearers and readers of his fourth sermon for the first Sunday in November that, with the seraphim, one flies securely up to heaven "when the wings of understanding and love, of knowledge and devotion, are joined in the flight. [Then] one will fly without end who [thus] flies toward eternity."[122]

VIII
The Chimaera Revisited[1]

If, indeed, I am seen to be either a monk or a sinner—which I am—my duty is not to teach but to mourn. Unlearned, as well, as I confess myself to be, if I presume to teach what I do not know, that would be an activity still less learned. To teach an unlearned person is not competent, a monk does not dare, a penitent does not desire. It is for these very reasons that I have gone fleeing far off and remain in the wilderness [see Ps 54:8] . . . .[2]

This passage is from a letter to Oger, a canon regular—a letter in which Bernard also shows a thorough command of and sensitivity to the art of literary composition.[3] Yet Bernard repeatedly insists that teaching is not the monk's function. He writes of the renegade monk, Radulf: "If he boasts of being a monk or hermit, and on that basis assumes for himself the liberty or office of preaching, he can and should know that a monk does not have the duty to preach but to mourn."[4] This from a monk who does not hesitate to preach to the clerics at Paris and to teach them their duties through his *On Conversion*.

Not teaching but praying is the monk's function:

"Pray for the things which promote the peace [Ps 121:6]" of the Church. Pray for the things which promote our salvation. Pray that I may see you once more, live with you once more, die in your presence. And so live that you may obtain that for which you pray.[5]

This from an abbot traveling on the business of the Church to his monks at Clairvaux. Bernard acknowledges that such non-monastic activities like that travel detract from his duty as abbot to preach to his monks. Returning from his third trip to Rome,[6] during which he preached and taught in support of Innocent II's claim to the papacy, Bernard tells his monks:

> Because you wish me to pursue the sermons on the Song [of Songs] I began a while back, I gladly take on the task, and I think better to patch on to the properly interrupted sermon than to begin something new. But I am afraid that a mind alienated by all that time away from the grandeur of the subject, a mind long preoccupied with matters so diverse and unworthy, will not grant what it ought.[7]

Bernard paints a picture of the ideal monastic life in a letter to the monks of Saint Jean d'Aulps:

> Our place is at the bottom, is humility. Our place is voluntary poverty, obedience, and joy in the Holy Spirit. Our place is under a master, under an abbot, under a rule, under discipline. Our place is to cultivate silence and exert ourselves in fasts, vigils, prayers, manual labor. Above all, our place is to keep that "more excellent way [1 Cor 12:31]" which is the way of love.[8]

No mention here of the mastery of literary exposition that the letter itself exhibits. Indeed, Bernard's masterful eulogy of his brother Gerard includes, as an apparent indication of monastic virtue, the observation that "he had no knowledge of learning [see Ps 70:15]...."[9] In the preface to Bernard's *On the Need for Loving God*, he seems apologetic at his venturing to write: "It has been your custom, [Cardinal Haimeric], to ask of me prayers, not questions; I am sure I am capable of neither."[10] Much of this is certainly rhetorical; one must ask how seriously one should take Bernard's criticism of monastic learning[11]— criticism always expressed in a most learned literary fashion.

We know of Bernard's criticism of monks who fondly recall their cunning in learned discussions conducted before entering the cloister.[12] Bernard's comments on monks who exhibit that learning is bitingly satirical:

> If the discussion turns to literature, [the monk], having found the opportunity to speak, brings forth old things and new [see Mt 13:52]. His sentences soar; his liquid words resound. He anticipates questions; he responds to those not questioning. He himself poses the questions, delivers the answers, and cuts off the unsatisfactory words of his fellow discussants. When, at the sound of the bell, it is necessary to interrupt the hour-long conversation, he seeks but a short pause. He asks permission to return, after that time, to his talk—not to edify anyone, but to display his knowledge.[13]

Rhetorical exaggeration is the stuff of satire, but it is hard to escape the impression that here, as elsewhere,[14] Bernard paints a picture of reality, though perhaps with over-bright colors. It is clear, as well, that Bernard exhibits his own literary skill in criticizing this exhibition of learning.

Questions of rhetoric aside, it is clear that Bernard's enthusiastic endorsement of literary and philosophical studies is directed to members of the clergy,[15] not to monks who have their own source of "learning" in contemplation.[16] The mastery of canon law, for example, which Bernard urges on clerics, he claims "has little relevance for us who are monks"[17]—despite the fact that he quotes canon law and keeps copies of canonical treatises in his possession.[18] But canon law seems a trifling concern when compared with Bernard's massive literary production and extensive philosophical and theological expositions—intellectual efforts appropriate to clergy but, apparently, not to monks. Perhaps this is part of the reason for Bernard's plaintive self-analysis: "My monstrous life, my troubled conscience, cries out to you. I am something like the chimaera of my age—neither cleric or lay. For I have cast off the life of the monk, though not the habit."[19]

A. The Writer

Though surely not monstrous, Bernard's literary output is certainly massive—as the nine hefty volumes of the critical edition of his works amply testify.[20] This edition contains some 128 liturgical sermons, 4 homilies in praise of the Virgin Mother, 86 sermons on the Song of Songs, 9 miscellaneous sermons, and 125 sermons on various subjects *(De diversis)*. In addition, there are 8 parables and some 358 "sentences" (notes on or for Bernard's sermons, ranging from fragments to full-blown expositions, made by Bernard himself or by his monks[21]). If my count of Bernard's surviving sermons is correct, the total is 718, and some of his sermons are lost to us.[22] One might well expect an abbot to preach to his monks, but Bernard's output is truly formidable. On one occasion, in his tenth sermon on Psalm 90, Bernard offers this explanation:

> ... If I preach to you many times more than is customary in our order, I do not do so out of presumption, but by the decision of my venerable brothers and fellow abbots. They have charged me to do what, nevertheless, they do not at all wish to allow indiscriminately to themselves. They know it is another matter for me; there is a unique need—for I should not preach to you this often if I could work with you.[23]

But Bernard's response to this permission is overwhelming.

Bernard's literary output is, of course, not confined to sermons. The last of the letters in the critical edition is numbered "547," and very few of the numbers preceding represent letters spuriously attributed to Bernard. In addition, there are eight treatises included in volume 3 of the critical edition; one more *(On Conversion)* is included with the sermons, and there are three more that are letters long enough to be counted as treatises. There are also four liturgical compositions extant, ranging from the *Office of Saint Victor* to the *Prologue to the Cistercian Antiphonary.* These works are not the accidental products of monastic piety; with the exception of some, perhaps most, of the *Sentences,* they exhibit a polished literary style and, often, considerable philosophical and theological sophistication.

Bernard's *Apology to Abbot William* is a polemic, cast in the form of a satire, heavily dependent on classical models. "...Bernard took great pains in its composition," submitting it to the examination of two friends and reworking it for final publication.[24] This is but one example of Bernard's "learned" literary method.[25] Jean Leclercq has described the process by which Bernard produced his works:

> ...The first sketch of a Bernardine writing was the result of a great art, but it did not satisfy the exacting requirements of its author. Bernard reread, listened anew, dictated corrections, and practiced that *emendatio* recommended by the literary tradition.... The variant readings of the successive and authentic collections of his works as they are preserved in manuscript form allow us to witness the author's labors and appreciate the improvements he made in his style. During the last five years of his life, this elderly abbot, who was also a very active man of the Church, took pains to review his own major works, letter by letter, in order to prepare a revised edition.[26]

If Bernard's task as an "unlearned" monk were merely to mourn, not teach, he was truly a chimaera.

In addition, Bernard's philosophical method is precise and painstaking, as his long and tightly reasoned arguments on God in the fifth book of *On Consideration* amply illustrate.[27] Then, too, at one point in his commentary on the Song of Songs, Bernard interrupts himself to launch into similarly extensive and closely reasoned arguments,[28] employing a considerable range of technical, philosophical vocabulary.[29] The use of such a vocabulary hardly lends credence to a notion that Bernard's philosophical work is merely an accidental expression of monastic meditation.[30]

Bernard's theological activity is likewise not an incidental byproduct of his religious preoccupations. The range of his theological writing is vast and includes significant contributions to Christology, anthropology, Mariology, angelology, ecclesiology, and sacramentology.[31] Bernard's theological method—as illustrated, for example, in his *Letter 77,* a treatise on baptism—has been aptly described by Hugh Feiss:

... Called on to address theological questions which had
arisen in the schools, Bernard employs the techniques of a
nascent scholasticism with impressive skill. He invokes the
authority of Scripture and the Fathers; he uses reason to
solve apparent contradictions among authorities, to create
dilemmas, to drive home arguments, and to rebut objections.
... Bernard does not attempt to draw any immediate spiritual
fruit from the opinions he supports. In this work he is content to argue for the truth with the considerable resources of
logic and erudition at his disposal.[32]

Theological discussions of this sort are also apt to intrude into
Bernard's sermons to his monks, as, for example, his discussion of
marriage in the *Sixty-sixth Sermon on the Song of Songs*.[33] Both the
subject and the method could be seen—perhaps by Bernard himself—
as inappropriate to the audience.

B. OBEDIENT RESPONSE

What possible motivation could Bernard have in engaging in the
learning proper, by his own definition, to clerics and not to monks?
One answer is that Bernard produces many of his treatises in response
to requests.[34] He writes the *Apology* at William of Saint Thierry's
"request, or rather on his orders."[35] The letter-treatise *On the Conduct and Duties of Bishops* is a response to a request from Archbishop Henry of Sens; Bernard gives his reasons for responding in
the preface:

> The good will of him who asks is flattering; the demands of
> that which is asked are frightening. Who am I that I should
> write to bishops? But who am I that I should disobey bish-
> ops? On one hand I am compelled to grant, on the other to
> deny, what I am asked. To write to such highly-placed per-
> sons is above me; to disobey them is beyond me. There is
> danger in both, but the greater seems to threaten on the side
> of disobedience.[36]

Bernard always insists, when justifying his literary production, on his duty of obedience to those in authority.

It is an obedient response to his cousin, the founder of the Knights Templar, which leads Bernard to write his *In Praise of the New Knighthood*.[37] Another urgent request by William of Saint Thierry is responsible for Bernard's treatise on the errors of Abelard.[38] It is in answer to the "many requests" of two monks at odds with their abbot that Bernard writes *On Precept and Dispensation*.[39] He even accepts the task of writing *Life of Malachy*, attempting what was for him a new genre, hagiography, and this because "...you, Abbot Congan, my reverend brother and dear friend, beseech me—you together with, since you write from Ireland, all the Church of the saints [see Si 31:11] which is there yours."[40] One of Bernard's relatives, who had followed him to Cîteaux and then to Clairvaux, was the instigator of *Steps of Humility and Pride:* "You asked me, Brother Godfrey, to treat more fully for you in a treatise what I had preached to the brothers."[41] And, as we have seen, it is in response to the Parisian scholar, Hugh of Saint Victor, that Bernard writes his letter-treatise *On Baptism*.[42]

Preaching sermons to his monks is Bernard's abbatial duty, but writing sermons and polishing them by editing and reediting is surely not. Yet Bernard undertakes, albeit reluctantly, the monumental task of composing his sermons on the Song of Songs at the request of a Carthusian friend, Bernard of Portes.[43] The task took some eighteen years and was unfinished at Bernard's death in 1153,[44] but Bernard's efforts were rewarded with a literary and spiritual masterpiece. As Jean Leclercq has written: "From the treasury of Holy Scripture he drew ideas and, equally, words which his genius and grace caused to sparkle. The beauty of the sermons on the Song of Songs explains their influence."[45]

But all this leaves an important question unanswered. Why does Bernard not refuse these many requests for literary activities? He does indeed respect the ecclesiastical authority of bishops and seeks to respond to the legitimate requests of those who hold it.[46] He writes Cardinal Haimeric, chancellor of the Roman Church:

> ... I know it has been my plan and purpose never to leave my
> monastery except on the business of my order—unless called

by the legate of the apostolic see or, certainly, by my own bishop. As you well know, a person of my humble state must obey any order of these authorities, except by the privilege of some higher authority.[47]

But the requests for Bernard's non-monastic activity do not all come from hierarchs, and, even when they do, Bernard is quite capable of a refusal. He writes another cardinal, the legate Hugh:

It was not my sloth, but a reason which cannot be held in contempt, which led me not to come as you commanded. The truth is that, with due reverence to you and to all good people, it is my firm intention never to leave my monastery except for reasons which I am not at all satisfied are present in this case—even with your permission to do so.[48]

Did Bernard ever refuse to write from, as well as leave, his monastery? He may have, but I am unaware of any such refusal—perhaps for the simple reason that a refusal would have demanded the same literary activity as acquiescence. Bernard does delay a response when the celebration of a liturgical feast demands more properly monastic activity.[49] But a delay is not a refusal. Nor is a protest—for example, that which Bernard makes to Abbot Guy and the monks of Montiéramey:

You ask me, my dear Abbot Guy, as do the brothers with you, to compose something you can solemnly recite or sing on the feast of Saint Victor, whose holy body rests in your midst. When I hesitate, you insist; when I offer excuses, you urge me on, ignoring my justifiable embarrassment. You even bring other petitioners to me, as if anyone could incline me to your wishes more cogently than your own desire. To properly decide this question, you ought to think not of your affection for me, but rather of my place in the Church.[50]

If Bernard protests against an action not fitting his function, he nevertheless performs it.

Are Bernard's protests rhetorical? They are indeed, and he quite self-consciously employs rhetoric in these protests. His protest in the prologue to *On the Need for Loving God* shows his sensitivity to the problem of sincerity within rhetorical discourse:

> ...To be frank, I see myself truly lacking those qualities which seem highly necessary [to the task]: diligence and talent. I acknowledge, nevertheless, that it is welcome that you ask for spiritual favors in return for material ones—if only you had desired these from someone richer than I. But, because it is the habit of both learned and ignorant to make excuses in this way, it is not easy to know whether the excuses stem from true ignorance or from modesty—unless tested by obedience to the task imposed. Accept from my poverty what I have, lest in my silence I be thought a philosopher.[51]

Bernard knows himself capable of the task. Rhetorical convention—to which both Bernard and his reader are obviously sensitive—demands that he excuse himself. And Bernard expertly tosses off an amusing line to cut through the standard rhetoric of protest. But this still leaves unattended Bernard's reasons for accepting the task.

C. LOVING CONCERN

In his *Sixty-fourth Sermon on the Song of Songs,* Bernard repeats a recurring refrain—but with a new twist:

> ...Paul says: "How can they preach unless they are sent [Rom 10:15]?" Now we know that the duty of a monk is not to teach but to mourn.... From this it is clear and certain that it is not fitting for a monk, not proper for a novice, to preach in public unless expressly sent.[52]

The issue is not *who* sends the monk, for, as we have seen, Bernard can cheerfully refuse the request of high ecclesiastical authorities. The critical question is *what* sends him to preach, teach, or write. There seem to be two reasons that Bernard cannot resist: concern for the Church and love for individual members of that Church.

Bernard does not refuse William of Saint Thierry's request for a work on monastic reform; he writes the *Apology*. He tells William why at the beginning of the work:

> Till now, if you had ordered me to write, I should have acquiesced only reluctantly or not at all. It is not that I care nothing about what I am commanded, but that I should not have presumed to do that of which I am ignorant. Now that the situation has become truly serious, my earlier modesty has vanished. Whether wisely or unwisely, I am compelled, to my distress, to give myself boldly to this necessity.[53]

Convinced of the necessity for action, Bernard will boldly undertake a task not proper to his calling as monk.

His concerns go beyond monastic reform. When convinced that the Church as a whole is in crisis, Bernard not only responds in person but with a flood of literary activity—indeed, the principal source for our knowledge of his involvement in the pressing questions of his time is the letters that he writes to identify those problems and offer solutions. He writes Pope Honorius II: "The tears of the bishops, the complaint of the whole Church, we [monks], however unworthy, who are also her sons, can in no way ignore. Of that which we see, we must speak. A great need draws us from the cloister into the public arena...."[54] The most pressing issues that arouse Bernard's extensive epistolary activity are the papal schism of 1130, about which he writes at least nine letters, and the Second Crusade and its aftermath, which occasion at least twelve letters—the numbers in both cases depend on how widely one casts the appropriate net. The urgency Bernard feels is well illustrated in two letters on the crusade, both written to fellow monks. To Peter the Venerable, abbot of Cluny: "I expect that the heavy and miserable sighs of the eastern Church have reached your ears and penetrated your heart.... If we harden our hearts, if we pay little heed to this misfortune and feel little pain at this grief, where is our love for our neighbors?"[55] And to Suger, abbot of Saint Denis: "The eastern Church now cries out in misery, so that whoever does not have complete compassion for her cannot be judged a true child of the Church."[56] Bernard feels no embarrassment in writing to monks and urging them to join him in responding to a crisis. Monks share the concerns and burdens of all the Church's children—to the extent that they must freely engage in physical or literary efforts to relieve the Church's stress and suffering.

Concern for others results in more than epistolary responses. Bernard's extensive excursus on the nature of God in the *Eightieth Sermon on the Song of Songs*[57] he justifies to his monks at the end of that sermon:

> Accepting the opportunity offered by our discussion of the difference between the image and the soul made in the image, I have believed it worthwhile to make this excursus, not only for their sake [that of Gilbert de la Porrée's followers] but also for yours. So that, if any of you had ever drunk of the stolen waters which seem so sweet [see Prv 9:17], they might take the antidote, vomit them up, and thus purge the stomach of the mind . . . .[58]

Bernard is willing to engage in philosophical discourse, even in a sermon to his monks, when called by what he considers great need. The same is true of theological discourse, when the occasion demands. Bernard explains the genesis of *On Grace and Free Choice* in this way:

> Once, when I was engaged in conversation, and commending [see Rom 5:8] the grace of God working in me, I acknowledged that, clearly, whatever was good in me was the product of grace's prevenient action, that I felt myself borne along by it, and that I would hope to be perfected by it. One of the bystanders asked: "What part do you play, then, and for what rewards or profit do you hope if God does everything?"[59]

The need to answer this knotty problem for the bystander—and for all pursuing the path to perfection—leads to Bernard's brilliantly argued and highly nuanced treatise, a work of true theological erudition. A fellow monk, William of Saint Thierry, had no qualms in requesting this work from Bernard,[60] but then, Bernard has no qualms in urging Aelred, monk of Rievaulx, to compose his treatise *The Mirror of Love*.[61] Theological, philosophical, and other literary activity is justified, even for the monk, by the need of the Church and her people.

Love is the motive that justifies, indeed compels, the monk's intellectual activity. Bernard poses the problem in writing to the prior, Guy, and his semi-eremetical band at the Grand Chartreuse:

> I feared to invade the very holy quiet which you possess in the Lord with my troublesome scribbling. I feared to connect your silence with the world, to interrupt your holy whispers with God, to inflict my musings on solitary ears, inwardly occupied with the celestial praises. I feared, above all, to disturb Moses on the mountain [see Ex 24:13–14], Elijah in the wilderness [see 1 K 19:4], or, surely, Samuel sleeping in the temple [see 1 Sm 3:3], if I should be thought here to interrupt with my conversation your most intent aspirations. ...Should I be so rash as to dare rousing the beloved resting sweetly in the arms of her Spouse until she wishes it [see Sg 2:7]? I think I should instantly hear from her: "Do not trouble me [Lk 11:7]"; "I to my beloved and my beloved to me, who feeds among the lilies [Sg 6:2]."[62]

Bernard's resolution of the tension between the retiring life of contemplation and the intellectual activity of the monk is straightforward:

> What I do not dare, love dares. She knocks with complete confidence on the door of her friend, never thinking she might be turned away [see Lk 11:7–8], she who knows herself the mother of friendships. She does not fear to disturb, for a little while, your leisure, however agreeable, for the sake

of her concerns. She, indeed, whenever she wishes, can make you withdraw from God . . . .[63]

The contemplative monk must respond to love, even when he does not respond to the urgency of authority or the demands of apparent need.

And Bernard does respond. He believes that "the gifts of learned and wise speech, of healing, of prophesy, and other similar gifts [see 1 Cor 12:8–10]—without which we can [surely] attain our own full spiritual well-being—are undoubtedly given us to be spent on our neighbors' welfare."[64] Bernard lovingly spends his gift of wise and learned speech on a vast number of fellow-members of God's family. Bernard's letters to members of each class in society and Church characterize this expenditure. To the abbot of the Cistercian house of Foigny:

> You wring your hands, my dear son Rainald, over your many tribulations, and by your pious complaints you rouse lamentation in me. I cannot but sorrow at your sorrowing; I cannot be other than troubled and full of anxiety to hear of your troubles and anxiety.[65]

On behalf of a cardinal:

> I commend to you a man noble in birth and in life, the abbot of Farfa, cardinal of the apostolic see. . . . It would seem rash that I, one so inconsequential, should dare to commend such a person to you, but his humility in asking me this excludes propriety. So, if "I have become foolish [2 Cor 12:11]," it is this humility which has made me agree to it.[66]

To a ruler, Queen Melisande of Jerusalem:

> Your husband the king is dead, the little king still incapable of bearing the weight of kingly affairs and of fulfilling his royal functions. All eyes look to you, and on you alone falls the whole burden of government. You must give proof of

courage and show yourself manly in your womanhood, acting in all you do with a spirit of counsel and fortitude [see Is
11:2]. You must arrange all things with prudence and mod-
eration, so that all who see you in action may look on you
more as a king than a queen, "lest it be said among the people [Ps 78:10]": "Where is the king of Jerusalem?" But, you
will say: "I am not up to that. These are weighty matters
beyond my ken...." I know, my daughter, I know how
weighty these matters are. But I know too that, although
"the surges of the sea are full of wonder, wonderful is the
Lord on high [Ps 92:4]." This matter is great, but "great is
the Lord, and great is his strength [Ps 146:5]."[67]

To a couple who are surely wealthy and, perhaps, members of the
middle class:

Bernard, abbot of Clairvaux, to his beloved Marius and his
wife. May you love one another and thus nourish one another
by placing first the love of Christ. Whatever you possess on
earth, it is certain that, sooner or later, you will lose it all
unless you take care to send it on to heaven by the hands of
the poor. Through them, dearest friends, "store up treasures
for yourselves in heaven, where moths cannot destroy them,
where thieves cannot break in and steal [Mt 6:20]"....[68]

Bernard's love goes out to members of all classes of society, and he
shows his loving concern, too, for the folk to whom they minister,
for the people to whom they provide justice, for the poor whose
need they can relieve.

For Bernard friendship is a special sort of love;[69] he uses his letters to reinforce that friendship. For example, he writes to Ermen-
garde, formerly countess of Brittany:

Would that, by the page now before you, I might lay open
my mind to you! Oh, if you could only read in my heart
what the finger of God has deigned to write there of love for
you! Then you would surely know what no tongue or pen is

sufficient to express: that which the spirit of God has been able to inscribe on my inmost and best part. Now I am present to you in spirit, though absent in body [see 1 Cor 5:3]. . . . You see, therefore, how you will always hold me fast. I acknowledge that I am never absent from you and will never leave you.[70]

Friendship is so important a part of love that, on one occasion, Bernard employs his literary skills on behalf of a friend of friend, even though Bernard judges his friend's friend unworthy:

I have done what you wished, and what I have done was not my concern at all—except that you wished it. For how do your lands, your plans, and your marriages concern me? Then too, that man, on whose behalf you pressed me to intercede with the duchess, I have always known as one intent from his youth on doing evil [see Gn 6:5, 8:21] and far removed from all good.[71]

And Bernard also uses his literary erudition to intercede with his friends on behalf of others. He writes to his "brother and friend Odo, abbot of the regular clerics of Beaulieu":

The savings of this man, which, so he says, he committed to you, it is neither good nor honorable for you to keep—if indeed that is what you do. He came to me to make his complaint because he had heard of the intimate and special friendship which exists between you and me.[72]

It seems Bernard's loving concern is not only for grand enterprises, such as crusades, or devastating crises in the Church such as the schism of 1130, it is also for the savings of folk who appear at his monastery with complaints of injustice.

Bernard's use of his dialectical and literary skills in issues great and small is prompted by a love that justifies all. Bernard's literary, philosophical, and theological activity is not a product of softheartedness or inconsistency; his motivation is thought out thoroughly: obedience, grave need, and, above all, love justify the monk's use of the skills Bernard ordinarily associates with the clergy. The contemplative, the bride of the Song of Songs, must respond to the love of the Bridegroom with whatever tools and talents she has been given. Bernard writes in his *Fifty-eighth Sermon on the Song of Songs:*

> When her Spouse plainly perceives that his dear one has rested some time on his own chest, he does not hesitate to entice her away again to what seems more useful. It is not that she is unwilling or that he himself is doing what he has forbidden. But, if she is enticed by her Spouse, this is because she receives from him the desire by which she is enticed, the desire for bringing forth fruit for her Spouse. For her, to live is the Spouse and to die is gain [see Phil 1:21].[73]

IX

The Abelard Affair

O n the octave day of Pentecost in the year 1140 or 1141,[1] a great gathering of dignitaries, both clerical and lay, assembled at Sens at the invitation of Henry, the archbishop, "to contribute by their presence to the honor and reverence paid to holy relics"[2] of which he had made an exposition.

> Among those attending were the glorious king of France, Louis, with William, the devout count of Nivern; the archbishop of Reims, with some of his suffragan bishops; and I [Henry of Sens] and my suffragans, with many devout abbots and wise and highly learned clerics. The abbot of Clairvaux was present, as was Master Peter with his supporters.[3]

The presence of Bernard of Clairvaux and Peter Abelard indicates that there was an additional and more important purpose for the gathering. For, at this council, many of Abelard's alleged theological positions were condemned. Abelard refused to answer the charges against him and appealed to Rome,[4] resulting in his censure by Pope Innocent II. The conclusion of the papal rescript reads:

> We, therefore, who are seen to sit, however unworthily, in the chair of blessed Peter—to whom was said by the Lord: "When you are converted, strengthen your brothers [Lk 22:32]"—having received the counsel of our brother bishops and cardinals, have condemned, by the authority of the holy canons, the articles sent us by your discretion and all the per-

verse teachings of Peter himself, together with their author. And we have imposed perpetual silence on him as a heretic. We decree also that followers and defenders of his error be cut off from the fellowship of the faithful and be bound with the chain of excommunication.[5]

Although this letter is addressed to the archbishops of Sens and Reims and their suffragans, the discretion to which Innocent refers is surely that of Bernard, who undoubtedly wrote the request for Innocent's action on behalf of Samson of Reims and his episcopal company.[6]

The history of the encounter between Abelard and Bernard tells much about Bernard's motivation. According to Edward Little, "there is no sure evidence that St. Bernard and Abelard were at odds, other than professionally in some particulars, before 1139, and there is some slight evidence that their relations were surely correct, and probably friendly."[7] But all this was to change in 1139, when William of Saint Thierry wrote to Geoffrey, bishop of Chartres and apostolic legate for France, and to Bernard. William alerted them to the dangers he had seen in those of Abelard's works he had read; William also offered a list of nineteen questionable propositions drawn from these works.[8] Bernard's response to William was cautious: "You know quite well that I am not accustomed to relying much on my own judgment, especially in matters so grave as these. I think it would be worth our while to meet somewhere and discuss the whole matter."[9]

After the discussion with William, Bernard then met with Abelard. Henry of Sens and his brother bishops were to tell the pope:

> He [Bernard] met the man [Abelard], at first privately, then accompanied by two or three witnesses, according to the precept of the Gospel [see Mt 18:15–16]. He admonished him, in a kind and friendly way, to restrain his students from [occupying themselves with] such matters and to correct his writings. He exhorted many of [Abelard's] students to repudiate and reject those works filled with poison, and to guard themselves against and refrain from teachings which would damage the catholic faith.[10]

According to Geoffrey of Auxerre, the meeting resulted in Abelard's compunction and his promise to correct his errors.[11] Whatever the truth of that, Abelard then petitioned the archbishop of Sens for a public disputation with Bernard.[12] At first Bernard hesitated, as he later told Pope Innocent:

> Then the archbishop of Sens wrote me, at his [Abelard's] request, fixing the day of the meeting at which, in his [the archbishop's] presence and that of his fellow bishops, he [Abelard] might, if he could, establish his perverse doctrines, against which I had dared to mutter. I refused, for I am but a lad [in such matters] and he a warrior from his youth [see 1 Sm 17:33]....[13]

But Bernard did indeed go to Sens, acting, as he would later relate,

> on the counsel of my friends, who, seeing how everyone was preparing as if for a spectacle, feared that my absence would be a cause of scandal to the people, that the strength of the adversary might be magnified, and that the error might be still more confirmed if there were no one to respond and refute it.[14]

This is the story of the proceedings of the council, as Bernard reports it:

> Besides the bishops and abbots there assembled, there were present many devout men, schoolmasters from various cities, many learned clerics, and the king. In the presence of all, standing face to face with my adversary, I produced certain articles excerpted from his works. When I began to read them, he refused to listen and walked out, appealing [to Rome] from the judges he himself had chosen—which I did not think permissible. Then the articles, having been examined by the decision of all, were found opposed to the faith, found contrary to the truth.[15]

Both before and after Abelard's appeal to Rome, Bernard presented his views of the case to the pope and to members of the papal curia. He was vehement in his denunciations: Abelard is a second Herod[16] and a new Goliath;[17] he is a persecutor of the faith and an enemy of Christ's cross;[18] he is a monk without a rule.[19] Bernard summed up his position on Abelard in a letter to Cardinal Guido:

> We have here in France a monk without a rule, a prelate without responsibility, an abbot without discipline, Peter Abelard, who disputes with youths and consorts with young women. In his books he puts stolen waters and hidden bread [see Prv 9:17] before his followers, and, in his discourses, he introduces "profane novelties of words [1 Tm 6:20]" and meanings. Unlike Moses, he does not approach alone "the dark cloud in which God was [Ex 20:21]," but with a great crowd and with his students. "Through streets and squares [Sg 3:2]" he leads disputations on the catholic faith: on the childbearing of the Virgin, on the sacrament of the altar, on the incomprehensible mystery of the holy Trinity. We have escaped the roaring of Peter the Lion [the antipope Anacletus II], only to encounter the hissing of Peter the Dragon.[20]

Bernard won his case, as the papal rescript shows,[21] and Abelard retired from his public career. At the invitation of Peter the Venerable, abbot of Cluny, Peter Abelard spent his last days at one of Cluny's dependant priories. Peter the Venerable later reported to Pope Innocent that Abelard had retracted his errors and had been reconciled with Bernard, who came to the priory to make his peace with the aging scholar.[22]

A. Abelard's Method

The traditional interpretation of Bernard's role in the condemnation of Abelard has been to assign to Bernard a deep-seated obscurantism. This point of view has been popular with scholars who have studied both men, and those scholars have been followed in their opinion by

historians of ideas. From these sources has come the notion of
Bernard's deeply rooted anti-intellectualism, a stance that has been
popularized in encyclopedias and textbooks.

The theory that Bernard was an intransigent obscurantist draws
some support from the analysis of Otto of Freising, who, as a twelfth-
century Cistercian, might be expected to cast his fellow Cistercian in
a favorable light. But Otto writes:

> The previously mentioned abbot [Bernard] was as zealous in
> his fervor for the Christian religion as he was somewhat cred-
> ulous in consequence of a habitual gentleness. So he was
> averse to teachers who put their trust in worldly wisdom and
> clung too much to human argument. If anything at variance
> with the Christian faith were told him concerning any one
> [of these teachers], he would readily give ear.[23]

It is far more than this word of caution that is expressed by modern
scholars. For example, Joseph McCabe, a biographer of Abelard,
considers that Bernard's

> mystic and unreasoning attitude brought him into funda-
> mental antagonism with Abelard. To him faith was the soul's
> first duty; reason might think itself fortunate if there were
> crumbs of knowledge in the accepted writings which it could
> digest. To reason, to ask a question, was honestly incompre-
> hensible and abhorrent to him.[24]

This represents a typical analysis from the turn of the last century.
But, later, in the middle of the twentieth century, even Étienne
Gilson, a scholar with great sympathy for Bernard—and one widely
read in Bernard's works—could still consider that the basis for the
contest with Abelard was that the application of dialectics to theology was foreign to Bernard's thought.[25] Although some recent scholarship has taken issue with this traditional interpretation,[26] it still
remains part of the popular and even general scholarly imagination.
For example, a recent, excellent history of the Church speaks of
twelfth-century "speculative discursive theology, which Bernard of

Clairvaux felt called upon to assail as arrogant learning *(stultilogia)* in Peter Abelard...."[27] A recent commentator on twelfth-century education has characterized the dispute between Abelard and Bernard as "a battle between two different and fundamentally irreconcilable approaches to the knowledge of the faith, one of which Bernard viewed as a serious danger to the Church."[28]

What does Bernard himself say of Abelard's method, of his application of the tools of dialectic to theology? Surprisingly little. The nineteen articles or propositions sent to Pope Innocent as an appendix to Bernard's letter on Abelard's errors contain no mention of Abelard's method.[29] But there are scattered references to Abelard's method in his accusatory letters to the pope and members of the papal curia. To the cardinal and papal chancellor, Haimeric, Bernard writes of Abelard:

> With his reason he labors to explore what the pious mind apprehends with a vigorous faith. The faith of the pious believes; it does not discuss. But this man, holding God suspect, does not wish to believe unless he can first investigate rationally. The prophet says: "Unless you believe, you will not understand [Is 7:9]." But this man contradicts willing faith, calling it levity and thus misusing that testimony of Solomon: "He who is hasty to believe is light of heart [Si 19:4]."[30]

One of the reasons Bernard hesitated to attend the Council of Sens, he reports to Pope Innocent, is because "I would judge it unworthy that faith's reason be agitated by the assaults of little minds; for faith's reason stands firm, supported by sure and stable truth."[31] To Stephen of Palestrina, Bernard complains of Abelard's teaching techniques:

> Green young students, newly weaned from the breasts of dialectic, and those who are barely able to keep down, so to speak, the first solid food of the faith, he introduces to the mystery of the holy Trinity, to the Holy of Holies, to the chamber of the King [see Est 2:16], and to him who "made darkness his hiding place [Ps 17:12]."[32]

There are two elements of importance here: first, the study—and, presumably, the use—of dialectics are not criticized; and second, Bernard seems to be setting limits to the use of logic in exploring the contents of the faith. Both positions are compatible with what we know of his teaching on these subjects.[33]

It is not the use of dialectics for which Bernard criticizes Abelard; what he attacks is Abelard's application of logic to subjects beyond its scope. This is a theme to which Bernard returns again and again. In his letter-treatise on Abelard's errors, Bernard tells Pope Innocent:

> Of all that is "in heaven above and on earth below [Dt 4:39]" there is nothing which he considers he does not know—except only the words "I do not know." He places his head in heaven [see Ps 72:9] and searches out the depths of God [see 1 Cor 2:10], and, returning to us, he brings back secret words which to speak is not allowed to humans [see 2 Cor 12:4]. He is ready to give reasons for everything [see 1 Pt 3:15], even for those things which are above reason, and thus he encroaches on reason and on faith. What could be more against reason than to attempt to transcend reason with reason? What could be more against faith than to be unwilling to believe what reason cannot attain?... But against this our theologian says: "What is the use of speaking about doctrine if what we wish to teach cannot be explained so as to be understood?" Thus he promises understanding to his hearers, even in those more sublime and sacred matters contained in the bosom of the faith....[34]

Bernard sees Abelard's approach as an assault not only on faith but also on reason. Abelard pretends, as Bernard sees it, to understand through reason what cannot be comprehended except through faith. This is a refrain repeated throughout Bernard's letter to Innocent: "It is no wonder if a man, who does not care what he says, should, when forcing his way into faith's hidden places, so irreverently attack and destroy the hidden treasures of piety, since he feels neither piously nor faithfully about the piety of faith."[35]

Abelard's misuse of the tools of logic is a theme repeated in Bernard's letters to the papal court. To the bishops and cardinals of the curia, he writes:

> The faith of simple folk is being ridiculed; God's hidden places are being torn open; questions on the loftiest matters are being audaciously aired; the Fathers are being reviled because they held that these things are better tasted than broken open. . . . Thus human ingenuity is usurping everything for itself, leaving nothing to faith. It is attacking matters higher than itself, prying into things more powerful than itself [see Si 3:22], forcing itself into divine matters, profaning rather than revealing the holy. That which is closed and sealed he does not merely open but tears asunder, and whatever he cannot penetrate he thinks worthless and unworthy of belief.[36]

Abelard's intellectual arrogance is also assailed in Bernard's letter to a professor become cardinal, Guido of Castello, who would later be elected pope and take the name Celestine II. More important for this story, Guido had been a student of Peter Abelard, of whom Bernard writes:

> He sees nothing through a mirror or in darkness, but sees everything face to face [see 1 Cor 13:12], walking in great matters and wonderful things above him [see Ps 130:1]. It would be better for him if he would know himself—as the title of his work [*Know Yourself*] suggests—and not overstep his limits but be wise in sobriety [see Rom 12:3].[37]

What Guido may have known, but Bernard did not, was that Abelard's position on the limits of logic paralleled Bernard's, and that Abelard expressed that stance with a vehemence that matched his opponent's. In his *Christian Theology*, Abelard writes:

> The arrogance of these [professors of dialectic] is so great that they hold that there is nothing which cannot be grasped

or expounded by their little reasons, and, contemptuous of all authority, they glory in believing only themselves.[38]

Abelard is convinced that beyond the limited scope of reason lies the exclusive domain of faith: "That which is beyond one's power to explicate, one should believe to one's advantage . . . ."[39] In the light of Abelard's position, one might conclude that Bernard attacks Abelard's stance on the relationship between faith and reason without appropriate investigation and, thus, proper information.

If Bernard does not know of Abelard's disavowal of the unlimited use of reason in matters of faith, he does know, through William of Saint Thierry, Abelard's definition of faith as an *aestimatio*. William writes to Bernard:

> . . . He proceeds in treating holy Scripture as he is accustomed to carry on in dialectics, with his own inventions, his recurring novelties. He is a critic of the faith, not a disciple. He is an amender of the faith, not an imitator. . . . [He defines] faith as an opinion [*aestimationem*] about things which are not seen.[40]

If *aestimatio* means "opinion," as William and Bernard think it does,[41] then the certainty of faith vanishes, as neither are prepared to allow. Bernard writes to Innocent:

> What, then, is this faith, which he dares to call opinion, except that he does not yet accept the Spirit, thus ignorant of the Gospel or thinking it a fable? "I know whom I have believed, and I am certain [2 Tm 1:12]"; thus cries out the apostle— and you [Abelard] launch at me: "Faith is an opinion"? . . . Faith is not opinion but certainty.[42]

If faith does not result in certainty, as Bernard believes Abelard holds, then reason is the sole source of certitude, which Bernard surely does not believe.

This is the basis of Abelard's methodological error, as Bernard sees it. It is not Abelard's use of dialectics in examining the truths of the faith—Bernard does this himself with great frequency and acuity.[43] The problem is that Abelard—so Bernard thinks—in defining faith as opinion, gives reason an unlimited role in the pursuit of truth—even the truths of faith, which exceed the scope of reason. Bernard writes of Abelard to Cardinal Ivo:

> He oversteps the boundaries which our Fathers set up in his disputations and writings on faith, on the sacraments, on the holy Trinity. He changes them one by one, as he wishes, either by addition or diminution. . . . He is a man going beyond his own limits, making Christ's cross meaningless by the wisdom of his words [see 1 Cor 1:17]. He is not ignorant of anything which is in heaven or on earth [see Dt 4:39]—except himself.[44]

Abelard does not know himself; he does not have the humility that makes rational investigations fruitful.[45] And thus Abelard flounders in error—and that is Bernard's overwhelming concern in assessing the theology of Abelard.

B. Abelard's Theology

Bernard is sure that Abelard's theology is not orthodox; the extent of the error is indicated in a letter to Cardinal Haimeric:

> ...This [Peter Abelard], in writing new dogmas, provides a means by which his virus may infect posterity and, by that means, he will be known "to all generations which are to come [Ps 70:18]." To say much with few words, our theologian, with Arius, arranges grades and steps in the Trinity, with Pelagius he places free choice above grace, with Nestorius, by dividing Christ, he excludes the human nature Christ assumed from the fellowship of the Trinity.[46]

Bernard repeats this virtually all-embracing condemnation, in almost the same words, in his letters to Haimeric's fellow-cardinals Stephen of Palestrina and Guido, to a fellow abbot, and, once more, to Haimeric himself.[47] The overwhelming emphasis in all these letters— and in many others written to refute Abelard—is on his errors, not his method. As Bernard's association of Abelard with the greatest of heresiarchs indicates, Abelard's works are filled with virtually all-encompassing errors: "Peter Abelard has now gone before the face of the Antichrist to prepare his ways [see Lk 1:76], speaking out on faith, on the sacraments, on the Father and the Son and the Holy Spirit, beyond what we have received [see Gal 1:9]."[48]

"When he speaks of the Trinity, he savors of Arius…",[49] so Bernard writes to Cardinal Guido. Bernard expands this accusation in his letter to the leaders of the papal curia:

> Read, if you please, Peter Abelard's book which he calls *On Theology*. . . . See how he speaks there of the holy Trinity, of the generation of the Son and the procession of the Holy Spirit, and innumerable other matters—directly opposing catholic ears and minds.[50]

But it is in his letter-treatise to Pope Innocent on Abelard's errors that Bernard explicates most fully his objections to Abelard's trinitarian theology:

> . . . He places degrees in the Trinity, modes in the Majesty, numbers in Eternity. He has determined God the Father is full power, the Son a certain power, and the Holy Spirit no power. He has thus determined the Son to be related to the Father as a certain power to power, as species to genus, as a material thing to matter, as human to animal, as a brazen seal to brass. Did Arius go farther?[51]

Bernard's criticism is of Abelard's misuse, not his use, of philosophical categories: "You see with how much awkwardness or impiety the invention of these similitudes descends."[52]

Bernard's objection is based on what he thinks is Abelard's misuse of the philosophical method and its categories and terminology:

He says that power pertains properly and specifically to the
Father, wisdom to the Son—which is surely false. For the
Father is most truly and is most soundly called wisdom and
the Son power, and what is common to both cannot be the
unique property of one or the other. There are surely other
names which cannot be given to one but rather to the other,
and therefore are peculiar to the one and not held in common with the other. . . . It is not so with power, not so with
wisdom, not so with much else which is said both of the
Father and the Son not specifically. . . .[53]

Bernard then quotes Abelard's position on the question:

"But no," he says, "we find that all power properly and
specifically pertains to the person of the Father as a unique
property, because not only can he alone effect all things, just
as with the other two persons, but he also has his existence
from himself and not from another. As he has his existence
from himself, so he has his power from himself."[54]

Bernard does not reject this use of the dialectical method in analyz-
ing the Trinity. He thinks, rather, that it betrays bad logic, and he
employs what he considers good logic to correct Aelred's logical
errors:

O second Aristotle! By the same reasoning—if, indeed, this
were reasoning—would not wisdom and benevolence pertain
properly to the Father, since the Father has his wisdom and
benevolence equally from himself and not from another, just
as he has his being and his power? If he does not deny this—
as he cannot rationally do—what, I ask, is he going to do
with that renowned partition of his, in which he has attributed power properly and specifically to the Father, wisdom
to the Son, and benevolence to the Holy Spirit? For one and
the same thing cannot appropriately be the unique property
of two, be the unique property of each.[55]

This is an attack on poor philosophy, not on the dialectical method, and Bernard continues by attacking Abelard's analogies:

> What he says he explains with clear examples, asserting that the power of discernment, which is the Son, is a kind of power, just as a human is a kind of animal and a brazen seal is a kind of brass. He asserts that this power of discernment is to the power of creation and discernment (that is, the Son to the Father) as human is to animal and a brazen seal to brass. He says: "Just as that of which a brazen seal is formed must be brass and that of which a human is formed must be animal— but not the converse—so divine wisdom, which is the power of discernment, must be formed of divine power, but not conversely." What follows from all this? Do you really wish to say—as your similitude, your preceding image, demands—that that of which the Son is formed must be the Father, that is, that he who is the Son must be the Father, but not conversely? If you say this, you are a heretic; if you do not say it, your similitude is meaningless.[56]

This argument is not the work of an obscurantist; not only does Bernard apply dialectical tools to a most complex theological question, he does so with great skill.

In his letter-treatise on Abelard's errors, Bernard uses the same dialectical tools and skill in arguing extensively against Abelard's position on the role of grace in the redemption of human beings.[57] Bernard reports to the pope that there are a whole host of additional errors in Abelard's works, but to answer them all would require "the work of many volumes; I speak here only of those about which I cannot keep silence."[58] He does enumerate some of them in urging the curial bishops and cardinals to read Abelard's works and

> discern how they run wild with a whole crop of sacrileges and errors: what he thinks about Christ's soul, Christ's person, Christ's descent into hell; about the sacrament of the altar, the power of binding and loosing, original sin, concu-

piscence; about the sin of pleasure, of weakness, and of ignorance; about the work of sin and willful sin.[59]

Bernard's concern is clearly with Abelard's errors, not his method.

Bernard has no quarrel with the method of the philosophers, but
that is not to say that he accepts uncritically all the content of their
works—and that is as true of Plato as of Abelard. One of the latter's
errors involves that of the former, Bernard writes to Innocent:

> ... He [Abelard] says that ... the Holy Spirit is the soul of the
> world, that the world, as Plato says, is a more excellent animal
> as it has a better soul in the Holy Spirit. Here, where he
> sweats torrents to make Plato a Christian, he proves himself a
> pagan.[60]

But Abelard's attempts to prove himself a pagan are matched, as
Bernard sees it, by Abelard's attempts to make himself a heretic: "In
his books and his actions he shows himself a fabricator of falsehood
and a cultivator of perverse dogmas, proving himself a heretic, not so
much by his error as by his perseverance in error and defense of it."[61]
Bernard knows that Abelard has been condemned before, and his
perseverance in error makes him all the more culpable:

> He was condemned at Soissons [in 1121], as were his works,
> before the legate of the Roman church. But, as if this con-
> demnation were not enough, he is again acting in a way
> which will earn him another condemnation, and his "latest
> error" is "worse than the first [Mt 27:64]."[62]

Error is not heresy, Bernard thinks; it is stubborn, willful perseverance in error that is heretical.[63]

Abelard's error has a social and ecclesial component as well.[64] A
recurrent theme in Bernard's accusatory letters is that "this man
has defiled the Church; he rubs off his rust on simple minds"[65]
—that "by the ferment of his corruption, he spoils the faith of the
simple ...."[66] Abelard is, of course, a monk,[67] and Bernard reserves

the most vehement of denunciations for monks who scandalize the faithful. In his eighth and last *Parable*, the "Story of the King and the Slave Whom He Loved," Bernard writes:

> Thus it is with the monk who, when he was in the world, slew his soul through sin. As if to make satisfaction for his sin, he has entered the monastic life and profession. If, by the negligence of his subsequent life, he scandalizes the souls of those living in the world and, as much as he can, kills them, he shuts himself off from all hope of favor. Indeed, for a two-fold sin he will be sentenced to a two-fold punishment.[68]

This may well be the reason why Bernard's condemnation of Abelard extends to his life and actions as well as his errors.[69]

Indeed, for Bernard, the fundamental problem underlying Abelard's errors is a moral and spiritual one. Like other "worldly-wise" philosophers,[70] he has succumbed to pride, the vice on which all intellectual errors are built:

> "I saw Satan falling from heaven like lightning [Lk 10:18]." So should he fall who walks among great matters and wonderful things above him [see Ps 130:1]. See, holy father [Innocent], what a stairway—rather, what a precipice—this one prepares for his own downfall.... Thus the foot of pride stumbles when it rushes in.[71]

Ignorance of one's capabilities or limitations is pride, which leads to error.[72] Coupled with this form of pride is the vanity that seeks recognition: "The one aim of all heretics has always been to gain glory for the singular extent of their knowledge."[73]

Leaving aside the question of Abelard's social and spiritual sins, Bernard's stance on Abelard's errors is clear. Bernard does not criticize Abelard's application of dialectics to theological matters; his complaint is that Abelard has applied logic where it is not applicable, and that that is illogical. Bernard presents an allegorical statement of this position in his fifth *Parable:*

Once the guardians of reason's citadel were overthrown, Blasphemy soon rose up against Faith. With the onrush of contradictions, commotions, confusions, and a crowd of others of that sort—each struggling with the other and laying claim to whatever each one wished—no reason was left rational . . . .[74]

Rational discourse must be just that: rational. The alternative is what Bernard rejects repeatedly and vehemently in Abelard's works: the error that, when held persistently and defiantly, becomes heresy.

C. An Afterword on Gilbert

Like Peter Abelard, Gilbert de la Porée had been a professor at Paris.[75] Unlike Peter Abelard, Gilbert was a bishop. Again, like Peter, Gilbert was to find a powerful adversary in Bernard of Clairvaux. Both encounters are related by Otto of Freising, Gilbert's following Abelard's. Otto writes of the outcome of the dispute with Gilbert, which was far different from Abelard's fate:

The bishop [Gilbert], accepting with due reverence the statement of the supreme pontiff [Eugenius III] and having been reconciled with his archdeacons [whose accusations had initiated the controversy], returned to his own diocese with his episcopal status unimpaired and in the fullness of honor. Whether the abbot of Clairvaux was deceived in this matter —because of the frailty of human weakness, being only a man—or the bishop, a very learned and well-known person, escaped condemnation by the Church by shrewdly concealing his true positions, it is not my task to discuss or decide.[76]

Whether or not Bernard suffered a defeat in this matter, as has been generally assumed,[77] remains to be seen.

There are two principal sources for Bernard's response to Gilbert's thought. The first is Bernard's extended treatment of the nature of God in Book 5 of *On Consideration*.[78] Since I have quoted this text extensively above,[79] I shall merely recall that Bernard's vocabulary is philosophic and his method dialectical. No criticism of Gilbert's method in approaching God and the Trinity is expressed or implied. It is Gilbert's conclusions that trouble Bernard:

> Indeed, he [God] is one, but not a composite. He does not consist of parts, like a body; he is not pulled in different directions by the affections, like the soul; he is not subject to forms, like everything made [see Jn 1:3], or to a form, as some see it . . . .[80]

The context of this quotation shows clearly that the "some" are Gilbert and his followers.[81]

Gilbert's teaching on God is also the subject of a large part of Bernard's *Eightieth Sermon on the Song of Songs*. There he cautions his readers:

> Withdraw yourselves, my dear ones, withdraw from those who teach new doctrines, who are not dialecticians but heretics, who most irreverently argue that the greatness by which God is great [see 2 Chr 2:5], and also the wisdom by which he is wise and the justice by which he is just, and, lastly, the divinity by which he is God, are not God.[82]

Bernard then quotes Gilbert—or what he believes is Gilbert's position[83] —only to refute him:

> "By divinity," they say, "he is God, but divinity is not God." Perhaps divinity does not deign to be God because it is what makes God what he is? But, if it is not God, what is it? For either it is God, or it is something which is not God, or it is nothing. Now you do not grant it to be God, and you do not grant, I think, that it is nothing. Rather, you indicate that it is so necessary for God to be God that, not only can God not be God in its absence, but also that by it he is. If it is something other than God, then it must either be less than God,

or greater, or equal. But how could it be less, if by it God is? There remains the necessity of acknowledging it is either greater or equal. But, if greater, it is itself the highest good; God is not. If it is equal to God, there are two highest goods, not one. Both of these the universal sense rejects.[84]

The "universal sense" here is not only the catholic faith but reason and the philosophical "sense" built upon it. Bernard then continues in the same vein—a dialectical vein—to consider the other attributes of God:

Now we discern the same of magnitude, goodness, justice, and wisdom as of divinity: they are one in God and with God. For good does not come from any other source than great, just or wise from any other source than great or good. In consequence, all these have no other source than God, and this source is also nothing other than he himself.[85]

The dialogue continues in the sermon. But perhaps these excerpts are enough to indicate that Bernard's objection is to what he believes is Gilbert's misuse of philosophical categories and methods, not to those categories and methods themselves.

Bernard affirms: "... There are clearly quite a few passages in that book [*On Boëthius' On the Trinity*] by the aforesaid bishop which can be seen to differ from faith's rectitude...."[86] Why, then, does not Bernard pursue Gilbert with the same vehemence with which he attacked Abelard? The answer, I believe, lies in Otto of Freising's account of Gilbert's submission to authority.[87] Bernard confirms this near the end of his sermon dealing with Gilbert:

But I am not in the least speaking against him personally. For in the same meeting [with the pope at Reims], in humbly acquiescing to the bishops' decisions, he condemned with his own mouth those passages properly found at fault. I am speaking for the sake of those who continue to transcribe and read his book, contrary to the apostolic promulgation forbidding this, contentiously persisting in following the bishop in those positions for which he himself does not stand and preferring to have him as their teacher in error rather than in correction.[88]

Again, it is not error, but persistence in error, that makes a heretic.[89] Since Gilbert has rejected his error, Bernard has no further quarrel with him.[90]

Abelard, Bernard, and Gilbert all thought that faith was a sure guide to the truth. They all believed reason was a proper tool in explicating the truths of the faith and in pursuing the truth independently. Bernard wove these common positions into a wide-ranging system based on his social, his ecclesial teaching. All the people of God have at their disposal faith and inspiration in determining reality and the proper way to react to it. Monks can glimpse the Truth in contemplation. Clerics can discover some of the truths they need to teach their people through literary analysis of Scripture and through rigorous application of the logic they learn in the schools. Lay folk can provide for the physical needs or wants of all society through learning their duties and skills and with the help of good counsel. However, none of these methods is the exclusive property of one class: monks and lay folk can apply logic to their needs, and the meditation or consideration which Bernard recommends to monks can be profitably employed by lay folk and clerics. Bernard's integrated view of the intellectual life matches his complex though consistent position on society—and is largely inspired by it. Fundamental to both is his deep exploration of the spiritual life of perfection in and toward God. His epistemological stance thus contributed mightily to the integration and integrity of twelfth-century life and culture.

Notes

Preface

1. *Papers of the Michigan Academy of Science, Arts, and Letters* 46 (1961) 493–501.

2. Jean Leclercq, "Saint Bernard in Our Times," trans. Garth L. Fowden. Published as a pamphlet by the Stubbs Society (Oxford: Impensis Roberti Lyle & prostant venales apud G.L.J.S.; Printed for the Society at The Holywell Press in Alfred Street, 1973), p. 9. Also in M. Basil Pennington (ed.), *Saint Bernard of Clairvaux: Studies Commemorating the Eighth Centenary of His Canonization,* CS 28 (Kalamazoo, Michigan: Cistercian Publications, 1977), pp. 13–14.

3. The reader who consults Bruno Scott James's translation of Bernard's letters, *The Letters of St. Bernard of Clairvaux* (published by Burns Oates in 1953, and by Cistercian Publications in 1998), should know that James's numbering system does not correspond to that of the critical edition (SBOp). Another potential source of confusion lies in the numbering of the Psalm references in this volume. Bernard used the Vulgate text of the Bible, and I have followed him in this. Through Psalm 8, the numbering is the same as in the King James, Revised Standard, and other Protestant versions— as well as in the newer Catholic editions. From Psalm 10 to 112, one should add one number to those given. The Vulgate Psalm 113 is contained in Psalms 114 and 115 of the newer versions. The Vulgate 114–115 become 116; 116–145 become 117–146. Psalms 146 and 147 of the Vulgate version are contained in Psalm 147—and the rest have the same numbering.

4. *Spiritual Teachings,* p. xvi.

I. Bernard and the Life of the Mind

1. See *Spiritual Teachings,* p. xiii.

2. See *Spiritual Teachings,* p. xiv.

3. See, for example, my "The Vocabulary of Contemplation in Aelred of Rievaulx' *On Jesus at the Age of Twelve, A Rule of Life for a Recluse,* and *On Spiritual Friendship,*" in E. Rozanne Elder (ed.), *Heaven on Earth: Studies in Medieval Cistercian History, IX,* CS 68 (Kalamazoo, Michigan: Cistercian Publications, 1983), p. 78. The same point is made in my "Images of Visitation: The Vocabulary of Contemplation in Aelred of Rievaulx' *Mirror of Love,* Book II," in John R. Sommerfeldt (ed.), *Erudition at God's Service: Studies in Medieval Cistercian History, XI,* CS 98 (Kalamazoo, Michigan: Cistercian Publications Inc., 1987), p. 168, n. 44.

4. For the various interprelations of "Renaissance" and "humanism," see Wallace K. Ferguson, *The Renaissance in Historical Thought: Five Centuries of Interprelation* (Cambridge: The Riverside Press, 1948), passim, but especially chapter 4, "The Rationalist Tradition in the Eighteenth Century," and chapter 7, "Burkhardt and the Formation of the Modern Concept," pp. 78–112 and 179–94.

5. Jean Leclercq writes: "If humanism consists in studying the classics for their own sake, in focusing interest on the type of ancient humanity, then the medieval monks are not humanists. But if humanism means the study of the classics for the reader's personal good, to enable him to enrich his personality, they are, in the fullest sense, humanists." *The Love of Learning and the Desire for God: A Study of Monastic Culture,* trans. Catherine Misrahi (New York: A Mentor Omega Book Published by the New American Library, 1962), p. 140.

6. See Leclercq, *Love of Learning,* pp. 140–41.

7. A classic statement of this sort of thinking is chapter 3, "What and How They Studied at the Universities," pp. 33–50 of James J. Walsh's *The Thirteenth, Greatest of Centuries,* 4th ed. (New York: Catholic Summer School Press, 1912).

8. A nuanced account of both tension and "peaceful coexistence" between humanism and scholasticism in the late Middle Ages can be found in Steven Ozment, *The Age of Reform, 1250–1550: An Intellectual and Religious History of Late Medieval and Reformation Europe* (New Haven: Yale University Press, 1980), pp. 305–9.

9. See Jean Leclercq, "Saint Bernard on the Church," *Downside Review* 85 (1967) 274.

10. See SC 57.3; SBOp 2:120–21; CF 31:97–98. See also III Sent 97; SBOp 6/2:155; CF 55:314.

11. SC 78.3; SBOp 2:268; CF 40:132.

12. See SC 25.2; SBOp 1:164; CF 7:51.

13. Pent 3.8; SBOp 5:176; CF 53:87.

14. SC 80.1; SBOp 2:277; CF 40:146.

15. SC 68.1; SBOp 2:196; CF 40:17.

16. See Ep 78.9; SBOp 7:207; James 115.

17. See SC 65.1; SBOp 2:172; CF 31:179.

18. See Mich 1.5; SBOp 5:297; Luddy 3:321. See also Thomas Renna, "The City in Early Cistercian Thought," *Cîteaux* 34 (1983) 5–19.

19. See SC 76.8; SBOp 2:259; CF 40:116–17.

20. Yves Congar offers an extensive list of bernardine references to the Church as the body of Christ in "Die Ekkesiologie des hl. Bernhard" in *Bernhard von Clairvaux,* p. 108, n. 32.

21. Ep 243.2; SBOp 8:131; James 391–92.

22. See *Spiritual Teachings,* p. 209. An earlier version of some of the material in this section may be found in my "The Social Theory of Bernard of Clairvaux," in Joseph F. O'Callaghan (ed.), *Studies in Medieval Cistercian History Presented to Jeremiah F. O'Sullivan,* CS 13 (Spencer, Massachusetts: Cistercian Publications, 1971), pp. 35–40. A good survey of Bernard's teaching on various vocations is Raphael Fritegotto's *De vocatione christiana s. Bernardi doctrina,* Studia Antoniana 15 (Roma: Pontificum Athenaeum Antonianum, 1961).

23. Abb 1; SBOp 5:288–89; Luddy 3:306–7. Bernard Jacqueline points out that Gregory the Great, following Origen and Augustine, makes the same distinction. See "Saint Grégoire le Grand et l'ecclésiologie de saint Bernard," *Coll* 36 (1974) 72.

24. Div 9.3; SBOp 6/1:119.

25. See Nat 1.7; SBOp 4:249; Luddy 1:388. The mercy of God extends even to those who have gravely sinned. See Ep 363.3; SBOp 8:313.

26. See Div 40.9; SBOp 6/1:242; Luddy 3:458. See also Par 6 (SBOp 6/2:294; CF 55:82) and V Nat 3.9 (SBOp 4:218–19; Luddy 1:340–41).

27. SC 12.11; SBOp 1:67; CF 4:86.

28. See SC 66.9; SBOp 2:183–84; CF 31:200.

29. See Csi 5.5.12; SBOp 3:476; CF 37:154.

30. Apo 3.5; SBOp 3:84–85; CF 1:38–39.

31. Apo 3.6; SBOp 3:86; CF 1:40.

32. Apo 3.5; SBOp 3:85; CF 1:40.

33. Apo 3.6–4.7; SBOp 3:86–87; CF 1:41.

34. Apo 4.8; SBOp 3:88; CF 1:43.

35. Apo 4.8; SBOp 3:88; CF 1:44.

36. Apo 4.9; SBOp 3:89; CF 1:44.

II. Mysticism: The Truth as Gift

1. An earlier version of this section, "Bernard of Clairvaux On the Truth Accessible Through Faith," was published in E. Rozanne Elder (ed.), *The Joy of Learning and the Love of God: Studies in Honor of Jean Leclercq*, CS 160 (Kalamazoo, Michigan; Spencer, Massachusetts: Cistercian Publications, 1995), pp. 239–51.

2. QH 10.1; SBOp 4:442–43; CF 25:192.

3. Csi 5.3.6; SBOp 3:471; CF 37:145.

4. SC 59.9; SBOp 2:140; CF 31:128.

5. SC 70.2; SBOp 2:209; CF 40:38. See also I Sent 12; SBOp 6/2:10; CF 55:121.

6. SC 28.7; SBOp 1:197; CF 7:94.

7. Bapt 3.13; SBOp 7:194. The translation follows that of Hugh Feiss in "*Bernardus Scholasticus:* The Correspondence of Bernard of Clairvaux and Hugh of Saint Victor on Baptism," in *Bernardus Magister*, p. 371.

8. Hum 4.15; SBOp 3:28; CF 13:43.

9. Tpl 3.5; SBOp 3:218; CF 19:135.

10. SC 76.6; SBOp 2:258; CF 40:115.

11. See Bapt 2.6 (SBOp 7:189; Feiss 365) and 5.18 (SBOp 7:198; Feiss 375).

12. SC 28.9; SBOp 1:198; CF 7:95.

13. SC 28.9; SBOp 1:198; CF 7:96.

14. Csi 5.3.5–6; SBOp 3:470–71; CF 37:144–45.

15. Csi 5.8.18; SBOp 3:482; CF 37:163.

16. Miss 4.8; SBOp 4:54; CF 18:54.

17. See *Spiritual Teachings*, pp. 9–11.

18. Pent 1.1; SBOp 5:160; CF 53:69.

19. Pent 1.1; SBOp 5:160–61; CF 53:69.

20. See V Nat 3.3; SBOp 4:213; Luddy 1:331.

21. Bapt 1.2; SBOp 7:186; Feiss 362. Bernard does not mean that all must undergo a baptism with water to be saved, as the rest of the letter-treatise makes clear.

22. See Ep 18.2; SBOp 7:67; James 53.

23. See SC 41.2; SBOp 2:29; CF 7:205.

24. See Hum 22.54; SBOp 3:57; CF 13:80.

25. Dil 3.9; SBOp 3:126; CF 13:101.

26. See SC 28.7; SBOp 1:196–97; CF 7:93–94. Faith so restores the human being that it is efficacious for salvation even without baptism. Even

martyrdom draws its efficacy from the faith that informs it. See Bapt 2.6 and 8; SBOp 7:189 and 191; Feiss 365 and 366–67. Faith, Bernard believes, surely sufficed for salvation before the institution of baptism. See Bapt 2.8; SBOp 7:190; Feiss 367.

27. See above, p. 12.

28. For a discussion of the soul's faculties of intellect and will, see *Spiritual Teachings*, pp. 7–11.

29. Dil 5.15; SBOp 3:131; CF 13:108.

30. Dil 11.32; SBOp 3:146; CF 13:123. The necessity of living out one's faith in loving service is discussed in *Spiritual Teachings*, pp. 173–81.

31. The primacy of grace in Bernard's soteriology is discussed in *Spiritual Teachings*, pp. 27–30 and 145–50.

32. SC 51.2; SBOp 2:84–85; CF 31–41.

33. SC 48.7; SBOp 2:71; CF 31:18.

34. Bapt 2.8; SBOp 7:191; Feiss 368.

35. SC 28.10; SBOp 1:198–99; CF 7:96.

36. Csi 2.6.13; SBOp 3:421; CF 37:63.

37. SC 31.9–10; SBOp 1:225; CF 7:132.

38. See Ep 18.2; SBOp 7:67; James 53.

39. Ep 366; SBOp 8:323–24; James 460. On Bernard's relations with Hildegard, see Jean Leclercq, *Women and Saint Bernard of Clairvaux*, trans. Marie-Bernard Saïd, CS 104 (Kalamazoo, Michigan: Cistercian Publications, 1989), pp. 62–67. An earlier version of the material in this section was published in my "Bernard on Charismatic Knowledge: The Truth as Gift," *CSQ* 32 (1997) 295–301.

40. SC 17.3; SBOp 1:99–100; CF 4:128. See III Sent 109; SBOp 6/2:181; CF 55:350.

41. See SC 42.11; SBOp 2:40; CF 7:219.

42. SC 25.9; SBOp 1:169; CF 7:57. See SC 26.2; SBOp 1:170–71; CF 7:60.

43. SC 15.1; SBOp 1:82; CF 4:105.

44. JB 11; SBOp 5:183; CF 53:95.

45. JB 4; SBOp 5:178; CF 53:90.

46. For the abbot's role as preacher, see my "Bernard of Clairvaux's Abbot: Both Daniel and Noah," in Francis R. Swietek and John R. Sommerfeldt (eds.), Studiosorum Speculum: *Studies in Honor of Louis J. Lekai, O.Cist.*, CS 141 (Kalamazoo, Michigan: Cistercian Publications, 1993), p. 357; and my "Bernard of Clairvaux as Sermon Writer and Sentence Speaker," the introduction to Bernard of Clairvaux, *The Sentences*, trans. Francis R.

Swietek, CF 55 (Kalamazoo, Michigan: Cistercian Publications, 2000), pp. 105–14.

47. See SC 57.5; SBOp 2:122; CF 31:99–100.

48. Ep 270.3; SBOp 8:180; James 419.

49. SC 22.3; SBOp 1:130–31; CF 7:15–16. See also Dil 27; SBOp 3:142–43; CF 13:119.

50. SC 7.8; SBOp 1:36; CF 4:44. See Pent 3.1; SBOp 5:171; CF 53:81.

51. See Div 29.1; SBOp 6/1:210.

52. SC 66.13; SBOp 2:187; CF 31:204. Bernard is responding to an inquiry on the source of the heretics' certainty made by Eberwin, the provost of Steinfeld (see PL 182:677).

53. Csi 2.1.3; SBOp 3:412–13; CF 37:50.

54. SC 49.5; SBOp 2:76; CF 31:26.

55. See SC 13.6; SBOp 1:72; CF 4:92.

56. For Bernard, miracles are not the index of sanctity; virtue is. See Mart 16; SBOp 5:410; Luddy 3:21–22.

57. Pent 3.8; SBOp 5:175; CF 53:86.

58. Csi 5.11.24; SBOp 3:486; CF 37:169.

59. SC 17.1; SBOp 1:98; CF 4:126.

60. SC 17.3; SBOp 1:100; CF 4:128.

61. The humility and love that ready one for contemplation (see *Spiritual Teachings*, pp. 234–36) are the same virtues enjoined on all (see *Spiritual Teachings*, pp. 45–63 and 89–93).

62. The fact that the best source for Bernard's definition of contemplation is the *On Consideration* does not disturb this pattern. The recipient of this treatise was, of course, Pope Eugenius III. But Eugenius was a Cistercian monk—indeed, had been a monk at Clairvaux.

63. See below, pp. 31–33 and 49–54.

64. SC 1.1; SBOp 1:3; CF 4:1.

65. SC 1.1; SBOp 1:3; CF 4:1.

66. Much of the material in this section is discussed more fully in *Spiritual Teachings*, pp. 215–49. Among the many secondary sources useful in—or that have influenced—my understanding of Bernard's teaching on contemplation are: Michael Casey, *Athirst for God: Spiritual Desire in Bernard's Sermons on the Song of Songs*, CS 77 (Kalamazoo, Michigan: Cistercian Publications, 1988); Joseph Bernhart, *Die philosophische Mystik des Mittelalters von ihren antiken Ursprüngen bis zur Renaissance*, Geschichte der Philosophie in Einzeldarstellungen 3, Die christliche Philosophie 14 (München: Verlag

Ernst Reinhardt, 1922); Louis Bouyer, *The Cistercian Heritage,* trans. Elizabeth A. Livingstone (London: A. R. Mowbray & Co. Limited, 1958); Ingeborg Brauneck, *Bernhard von Clairvaux als Mystiker* (Hamburg: G. H. Nolte, 1935); George Boswell Burch, "Introduction" to *The Steps of Humility by Bernard, Abbot of Clairvaux* (Cambridge, Massachusetts: Harvard University Press, 1942), pp. 3–112; Cuthbert Butler, *Western Mysticism: The Teaching of SS. Augustine, Gregory and Bernard on Contemplation and the Contemplative Life, with Afterthoughts,* 2nd ed. (London: Arrow Books, 1960); Étienne Gilson, *The Mystical Theology of Saint Bernard,* trans. A. H. C. Downes (London, New York: Sheed & Ward, 1940; reprinted as CS 120, Kalamazoo, Michigan: Cistercian Publications, 1990); Erich Kleineidam, "Wissen, Wissenschaft, Theologie bei Bernhard von Clairvaux," in *Bernhard von Clairvaux,* pp. 128–67; Jean Leclercq, *Bernard of Clairvaux and the Cistercian Spirit,* trans. Claire Lavoie, CS 16 (Kalamazoo, Michigan: Cistercian Publications, 1976); Leclercq, *Saint Bernard mystique* (n.p.: Desclée De Brouwer, 1948); Robert Linhardt, *Die Mystik des heiligen Bernhard von Clairvaux* (München: Verlag Natur u. Kultur, 1923); Bernard McGinn, *The Growth of Mysticism,* The Presence of God: A History of Western Christian Mysticism 2 (New York: Crossroad, 1994), pp. 158–224; Pierre Pourrat, *Christian Spirituality in the Middle Ages,* trans. S. P. Jacques (Westminster, Maryland: The Newman Press, 1953); Joseph Ries, *Das geistliche Leben in seinen Entwicklungsstufen nach der Lehre des hl. Bernhard* (Freiburg i. Br.: Herder, 1906); and Goswinus Verschelden, "Het Kennisaspect van Bernardus' Godservaring," in *Sint Bernardus van Clairvaux,* pp. 65–88. The best introductions are in the works by Gilson, Leclercq, and McGinn. See also my "The Epistemological Value of Mysticism in the Thought of Bernard of Clairvaux," in John R. Sommerfeldt (ed.), *Studies in Medieval Culture [1]* (Kalamazoo, Michigan: Western Michigan University, 1964), pp. 48–58; "Bernard of Clairvaux: The Mystic and Society," in E. Rozanne Elder (ed.), *The Spirituality of Western Christendom,* CS 30 (Kalamazoo, Michigan: Cistercian Publications Inc., 1976), pp. 72–84 and 194–96; and "Bernard as Contemplative," in *Bernardus Magister,* pp. 73–84.

    67. Csi 2.2.5; SBOp 3:414; CF 37:52.

    68. Csi 2.2.5; SBOp 3:414; CF 37:52.

    69. See SC 31.4; SBOp 1:221; CF 7:127.

    70. See SC 31.6; SBOp 1:223; CF 7:128–29.

    71. Dil 10.27; SBOp 3:142; CF 13:119.

    72. Dil 10.27; SBOp 3:142; CF 13:119.

    73. Dil 10.27; SBOp 3:142; CF 13:119.

74. For Bernard's tripartate analysis of the soul, see *Spiritual Teachings*, pp. 7–16. For the effect of contemplation on the will and feelings, see *Spiritual Teachings*, pp. 244–47.

75. SC 23.11; SBOp 1:145–46; CF 7:35.

76. SC 22.8; SBOp 1:134; CF 7:20.

77. See SC 8.3–4; SBOp 1:37–38; CF 4:46–47.

78. SC 23.12–14; SBOp 1:146–47; CF 7:36–37.

79. Contemplatives are thus "learned," *docti;* those who pursue truth through reason are also "learned." The significance of this will be discussed below, p. 72.

80. See SC 69.2; SBOp 2:203; CF 40:28.

81. SC 8.6; SBOp 1:39–40; CF 4:49–50.

82. See Hum 7.21; SBOp 3:32; CF 13:49.

83. SC 8.9; SBOp 1:41; CF 4:52. In contemplation, the feelings, too, are purged of pain and filled with pleasure; see *Spiritual Teachings*, pp. 244–46.

84. See Div 29.1; SBOp 6/1:210; Luddy 3:496.

85. SC 49.4; SBOp 2:75; CF 31:24–25.

86. Even the humility and love that prepare the soul's intellect and will for the contemplative embrace are the result of God's gifts. See *Spiritual Teachings*, pp. 49–50 and 145–50.

87. Hum 8.22; SBOp 3:33; CF 13:50–51.

88. See SC 69.2; SBOp 2:202; CF 40:28.

89. SC 74.5; SBOp 2:242; CF 40:89.

90. See SC 1.11; SBOp 1:7–8; CF 4:6–7.

91. SC 1.12; SBOp 1:8; CF 4:7.

92. SC 3.5; SBOp 1:17; CF 4:19.

93. SC 46.1; SBOp 2:56; CF 7:241.

94. See SC 9.2; SBOp 1:43; CF 4:54.

95. SC 85.12; SBOp 2:315; CF 40:208–9.

96. SC 3.1; SBOp 1:14; CF 4:16.

97. See SC 69.8; SBOp 2:207; CF 40:35.

98. SC 85.13; SBOp 2:315–16; CF 40:209.

99. See SC 52.2; SBOp 2:91; CF 31:50–51.

100. See *Spiritual Teachings*, pp. 226–27.

101. On the social effects of contemplation, see *Spiritual Teachings*, pp. 248–49, and below, p. 119.

III. Humanism: Beauty and the Pursuit of Truth

1. For a survey of the curriculum offered in the schools of the High Middle Ages, the eleventh through thirteenth centuries, see John W. Baldwin, *The Scholastic Culture of the Middle Ages, 1000–1300* (Lexington, Massachusetts: D. C. Heath and Company, 1971), pp. 59–77.

2. The vast literature on this question defies citation or even enumeration. I have tried to ascertain Bernard's attitude toward the dialectic of the schools in "Abelard and Bernard of Clairvaux," *Papers of the Michigan Academy of Science, Arts, and Letters* 46 (1961) 493–501. See also my "The Intellectual Life According to Saint Bernard," *Cîteaux* 25 (1974) 249–56.

3. Among the many studies of Bernard's use of rhetorical devices—and of his style and method of composition in general—are: Elizabeth T. Kennan, "Antithesis and Argument in the *De consideratione*," in M. Basil Pennington (ed.), *Bernard of Clairvaux: Studies Presented to Dom Jean Leclercq,* CS 23 (Washington, D.C.: Cistercian Publications, 1973), pp. 91–109; Kennan, "Rhetoric and Style in the *De consideratione*," in John R. Sommerfeldt (ed.), *Studies in Medieval Cistercian History II,* CS 24 (Kalamazoo, Michigan: Cistercian Publications, 1976), pp. 40–48; Jean Leclercq, "L'art de la composition dans les sermons de s. Bernard," in his *Recueil d'études sur saint Bernard et ses écrits* 3 (Roma: Edizioni de storia e letteratura, 1969), pp. 105–62 (reprinted from *Revue Bénédictine* 76 [1966] 87–115); Leclercq, "Sur le caractère litteraire des sermons de s. Bernard," in *Recueil* 3:163–210 (reprinted from *Studi medievali* 7 [1966] 701–44); Christine Mohrmann, "Le style de saint Bernard," in *S. Bernardo: Pubblicazione commemorativa nell'VIII centenario della sua morte,* Pubblicazione dell'Università Cattolica del S. Cuore, nuova serie 46 (Milano: Società Editrice "Vita e Pensiero," 1954), pp. 166–84; Dorette Sabersky, "The Compositional Structure of Bernard's Eighty-fifth Sermon on the Song of Songs," in E. Rozanne Elder (ed.), *Goad and Nail: Studies in Medieval Cistercian History X,* CS 84 (Kalamazoo, Michigan: Cistercian Publications, 1985), pp. 86–108; Sabersky, "*Nam iteratio, affectionis expressio est:* Zum Stil Bernhards von Clairvaux," *Cîteaux* 36 (1985) 5–20; and Emero Stiegman, "The Literary Genre of Bernard of Clairvaux's *Sermones super Cantica canticorum*," in John R. Sommerfeldt (ed.), *Simplicity and Ordinariness: Studies in Medieval Cistercian History IV,* CS 61 (Kalamazoo, Michigan: Cistercian Publications, 1980), pp. 68–93.

4. Some of the material in this chapter was published, in an earlier form, in my "Bernard and the Trivial Arts: A Contemplative's Thoughts on

Literature and Philosophy," in E. Rozanne Elder (ed.), *Praise No Less Than Charity: Studies in Honor of M. Chrysogonus Waddell, Monk of Gethsemani Abbey,* CS 193 (Kalamazoo, Michigan: Cistercian Publications, 2002), pp. 141–59.

5. See above, p. 7.

6. See Abb 6; SBOp 5:292; Luddy 3:311–12.

7. See SC 25.2; SBOp 1:163–64; CF 7:51.

8. See SC 23.2 (SBOp 1:140; CF 7:27), SC 85.13 (SBOp 2:315; CF 40:209), and SC 9.8 and 9 (SBOp 1:47; CF 4:59–60).

9. See Ep 238.2; SBOp 8:116–17; James 278.

10. See Csi 1.5.6 (SBOp 3:400; CF 37:33–34) and SC 18.3 (SBOp 1:104; CF 4:134).

11. See Mor 10–11; SBOp 7:108–9.

12. See, for example, Csi 2.6.13 (SBOp 3:420; CF 37:62) and Csi 4.2.3 (SBOp 3:451; CF 37:113).

13. See SC 77.5; SBOp 2:264; CF 40:125–26.

14. See Csi 2.6.9; SBOp 3:416–17; CF 37:56–57.

15. See SC 46.2; SBOp 2:56–57; CF 7:241–42.

16. See SC 77.3; SBOp 2:263; CF 40:123.

17. SC 76.10; SBOp 2:260–61; CF 40:119–20. See III Sent 13; SBOp 6/2:72; CF 55:199.

18. Ep 200.2; SBOp 8:58; James 337.

19. Ep 250.2; SBOp 8:146; James 401–2.

20. See SC 76.9; SBOp 2:259–60; CF 40:117–18.

21. See SC 41.6; SBOp 2:32; CF 7:208.

22. See SC 76.7; SBOp 2:258; CF 40:115.

23. See Csi 4.4.12; SBOp 3:458; CF 37:124.

24. See Ep 348.3 (SBOp 8:293; James 333) and Ep 180 (SBOp 7:402; James 301).

25. See Ep 358 (SBOp 8:303; James 374) and Conv (SBOp 4:107–8; CF 25:68).

26. See Csi 4.7.23 (SBOp 3:466; CF 37:138) and V Mal 8.16 (SBOp 3:325–26; CF 10:34).

27. See Ep 257.2 (SBOp 8:166; James 412) and Ep 95 (SBOp 7:245; James 240).

28. See Ep 189.5 (SBOp 8:16; James 320) and Par 6 (SBOp 6/2:294; CF 55:83–84).

29. See Par 6 (SBOp 6/2:287; CF 55:73) and SC 65.1 (SBOp 2:172; CF 31:180).

30. See SC 64.8; SBOp 2:170; CF 31:175.

31. Ep 104.1; SBOp 7:261; James 152.

32. SC 36.2; SBOp 2:4; CF 7:174.

33. See SC 18.3; SBOp 1:104; CF 4:134.

34. Ep 6.2; SBOp 7:30; James 25.

35. SC 64.8; SBOp 2:170; CF 31:175.

36. SC 66.12; SBOp 2:186–87; CF 31:204.

37. Csi 3.1.3; SBOp 3:433; CF 37:82.

38. Ep 174.1; SBOp 7:388; James 289–90.

39. See Thomas Renna, "St Bernard and the Pagan Classics: An Historical View," in E. Rozanne Elder and John R. Sommerfeldt (eds.), *The Chimaera of His Age: Studies on Bernard of Clairvaux; Studies in Medieval Cistercian History V,* CS 63 (Kalamazoo, Michigan: Cistercian Publications Inc., 1980), pp. 125–26.

40. An extended treatment of the material in the following two paragraphs may be found in my "Bernard of Clairvaux and Scholasticism," *Papers of the Michigan Academy of Science, Arts, and Letters* 48 (1963) 266–70. See also Kleineidam, "Wissen, Wissenschaft, Theologie bei Bernhard von Clairvaux," in *Bernhard von Clairvaux,* pp. 128–31; and Nikolaus Häring, "Saint Bernard and the *Litterati* of His Day," *Cîteaux* 25 (1974) 199–222.

41. Ep 125.1; SBOp 7:307–8; James 190.

42. Ep 24; SBOp 7:76–77; James 59–60.

43. Ep 410; SBOp 8:391; James 508.

44. Ep 361; SBOp 8:307–8; James 459.

45. Ep 205; SBOp 8:64; James 345.

46. Kleineidam, "Wissen," p. 131.

47. Ep 362.1; SBOp 8:309–10; James 387.

48. See Horace K. Mann, *The Lives of the Popes in the Middle Ages,* 2nd ed. (London: Kegan Paul, Trench, Trubner & Co., Ltd.; St. Louis, Mo.: B. Herder Book Co., 18 vols., 1914–1932), 9:131–37.

49. In 1078, Pope Gregory VII insisted that all bishops should maintain a school in their cathedrals for the study of the *artes litterarum.* See R. W. Southern, "The Schools of Paris and the School of Chartres," in Robert L. Benson and Giles Constable (eds.), *Renaissance and Renewal in the Twelfth Century* (Cambridge, Massachusetts: Harvard University Press, 1982), p. 117 (see also note 117 on that page).

50. Jean Marilier, "Les premières années; Les études à Châtillon," in *Bernard de Clairvaux,* p. 20.

51. William of Saint Thierry, *Vita prima* 1.1.3; PL 185:228.

52. Marilier, "Premières années," p. 22. See Gillian R. Evans, "The Classical Education of Bernard of Clairvaux," *Cîteaux* 33 (1982) 121–34. See, too, Evans's *The Mind of St. Bernard of Clairvaux* (Oxford: Clarendon Press, 1983), pp. 37–49.

53. William of Saint Thierry, *Vita prima* 1.1.3; PL 185:228.

54. Bernard Jacqueline, "Répertoire des citations d'auteurs profanes dans les oeuvres de saint Bernard," in *Bernard de Clairvaux,* pp. 549–54.

55. See Leclercq, *Bernard of Clairvaux and the Cistercian Spirit,* p. 32.

56. Conv 8.14; SBOp 4:88; CF 25:48. The "wise man" is Böethius.

57. Pre 15.42; SBOp 3:283; CF 1:135. The author cited is Horace.

58. Div 41.6; SBOp 6/1:248. Ovid is the poet.

59. Apo 12.28; SBOp 3:104; CF 1:64. The interrogator is Perseius.

60. Ep 256.1; SBOp 8:163; James 471. This time the "wise man" is Seneca.

61. Ep 74; SBOp 7:181; James 108.

62. O Asspt 11; SBOp 5:270; Luddy 3:273.

63. JB 12; SBOp 5:184; CF 53:96.

64. Div 100; SBOp 6/1:367.

65. This phrase, and much of what follows, is borrowed from Jean Leclercq's article "The Love of Beauty as a Means and an Expression of the Love of Truth," *Mittellateinisches Jahrbuch* 16 (1981) 62–72, especially pp. 63–65.

66. SC 37.2; SBOp 2:9; CF 7:182.

67. Leclercq, "Love of Beauty," p. 63.

68. William of Saint Thierry, *Vita prima* 1.1.3; PL 185:228.

69. Ep 89.1; SBOp 7:235; James 137–38.

70. Ep 123; SBOp 7:304; James 186. See Ep 408 (SBOp 8:389; James 507) where Bernard recommends a young man for entrance into a community of regular canons because he is "learned in letters." See also II Sent 15; SBOp 6/2:28; CF 55:143.

71. Ep 398.2; SBOp 8:378; James 502; CF 1:181. See *Spiritual Teachings,* pp. 166–67.

72. Ep 398.1; SBOp 8:377; James 501; CF 1:180.

73. SC 40.2; SBOp 2:25; CF 7:200. See Agustín M. Altisent, "Inteligencia y cultura en la vida espiritual, segun los 'Sermones super Cantica' de S. Bernardo," in *Los monjes y los estudios: IV semana de estudios monasticos, Poblet 1961* (Poblet: Abadía de Poblet, 1963), pp. 147–62, especially pp. 154–56.

74. SC 36.3; SBOp 2:5; CF 7:175–76.

75. See SC 37.2; SBOp 2:9–10; CF 7:182. See also QH 9.5; SBOp 4:439; CF 25:187. Bernard offers the example of Malachy of Armagh as one whose motivation for study was early on tainted by undirected enthusiasm ("he was panting for advanced studies"), but who later put his studies in proper perspective. See V Mal 1.2; SBOp 3:311; CF 10:17.

76. SC 36.1; SBOp 2:3–4; CF 7:174. As another example, Bernard gives the case of his saintly brother Gerard, who "had no knowledge of letters [see Ps 70:15]." SC 26.7; SBOp 1:175; CF 7:66.

IV. Scholasticism: The Roles of Reason

1. SC 36.1; SBOp 2:4; CF 36:174.

2. As well as for all charged with instruction of the people of God, such as abbots. Since Bernard was, of course, an abbot, his own use of dialectic is pertinent to this discussion. See below, pp. 45–50.

3. Pent 3.3; SBOp 5:172; CF 53:82–83.

4. I Nov 2.3; SBOp 5:309; Luddy 2:351.

5. SC 31.3; SBOp 1:221; CF 7:126. See also SC 22.6; SBOp 1:132–33; CF 7:18.

6. Bapt 1.2; SBOp 7:186; Feiss 362.

7. SC 5.1; SBOp 1:21–22; CF 4:25.

8. SC 5.4; SBOp 1:23; CF 4:27. The body also serves as a means of communicating the truths acquired through it. See SC 5.5; SBOp 1:23; CF 4:28.

9. Gra 3; SBOp 3:167; CF 19:57.

10. SC 5.8; SBOp 1:24–25; CF 4:29–30.

11. Csi 5.1.2–2.3; SBOp 3:468; CF 37:141–42.

12. Csi 5.2.4; SBOp 3:469; CF 37:142–43.

13. Bernard distinguishes the faculty of reason (the intellect) and the method of reason (logic). Here the discussion is primarily of the method; the faculty is discussed more fully in *Spiritual Teachings,* pp. 8–9.

14. Csi 2.4.7; SBOp 3:415; CF 37–54. The passage in which this definition occurs is quoted in *Spiritual Teachings,* p. 15.

15. Hum 21; SBOp 3:32; CF 13:48–49.

16. Csi 5.3.5; SBOp 3:470; CF 37:144.

17. V Nat 3.2; SBOp 4:212; Luddy 1:329–30.

18. V Nat 3.8; SBOp 4:217; Luddy 1:338.

19. Ded 1.6; SBOp 5:374; Luddy 2:392. See Luke Anderson, "Wisdom

and Eloquence in St Bernard's *In dedicatione ecclesiae sermo primus*," in John R. Sommerfeldt (ed.), *Erudition at God's Service: Studies in Medieval Cistercian History XI*, CS 98 (Kalamazoo, Michigan: Cistercian Publications Inc., 1987), p. 126.

20. See Csi 5.2.4; SBOp 3:469; CF 37:143.

21. See Csi 5.3.5; SBOp 3:470; CF 37:144.

22. See Csi 5.3.6; SBOp 3:471; CF 37:145.

23. Csi 5.3.6; SBOp 3:471; CF 37:145.

24. SC 66.12; SBOp 2:186; CF 31:203.

25. See OS 4.4; SBOp 5:358; Luddy 3:337.

26. See Dil 8.17; SBOp 3:133; CF 7:109–10.

27. Miss 4.4; SBOp 4:50; CF 18:49.

28. Csi 5.12.26; SBOp 3:489; CF 37:173. See I Sent 25; SBOp 6/2:16; CF 55:128.

29. This is one of Bernard's objections to Abelard's work. See below, pp. 126–29.

30. SC 36.2; SBOp 2:5; CF 7:175.

31. The attempt to read Bernard "philosophically"—as opposed to "theologically"—and the effort to differentiate Bernard's philosophical positions from his theological conclusions has led to serious misunderstanding of his thought. See *Spiritual Teachings*, pp.18–19, n. 11.

32. See SC 48.6; SBOp 2:71; CF 31:17–18.

33. See Anselm of Canterbury, *Proslogion* 1, lines 2–3 on p. 104 (Latin text) of M. J. Charlesworth (trans.), *St. Anselm's* Proslogion *with* A Reply on Behalf of the Fool *by Gaunilo and* The Author's Reply to Gaunilo (Oxford: At the Clarendon Press, 1965).

34. An introduction to this question is offered in my "Bernard of Clairvaux and Scholasticism," pp. 270–75.

35. Csi 5.6.13; SBOp 3:477–78; CF 37:156. Sofia Vanni Rovighi gives a parallel passage from Anselm of Canterbury's *Monologion* 6 in "S. Bernardo e la filosofia," in *S. Bernardo*, p. 140, n. 2.

36. Csi 5.7.15; SBOp 3:479; CF 37:158.

37. See note 9 on p. 204 of John D. Anderson and Elizabeth T. Kennan's translation of Csi in CF 37. Bernard writes: "Quo nihil melius cogitare potest" (SBOp 3:479, line 3). Anselm writes: "...Aliquod quo maius nihil cogitare potest...." See his Proslogian 2; Charlesworth, p. 116, lines 6–7.

38. See Burch, "Introduction," p. 42, n. 2.

39. Csi 5.7.15; SBOp 3:479; CF 37:158.

40. Csi 5.7.16; SBOp 3:479–80; CF 37:159–60.

41. See SC 31.1; SBOp 1:219; CF 7:124. See III Sent 113; SBOp 6/2:197; CF 55:373.

42. See SC 6.1; SBOp 1:26; CF 4:32.

43. See Csi 5.6.14; SBOp 3:478; CF 37:157.

44. Csi 5.6.13; SBOp 3:477; CF 37:155.

45. Csi 5.6.13; SBOp 3:477; CF 37:155–56.

46. See Csi 5.6.14; SBOp 3:478; CF 37:156–57.

47. Dil 2.6; SBOp 3:123–24; CF 13:98. See Luke Anderson, "The Appeal to Reason in St Bernard's *De diligendo Deo* (II:2–6)," in *The Chimaera of His Age*, pp. 32–39.

48. Dil 2.4; SBOp 3:122; CF 13:96.

49. QH 14.1; SBOp 4:468–69; CF 25:229.

50. See Gra 5.14; SBOp 3:176; CF 19:70.

51. See Pre 5.11 (SBOp 3:261; CF 1:113), Gra 2.4 (SBOp 3:168; CF 19:58–59), and, especially, Tpl 11.19 (SBOp 3:230; CF 19:155). For a more complete exposition of Bernard's view of the effects of the misdirection of the will, see *Spiritual Teachings*, pp. 21–26.

52. Mart 3; SBOp 5:401; Luddy 3:5–6.

53. Csi 2.4.7; SBOp 3:415; CF 37:54.

54. Csi 5.12.25; SBOp 3:487; CF 37:170.

55. See Dil 7.18 (SBOp 3:134–35; CF 13:111) and III Sent 105 (SBOp 6/2:170–71; CF 55:334).

56. Csi 3.4.15; SBOp 3:442; CF 37:98.

57. Dil 5.15; SBOp 3:131; CF 13:107–8.

58. See III Sent 73; SBOp 6/2:112; CF 55:254.

59. See above, p. 32.

60. See Ep 213; SBOp 8:73; James 354.

61. See V Mal 18.42; SBOp 3:348; CF 10:56–57.

62. Csi 4.5.16; SBOp 3:461; CF 37:129.

63. Par 2.4; SBOp 6/2:270; CF 55:35.

64. Csi 3.2.7; SBOp 3:435; CF 37:86.

65. SC 46.2; SBOp 2:57; CF 7:241–42.

66. V Mal 7; SBOp 3:315–16; CF 10:22.

67. V Mal 32; SBOp 3:340; CF 10:48.

68. V Mal 33; SBOp 3:340; CF 10:49.

69. V Mal 34; SBOp 3:340; CF 10:49.

70. V Mal 6; SBOp 3:315; CF 10:21. It seems likely that Bernard's knowledge of canon law was not casually acquired. Some scholars have seen

Bernard using parts of Ivo of Chartres's canonical treatise, the *Parnormia*, in his *De praecepto et dispensatione*. See G. Paré et al., *La renaissance du XIIe siècle: Les écoles et l'enseignement*, Publications de l'Institut d'Études Médié-vales d'Ottawa 3 (Paris: J. Vrin, 1933), p. 288.

71. Csi 1.10.13; SBOp 3:408; CF 37:43–44.

72. Csi 3.2.8; SBOp 3:436; CF 37:88. See Bede Lackner, "Saint Bernard: On Bishops and Rome," *The American Benedictine Review* 40 (1989) 380–82.

73. Ep 61; SBOp 7:154; James 89.

74. Hayden V. White is clearly wrong in asserting that Bernard "neither knew, nor cared about canon law." See "The Gregorian Ideal and St. Ber-nard of Clairvaux," *Journal of the History of Ideas* 21 (1960) 337. Elizabeth Kennan has thoroughly refuted White's position in "The 'De considera-tione' of St. Bernard of Clairvaux and the Papacy in the Mid-twelfth Cen-tury: A Review of Scholarship," *Traditio* 23 (1967) 73–115, especially pp. 93–94 and 105.

75. See Abb 6; SBOp 5:292; Luddy 3:311–12.

76. See above, p. 32.

V. Common-sense Consideration and Counsel

1. See Csi 5.2.4; SBOp 3:469; CF 37:142–43.

2. Bernard uses the terms interchangeably. For an example of his use of "meditation," see And 1.10; SBOp 5:433; Luddy 3:50.

3. Csi 2.2.5; SBOp 3:414; CF 37:52.

4. SC 22.2; SBOp 1:130; CF 7:15.

5. See Csi 2.3.6; SBOp 3:414; CF 37:52. See *Spiritual Teachings*, pp. 68–75.

6. Csi 1.7.8; SBOp 3:403–4; CF 37:38.

7. *Spiritual Teachings*, p. 75.

8. See OS 1.5; SBOp 5:330; Luddy 3:335–36.

9. See SC 1.9; SBOp 1:7; CF 4:5.

10. SC 67.7; SBOp 2:193; CF 40:11.

11. V Mal 32; SBOp 3:339; CF 10:48. I have translated *contemplandi* as "meditation." Bernard explains the interchangeability of the terms in Csi 2.2.5; SBOp 3:414; CF 37:52. For Bernard's meaning of "contemplation," properly understood, see *Spiritual Teachings*, pp. 215–20, and above, p. 23.

12. See *Spiritual Teachings*, pp. 80–81, and the texts quoted there.

13. On the effort needed for meditation, see SC 22.2; SBOp 1:130; CF 7:15. For the action of the Holy Spirit in meditation, see SC 51.2; SBOp 2:84; CF 31:40.

14. Csi 1.5.6; SBOp 3:400; CF 37:33.

15. Csi 2.6.13; SBOp 3:420; CF 37:61. See also Csi 3.2.10 (SBOp 3:437; CF 37:90) and Csi 3.4.15 (SBOp 3:442; CF 37:98).

16. Csi 5.1.1; SBOp 3:467; CF 37:139.

17. Pasc 3.1; SBOp 5:103–4; Luddy 2:200.

18. Pasc 3.1–2; SBOp 5:104; Luddy 2:200–201.

19. Ep 289.2; SBOp 8:206; James 347.

20. Ep 289.2; SBOp 8:206; James 347–48.

21. See Csi 3.4.15; SBOp 3:442; CF 37:98.

22. Pasc 3.4; SBOp 5:106–7; Luddy 2:203–4.

23. Pasc 3.4; SBOp 5:107; Luddy 2:204–5.

24. Ep 28.2; SBOp 7:82; James 62–63.

25. Mor 2; SBOp 7:102.

26. See Csi 4.4.9; SBOp 3:456; CF 37:121.

27. Csi 4.4.9; SBOp 3:456; CF 37:121–22.

28. That some members of the papal curia were receptive to bribery is apparent in Csi 3.3.13; SBOp 3:441; CF 37:95.

29. Csi 4.4.12; SBOp 3:457; CF 37:124.

30. Ep 8.4; SBOp 7:49; James 40.

31. Ep 305; SBOp 8:222; James 441.

32. Ep 237.3; SBOp 8:115; James 386. Bernard also writes Cardinal Robert Pullen, urging him to provide Eugenius with good counsel. See above, p. 35.

33. Mor = Ep 42; in SBOp 7:100–131.

34. *Speculum paparum* is White's happy phrase. See Hayden V. White, *The Conflict of Papal Leadership Ideals from Gregory VII to Bernard of Clairvaux with Special Reference to the Schism of 1130* (unpublished Ph.D. dissertation, The University of Michigan, 1955), p. 546. Although I have adopted White's phrase, I disagree with him about its meaning. See my "Charismatic and Gregorian Leadership in the Thought of Bernard of Clairvaux," in *Bernard of Clairvaux: Studies Presented to Dom Jean Leclercq*, pp. 73–90.

35. Ep 164.1; SBOp 7:372; James 249–50.

36. Ep 226.1–2; SBOp 8:95–96; James 372–73.

37. Ep 377, praef.; SBOp 8:340; James 475.

38. Ep 342.1; SBOp 8:284; James 457.

39. Ep 342.1; SBOp 8:284; James 457.

40. Ep 221.1; SBOp 8:84; James 364. In the same letter, Bernard threatens Louis with the disgrace of exposure if he does not change his ways. See Ep 221.3; SBOp 8:85; James 365.

41. Ep 304; SBOp 8:221; James 440.

42. Ep 371; SBOp 8:331; James 474.

43. Ep 364.2; SBOp 8:319; James 470.

44. See Henry-Bernard De Warren, "Bernard, les princes et la société féodale," in *Bernard de Clairvaux,* pp. 649–57.

45. Ep 271; SBOp 8:181; James 419.

46. For Bernard's correspondence with the women of his world, see Leclercq, *Women and Saint Bernard of Clairvaux,* passim. See also Edith Russel, "Bernard et les dames de son temps," in *Bernard de Clairvaux,* pp. 411–25.

47. Ep 121; SBOp 7:301–2; James 184–85.

48. Ep 121; SBOp 7:302; James 185.

49. Ep 206; SBOp 8:65; James 345.

50. Ep 289.1; SBOp 8:205; James 347.

51. Ep 354; SBOp 8:298; James 346.

52. Ep 534; SBOp 8:499; James 267.

53. Ep 244.2–3; SBOp 8:135–36; James 394–95. A similar letter is sent to Louis VII of France; see Ep 221.2; SBOp 8:85; James 365.

54. See Ep 222.5; SBOp 8:89; James 368. For other examples of the effects of evil counsel, see Ep 38.2 (SBOp 7:96–97; James 72–73) and Ep 128 (SBOp 7:321–22; James 199).

55. The implications of this are discussed in my "Charismatic and Gregorian Leadership in the Thought of Bernard of Clairvaux," in *Bernard of Clairvaux: Studies Presented to Dom Jean Leclercq,* passim.

56. Ep 242.2–3; SBOp 8:129; James 390.

57. Ep 243.5; SBOp 8:133; James 393.

58. Miss 3.11; SBOp 4:44; CF 18:42. See also SC 66.11; SBOp 2:185–86; CF 31:202–3.

59. Tpl 4.8; SBOp 3:221; CF 19:141.

60. SC 26.7; SBOp 1:175; CF 7:66.

VI. The Relationship Between the Paths to Truth

1. See above, pp. 12–17.

2. See above, pp. 17–22.

3. See above, pp. 60–62.

4. See above, pp. 62–67.

5. See *Spiritual Teachings*, pp.152–57.

6. Adv 3.5; SBOp 4:178; Luddy 1:27. See Jean Leclercq, "St. Bernard and the Formative Community," *CSQ* 14 (1979) 99–119. See also, Leclercq, "Spiritual Guidance and Counseling According to St Bernard," in John R. Sommerfeldt (ed.), *Abba: Guides to Wholeness and Holiness East and West*, CS 38 (Kalamazoo, Michigan: Cistercian Publications, 1982), pp. 64–87.

7. See above, pp. 58–59.

8. See above, pp. 57–58.

9. RB 48. See Par 7; SBOp 6/2:300; CF 55:95–96.

10. See *Spiritual Teachings*, pp. 75–77.

11. See above, pp. 45–50.

12. See above, pp. 31–33.

13. See above, pp. 22–29.

14. See PP 1.2 (SBOp 5:189; Luddy 3:195), SC 8.7 (SBOp 1:40; CF 4:50–51), and III Sent 30 (SBOp 6/2:84; CF 55:216). See also, *Spiritual Teachings*, pp. 248–49.

15. See above, p. 25, and *Spiritual Teachings*, pp. 241–43.

16. "Epistemological and Social Hierarchies: A Potential Reconciliation of Some Inconsistencies in Bernard's Thought," *Cîteaux* 31 (1980) 85–86 and 92. This article was reprinted in Marian Leathers Kuntz and Paul Grimley Kuntz (eds.), *Jacob's Ladder and the Tree of Life: Concepts of Hierarchy and the Great Chain of Being*, American University Studies, Series 5, Philosophy 14 (New York, Bern, Frankfurt am Main, Paris: Peter Lang, 1987), pp.141–51.

17. See *Spiritual Teachings*, pp. 5–6, 24–25, and 35–37.

18. SC 23.14; SBOp 1:147; CF 7:37. See above, p. 25.

19. SC 36.2; SBOp 2:4; CF 7:174. Bernard's word here is *litterati*, but he immediately equates this word with *docti*.

20. Tpl 4.8; SBOp 3:221; CF 19:141.

21. Csi 5.2.3; SBOp 3:468–69; CF 37:141–42.

22. On the rarity and brevity of the contemplative experience, see *Spiritual Teachings*, p. 220, quoting Csi 5.14.32 (SBOp 3:493; CF 37:178), SC 23.15 (SBOp 1:148; CF 7:38), and SC 85.13 (SBOp 2:316; CF 40:209–10).

23. See *Spiritual Teachings*, pp. 248–49.

24. In Gra 5.15 (SBOp 3:177; CF 19:71), Bernard declares that only in contemplation can one find freedom of pleasure in this life, "though only

in part [see 1 Cor 13:9–10], in a scarcely satisfying part, and on the rarest occasions." Again, I believe, this shows that Bernard thinks God's gifts are greater than human efforts.

25. By me, at any rate. See "Epistemological and Social Hierarchies," p. 90.

26. Csi 5.14.32; SBOp 3:493; CF 37:179.

27. Csi 5.13.27; SBOp 3:489; CF 37:173.

28. SC 28.9; SBOp 1:198; CF 7:95.

29. SC 76.6; SBOp 2:257–58; CF 40:115. See Csi 5.8.18; SBOp 3:482; CF 37:163.

30. SC 33.3; SBOp 1:235; CF 7:146–47.

31. V Nat 3.10; SBOp 4:219; Luddy 1:341.

32. Csi 5.3.6; SBOp 3:471; CF 37:145.

33. Csi 5.3.6; SBOp 3:471; CF 37:145.

34. Csi 5.3.5; SBOp 3:470; CF 37:144.

35. Bernard sometimes speaks of faith illuminating a fallen reason. But "reason" in these cases is the faculty of the intellect, not the rational method. See, for example, Div 11.1–2 and 4; SBOp 6/1:262–64.

36. Csi 5.3.5; SBOp 3:470; CF 37:144.

37. Csi 5.3.6; SBOp 3:471; CF 37:145.

38. Csi 5.3.5; SBOp 3:470; CF 37:144. See Ep 123; SBOp 7:304; James 186.

39. Csi 5.3.6; SBOp 3:471; CF 37:145.

40. SC 36.7; SBOp 2:8; CF 7:179.

41. SC 37.1; SBOp 2:9; CF 7:181.

42. SC 36.1; SBOp 2:3; CF 7:173–74.

43. Csi 5.4.7; SBOp 3:472; CF 37:146–47.

44. SC 5.7; SBOp 1:24; CF 4:29.

45. SC 5.6; SBOp 1:23–24; CF 4:28–29.

46. See *Spiritual Teachings,* pp. 21–22, quoting Gra 9.28 (SBOp 3:185; CF 19:84) and Gra 7:21–22 (SBOp 3:182; CF 19:79).

47. See *Spiritual Teachings,* p. 39, n. 5, citing SC 80–82 (SBOp 2:277–98; CF 40:145–79) and Nat 2.3 (SBOp 4:253; Luddy 1:392).

48. SC 81.11; SBOp 2:291; CF 40:168–69. I am grateful to Luke Anderson for reminding me of this passage with his paper, "The Postlapsarian Influence on Bernard's Doctrine of *Imago Dei* in his *Super Cantica,*" read at the 1991 Cistercian Conference, held in conjunction with the Twenty-sixth International Medieval Congress in Kalamazoo, Michigan.

49. SC 17.3; SBOp 1:100; CF 4:128.

50. See Ep 174.1 (SBOp 7:388; James 289–90), quoted above, p. 33.

51. Csi 5.3.6; SBOp 3:470–71; CF 37:144–45.

52. Hum 6; SBOp 3:21; CF 13:35.

53. Hum 7; SBOp 3:21; CF 13:35–36.

54. Hum 8; SBOp 3:22; CF 13:36.

55. Hum, retractatio; SBOp 3:15; CF 13:25.

56. Hum, retractatio; SBOp 3:15; CF 13:25. See also Sept 2.2; SBOp 4:350; Luddy 2:64.

VII. Inconsistency and Order

1. The titles of three chapters of my doctoral dissertation not coincidentally include the phrase "inconsistency and order." See *Consistency of Thought in the Works of Bernard of Clairvaux: A Study of Mystical Leadership in the Twelfth Century* (unpublished doctoral dissertation, The University of Michigan, 1960).

2. "Epistemology, Education, and Social Theory in the Thought of Bernard of Clairvaux," in *Saint Bernard of Clairvaux,* p. 169.

3. See, for example, Leclercq's "The Making of a Masterpiece," the introduction to Bernard of Clairvaux, *On the Song of Songs IV,* CF 40 (Kalamazoo, Michigan: Cistercian Publications, 1980), pp. ix–xxiv, especially pp. xi–xvi.

4. I believe the latter is what Jean Leclercq meant by his oral response to one of my presentations on the question; he said: "Saint Bernard was as inconsistent as he wished to be."

5. Goswinus Verschelden, "Het Kennisaspect van Bernardus' Godservaring," in *Sint Bernardus van Clairvaux,* p. 66.

6. William of Saint Thierry, *Vita prima* 1.23; PL 185:240.

7. Ep 523; SBOp 8:487; James 246. The letter also appears in A. Hoste and C. H. Talbot (eds.), *Aelredi Rievallensis opera omnia,* CCCM 1 (Turnhouti: Typographi Brepols Editores Pontificii, 1971), pp. 3–4. It is translated from that edition in CF 17:69–72. Anselme Dimier has shown how a literal reading of texts such as these has resulted in a common misinterpretation of the early Cistercian view on work and study. He gives some telling examples from the historiography on the question; the authors cited all assert that the first Cistercians devoted themselves exclusively to manual labor and were the "enemies of study." See "Les premiers Cisterciens: Etaient-ils ennemis des études?" in *Los monjes y los estudios,* pp. 119–46, especially pp. 119–21.

8. Ep 523; SBOp 8:487; James 246–47.

9. Ep 106.2; SBOp 7:266–67; James 155–56.

10. Ep 108.2; SBOp 7:278; James 166.

11. Ep 412.2; SBOp 8:395; James 509.

12. Geoffrey of Auxerre, *Sancti Bernardi abbatis Clarae-Vallensis vita et res gestae* [*Vita prima,* libri 3–5] 2.10; PL 185:327.

13. Ep 104.1; SBOp 7:261; James 152.

14. SC 2.8; SBOp 1:13; CF 4:14.

15. See above, pp. 34–38.

16. See Charles Dumont, "Aelred of Rievaulx: His Life and Works," the introduction to Aelred of Rievaulx, *The Mirror of Charity,* CS 17 (Kalamazoo, Michigan: Cistercian Publications, 1990), pp. 64–65. See, too, André Wilmart, "L'instigateur du *Speculum caritatis* d'Aelred, abbé de Rievaulx," *Revue d'ascétique et de mystique* 14 (1933) 369–95.

17. Bernard was the abbot of Clairvaux, the founding abbey, the "mother house," of Rievaulx, and thus charged by the Cistercian statutes with its annual "visitation," a supervisory and supportive visit to the "daughter house." For more on this practice, see Louis J. Lekai, *The Cistercians: Ideals and Reality* (Kent, Ohio: The Kent State University Press, 1977), p. 28.

18. Par 7; SBOp 6/2:298; CS 55:92.

19. Par 7; SBOp 6/2:297; CS 55:91.

20. Ep 108.3; SBOp 7:278; James 166.

21. Ep 412.1; SBOp 8:394; James 508.

22. See Ep 105; SBOp 7:265; James 155.

23. See Ep 112:1–2; SBOp 7:286–87; James 171–72.

24. See Ep 515; SBOp 8:474; James 309.

25. For a discussion of Bernard as recruiter, see Marion Risetto, "Fish for the Pond: The Recruitment Letters of Bernard of Clairvaux," *Word and Spirit: A Monastic Review* 12 (1990) 148–61.

26. See Ep 408 (SBOp 8:389; James 507), Ep 442 (SBOp 8:420; James 518), Ep 422 (SBOp 8:406; James 515), Ep 110 (SBOp 7:282–83; James 169), Ep 104 (SBOp 7:261–63; James 152–54), Ep 105 (SBOp 7:264–65; James 154–55), Ep 106 (SBOp 7:265–67; James 155–56), Ep 107 (SBOp 7:267–76; James 158–65), Ep 108 (SBOp 7:277–79; James 165–67), Ep 411 (SBOp 8:392–94; James 156–58), Ep 412 (SBOp 8:394–95; James 508–9), and Ep 415 (SBOp 8:398–99; James 511).

27. QH 4.3; SBOp 4:399; CF 25:137.

28. Henry later became abbot of two Cistercian houses—and eventually was chosen archbishop of York. See SBOp 7:265, n. 13.

29. Ep 106.1; SBOp 7:265; James 155.

30. Conv 19:32; SBOp 4:109; CF 25:69.

31. See Conv 19:32; SBOp 4:109; CF 25:69–70.

32. See Conv 19:32; SBOp 4:109–10; CF 25:70–71.

33. In his *Vita prima,* Geoffrey tells us there were three (see above, p. 84). Elsewhere he reports there were twenty-one. See *Fragmenta de vita et miraculis s. Bernardi* 9, ed. Robert Lechat in *Analecta Bollandiana* 50 (1932) 115–16.

34. Conv 21.37; SBOp 4.113; CF 25:75.

35. Ep 319.1; SBOp 8:252; James 244.

36. Geoffrey of Auxerre, *Fragmenta* 9; p. 116.

37. Conv 13.25; SBOp 4:99–100; CF 25:60–61.

38. See my "The Intellectual Life According to Saint Bernard," *Cîteaux* 25 (1974) 249–56.

39. Ep 104.2; SBOp 7:262; James 152–53.

40. Ep 104.2; SBOp 7:262; James 153.

41. Csi 5.3.6; SBOp 3:471; CF 37:145.

42. Asc 4.4; SBOp 5:140–41; CF 53:46–47.

43. Asc 4.5; SBOp 5:141; CF 53:47.

44. SC 16.9; SBOp 1:94; CF 4:120–21. Bernard uses almost the same words in Div 40.6; SBOp 6/1:239; Luddy 3:453.

45. See SC 23.14; SBOp 1:147–48; CF 7:37–38.

46. Quoted above, pp. 32–33.

47. SC 36.2; SBOp 2:4–5; CF 7:174–75.

48. See *Spiritual Teachings,* pp. 53–63.

49. See *Spiritual Teachings,* p. 53, quoting Hum 1.2 (SBOp 3:26–27; CF 13:42) and citing Div 47 (SBOp 6/1:267).

50. See above, pp. 32–33, quoting SC 36.2; SBOp 2:4; CF 7:174.

51. SC 9.7; SBOp 1:46; CF 4:58–59.

52. See *Spiritual Teachings,* pp. 89–93.

53. SC 8.5; SBOp 1:38; CF 4:48.

54. Div 73; SBOp 6/1:311–12.

55. SC 69.2; SBOp 2:203; CF 40:28.

56. See *Spiritual Teachings,* pp. 95–101.

57. See Dil 2.5; SBOp 3:123; CF 13:97.

58. SC 37.5; SBOp 2:11–12; CF 7:184.

59. Hum 28; SBOp 3:38; CF 13:57. See Jean Leclercq, "*Curiositas* and the Return to God in St Bernard of Clairvaux," *CSQ* 25 (1990) 92–100. See also Richard Newhauser, "The Sin of Curiosity and the Cistercians," in *Erudition at God's Service,* pp. 71–95, especially pp. 75–83.

60. Hum 28; SBOp 3:38; CF 13:57. See III Sent 98; SBOp 6/2:161; CF 55:320–21.

61. See Hum 39; SBOp 3:46; CF 13:66–67.

62. See Barton R. V. Mills, "Introduction" to *Saint Bernard: The Twelve Degrees of Humility and Pride* (London: Society for Promoting Christian Knowledge; New York, Toronto: The Macmillan Co., 1929), p. xiv. Gilson builds on this observation in "Curiositas," his useful appendix to *The Mystical Theology of Saint Bernard*, pp. 155–57.

63. For the "philosophic" consequences of Bernard's teaching on curiosity, see Josef Reiter, "Bernard de Clairvaux, philosophe malgré lui entre coeur et raison?," in Rémi Brague (ed.), *Saint Bernard et la philosophie* (Paris: Presses Universitaires de France, 1993), pp. 14–15.

64. See Hum 1; SBOp 3:16; CF 13:29.

65. See Hum, *praefatio;* SBOp 3:16; CF 13:28.

66. Conv 10; SBOp 4:82–83; CF 25:43.

67. Conv 10; SBOp 4:83; CF 25:43.

68. Conv 14; SBOp 4:88; CF 25:48.

69. Ep 385.3; SBOp 8:352; James 491–92.

70. Dil 2.4; SBOp 3:122; CF 13:96.

71. QH 8.5; SBOp 4:429; CF 25:174.

72. See Michael Casey, "The Last Two Parables by Bernard of Clairvaux," *CSQ* 22 (1987) 41, citing Sept 2.2; SBOp 4:31; Luddy 2:66.

73. V Nat 2.3; SBOp 4:206; Luddy 1:320.

74. William of Saint Thierry, *Vita prima* 1.4.20; PL 185:238D.

75. SC 32.8; SBOp 1:231; CF 7:140–41.

76. SC 6.6; SBOp 1:28; CF 4:35.

77. SC 36.3; SBOp 2:5; CF 7:176. See III Sent 57 (SBOp 6/2:97; CF 55:233) and III Sent 108 (SBOp 6/2:179–80; CF 55:348).

78. Div 14.2; SBOp 6/1:135. As Emero Stiegman observes, "What Bernard calls curiosity is, not intellectual vitality, but an outward movement that lessens concern for God's power in the soul." See "Saint Bernard: The Aesthetics of Authenticity," in Meredith Parsons Lillich (ed.), *Studies in Cistercian Art and Architecture II*, CS 69 (Kalamazoo, Michigan: Cistercian Publications Inc., 1984), p. 8.

79. Hum 38; SBOp 3:45; CF 13:66.

80. Hum 29; SBOp 3:39; CF 13:58.

81. See *Spiritual Teachings*, pp. 103–7.

82. Hum 29; SBOp 3:39; CF 13:58.

83. See Kleineidam, "Wissen," p. 142.

84. See above, pp. 76–77.

85. Ded 2.4; SBOp 5:378; Luddy 2:398–99.

86. See above, pp. 40–45.

87. See Csi 5.3.5; SBOp 3:470; CF 37:144.

88. PP 1.3; SBOp 5:189–90; CF 53:101. See Reiter, "Bernard ... philosophe," pp.15–16.

89. See Baldwin, *Scholastic Culture,* pp. 66–67.

90. See above, p. 36.

91. See above, p. 34.

92. See above, pp. 34–35.

93. SC 36.1; SBOp 2:4; CF 7:174.

94. Pent 3.3; SBOp 5:173; CF 53:83.

95. Pent 3.5; SBOp 5:173; CF 53:84.

96. See IV p P 3; SBOp 5:203; CF 53:116.

97. SC 79.4; SBOp 2:274; CF 40:140. See III Sent 111; SBOp 6/2:191; CF 55:365.

98. SC 58.7; SBOp 2:131; CF 31:114.

99. SC 33.8; SBOp 1:239; CF 7:151–52.

100. SC 79.4; SBOp 2:274; CF 40:140.

101. SC 41.1; SBOp 2:29; CF 7:205.

102. Div 40.1; SBOp 6/1:235; Luddy 3:444.

103. Div 7.1; SBOp 6/1:108.

104. SC 22.10; SBOp 1:136; CF 7:23.

105. See Div 40.1; SBOp 6/1:108, quoted above on this page.

106. SC 43.4; SBOp 2:43; CF 7:223.

107. See Csi 3.4.15; SBOp 3:442; CF 37:98. On "philosophy" as the sum total of Christian wisdom, see M.-D. Chenu, *Nature, Man, and Society in the Twelfth Century: Essays on New Theological Perspectives in the Latin West,* trans. Jerome Taylor and Lester K. Little (Chicago, London: The University of Chicago Press, 1968), p. 62.

108. Csi 1.9.12; SBOp 3:407; CF 37:42.

109. Csi 5.2.3; SBOp 3:468; CF 37:142.

110. Csi 1.8.9; SBOp 3:405; CF 37:39.

111. See Csi 2.4.7 (SBOp 3:415; CF 37:54) and Ded 5.7 (SBOp 5:393; Luddy 2:425).

112. OS 4.4; SBOp 5:358; Luddy 3:377.

113. OS 4.5; SBOp 5:358; Luddy 3:377. Bernard supports study of the works of the "wise of the world" in Ep 24; SBOp 7:76–77; James 59–60.

114. Pent 3.4; SBOp 5:173; CF 53:83.

115. SC 4.4; SBOp 1:20; CF 4:24.
116. SC 80.3; SBOp 2:278; CF 40:148.
117. SC 80.5; SBOp 2:280; CF 40:151.
118. See Csi 5.6.14; SBOp 3:478; CF 37:157.
119. Dil 7.22; SBOp 3:137; CF 13:114.
120. See Dil 12.35; SBOp 3:149; CF 13:127. See also Div 80.1; SBOp 6/1:320.
121. I Nov 5.1; SBOp 5:318; Luddy 2:368. See also V Nat 3.8; SBOp 4:217–18; Luddy 1:338–39. Bernard's use of Aristotelian categories and his reliance on sense data (see above, pp. 42–43) lead me to question David Bell's assessment of Bernard as a platonist. See "Plato Monasticus: Plato and the Platonic Tradition Among the Cistercians," in Mark Joyal (ed.), *Studies in Plato and the Platonic Tradition: Essays Presented to John Whittaker* (Aldershot, Brookfield, Singapore, Sidney: Ashgate, 1997), p. 87. Despite my quibble on this point, the article is a splendid introduction to the stance toward ancient philosophy adopted by the whole range of early Cistercians.
122. I Nov 4.2; SBOp 5:316; Luddy 2:363–64.

VIII. The Chimaera Revisited

1. This is also the title of an article of mine which appeared in *Cîteaux* 38 (1987) 5–13, and which attempted to explain Bernard's views on his own non-monastic activity, both ecclesial and intellectual.
2. Ep 89.2; SBOp 7:236; James 138.
3. See Ep 89.1; SBOp 7:239; James 137–38; quoted above, p. 37.
4. Ep 365.1; SBOp 8:321; James 465.
5. Ep 144.4; SBOp 7:346; James 215.
6. So Bernard says at the beginning of SC 24.1; SBOp 1:151; CF 7:42.
7. SC 24.1; SBOp 1:151; CF 7:42.
8. Ep 142.1; SBOp 7:340; James 220.
9. SC 26.7; SBOp 1:175; CF 7:66.
10. Dil, *prologus;* SBOp 3:119; CF 13:91.
11. How learning is inappropriate to monks is discussed by Bede K. Lackner in "The Monastic Life According to Saint Bernard," in *Studies in Medieval Cistercian History II,* pp. 59–61.
12. See above, p. 91, quoting SC 16.9; SBOp 1:94; CF 4:120–21.
13. Hum 41; SBOp 3:48; CF 13:69.
14. Jean Leclercq has discussed thoroughly the use of rhetorical exaggeration in Bernard's satire of Cluniac customs in the *Apology.* See

Leclercq's "Introduction" to *St Bernard's Apology to Abbot William*, CF 1:15–23.

15. See above, p. 54.

16. For the "learning" appropriate to each calling in the Church, see above, p. 72.

17. Pre 57; SBOp 3:291; CF 1:147.

18. See Leclercq, *Bernard of Clairvaux and the Cistercian Spirit*, p. 91.

19. Ep 250.4; SBOp 8:147; James 402.

20. Information on the Latin and English versions of the works mentioned below can be found in the bibliography.

21. See Jean Leclercq, *Monks and Love in Twelfth-Century France: Psycho-Historical Essays* (Oxford: at the Clarendon Press, 1979), pp. 86–87. See also my "Bernard of Clairvaux as Sermon Writer and Sentence Speaker," in CF 55:113–14.

22. See Leclercq, *Études sur saint Bernard et le text de ses écrits* (= ASOC 9 [1953] fasc. 1–2) (Roma: Apud Curiam Generalem Sacri Ordinis Cisterciencis, 1953), pp. 50–55.

23. QH 10.6; SBOp 4:447; CF 25:198–99.

24. See Leclercq, "Introduction" to *St Bernard's Apology*, pp. 3–30. The quotation is from p. 23.

25. The introductions to the translations found in the CF series are filled with further examples.

26. Leclercq, *Bernard of Clairvaux and the Cistercian Spirit*, p. 32.

27. See above, pp. 45–47.

28. See above, p. 46.

29. See Kleineidam, "Wissen," p. 147.

30. See my "Bernard of Clairvaux and Scholasticism," p. 277.

31. For a more extended discussion, with bibliography, see my "Bernard of Clairvaux and Scholasticism," pp. 272–75.

32. Feiss, p. 359. Bernard's influence on leading thinkers of his own time and of later ages is an indication of how seriously they took his contributions. See my "Bernard of Clairvaux and Scholasticism," pp. 275–77 (with bibliography), and the following articles in *Bernardus Magister*: Feiss (pp. 349–78); Bernard McGinn, "*Alter Moyses:* The Role of Bernard of Clairvaux in the Thought of Joachim of Fiore" (pp. 429–48); Mark D. Jordan, "Thomas [Aquinas] on Bernard and the Life of Contemplation" (pp. 449–60); William A. Frank, "*Sine proprio:* On Liberty and Grace, A Juxtaposition of Bernard of Clairvaux and John Duns Scotus" (pp. 461–78); Raymond D. DiLorenzo, "Dante's Saint Bernard and the Theology of Liberty in the *Commedia*" (pp. 497–514); Franz Posset, "*Divus Bernhardus:* Saint

Bernard as Spiritual and Theological Mentor of the Reformer Martin Luther" (pp. 515–30); and A. N. S. Lane, "Bernard of Clairvaux: A Forerunner of John Calvin?" (pp. 531–43).

33. See SC 66.1–7 and 10; SBOp 2:178–83 and 184–85; CF 31: 190–98 and 201–2.

34. For an extensive discussion of these requests, see Jean Leclercq, "Introduction" to *Bernard of Clairvaux: Selected Works,* in the series The Classics of Western Spirituality (New York, Mahwah, N.J.: Paulist Press, 1987), pp. 13–26.

35. Leclercq, "Introduction" to *St Bernard's Apologia,* p. 6. Bernard also wrote his treatise *On Grace and Free Choice* at William's behest. See Gra, *prologus;* SBOp 3:165.

36. Mor, *praefatio;* SBOp 7:100.

37. Leclercq, "Introduction" to *Selected Works,* p. 19.

38. See below, p. 121.

39. Pre, *praefatio;* SBOp 3:253; CF 1:103.

40. V Mal, *praefatio;* SBOp 3:309; CF 10:13.

41. Hum, *praefatio;* SBOp 3:16; CF 13:28.

42. See Feiss, p. 360.

43. Leclercq, "Introduction" to *Selected Works,* p. 21.

44. Leclercq, *Bernard of Clairvaux and the Cistercian Spirit,* p. 28.

45. Jean Leclercq, "Saint Bernard écrivain," in his *Recueil d'études sur saint Bernard et ses écrits* 1 (Roma: Edizioni di storia e letteratura, 1962), p. 351. Reprinted from *Revue Bénédictine* 70 (1960) 590.

46. See above, pp. 109–10.

47. Ep 48.3; SBOp 7:139; James 81.

48. Ep 17; SBOp 7:65; James 51.

49. See Ep 86.1; SBOp 7:223; James 127.

50. Ep 398.1; SBOp 8:377; James 501; CF 1:180.

51. Dil, *prologus;* SBOp 3:120; CF 13:91. Bernard's response to a request by Oger of Mount-Saint-Eloi shows his ability and willingness to engage in playful jest—and his complete awareness of the games he is playing. See Ep 87.12; SBOp 7:231; James 134–35. Jean Leclercq translates and comments on this text in "The Theme of Jesting in St Bernard and His Contemporaries," *CSQ* 9 (1974) 7–21.

52. SC 64.3; SBOp 2:168; CF 31:171–72.

53. Apo 1; SBOp 3:81; CF 1:33.

54. Ep 46; SBOp 7:135; James 77.

55. Ep 364.1; SBOp 8:318; James 469.

56. Ep 380; SBOp 8:344; James 478.

57. See below, pp. 136–37.

58. SC 80.9; SBOp 2:283; CF 40:155.

59. Gra 1; SBOp 3:165; CF 19:53.

60. See Bernard McGinn, "Introduction" to *On Grace and Free Choice*, in The Works of Bernard of Clairvaux 7; Treatises 3; CF 19 (Kalamazoo, Michigan: Cistercian Publications Inc., 1977), p. 14.

61. See above, pp. 82–83.

62. Ep 11.1; SBOp 7:52–53; James 42.

63. Ep 11.2; SBOp 7:53; James 42.

64. SC 18.1; SBOp 1:103; CF 4:133.

65. Ep 73.1; SBOp 7:179; James 106.

66. Ep 448; SBOp 8:425; James 519–20.

67. Ep 354; SBOp 8:298; James 346.

68. Ep 421; SBOp 8:405; James 514.

69. See *Spiritual Teachings*, pp. 107–11.

70. Ep 116; SBOp 7:296; James 181.

71. Ep 443; SBOp 8:421; James 518.

72. Ep 407; SBOp 8:388; James 506–7.

73. SC 58.1; SBOp 2:127; CF 31:108.

IX. The Abelard Affair

1. There has been some dispute about the date. The question seemed to have been settled by Vancandard in favor of 1140. See E. Vancandard, *Vie de saint Bernard*, 4th ed. (Paris: Victor Lecoffre, 2 vols., 1927) 2:146, n. 1. See also Piero Zerbi, "San Bernardo di Chiaravalle e il Concilio di Sens," in *Studi su s. Bernardo di Chiaravalle nell'octavo centenario della canonizzatione, Convegno internazionale Certosa di Firenze: (6–9 novembre 1974)*, Bibliotheca cisterciensis 6 (Roma: Editiones Cistercienses, 1975), p. 49. But, more recently, Peter Dinzelbacher has argued for the later date. See his *Bernhard von Clairvaux: Leben und Werk des berühmten Zisterziensers*, Gestalten des Mittelalters und der Renaissance (Darrmstadt: Wissenschaftliche Buchgesellschaft, 1998), p. 430, n. 231. A survey of the scholarship on the question is in Constant J. Mews's "The Council of Sens (1141): Abelard, Bernard, and the Fear of Social Upheaval," *Speculum* 77 (2002) 345–54.

2. Henry of Sens et al., *Epistola ad Innocentium pontificum*, 2; PL 182:541.

3. Henry of Sens et al., *Epistola*, 3; PL 182:542.

4. Accounts by eyewitnesses include Henry's letter; Samson, archbishop of Reims, et al., *Epistola ad Innocentium* (SBOp 8:41–43); and Bernard's Ep 189.4 (SBOp 8:14–15). Peter Berengar of Poitiers wrote an account from a point of view extremely critical of Bernard in his *Apologeticus contra Bernardum, Claraevallensem abbatem, et alios qui condemnaverunt Petrum Abaelardum*, to be found in PL 178:1858–70. A contemporary, though not eyewitness account is Otto of Freising's *Gesta Friderici I. imperatoris* 1:49–51, in G. Waitz and B. de Simpson (eds.), *Monumenta Germaniae historica, Scriptores rerum Germanicarum in usum scholarium...*, 46, 3rd ed. (Hannover, Leipzig: Impensis Bibliopolii Hahniani, 1912), pp. 68–74. This work has been translated by Charles Christopher Mierow in *The Deeds of Frederick Barbarossa*, Records of Civilization, Sources and Studies (reprint New York: W. W. Norton & Company, Inc., 1966); see pp. 82–88. See also Geoffrey of Auxerre, *Vita prima* 3.5.13; PL 185:310–12. An excellent account of the events at Sens is by Edward Little, "Bernard and Abelard at the Council of Sens, 1140," in *Bernard of Clairvaux: Studies Presented to Dom Jean Leclercq*, pp. 55–71. Other important articles that comment on the controversy include: Arthur Michael Landgraf, "Probleme um den hl. Bernhard von Clairvaux," *Cistercienser-Chronik* 61 (1954) 1–16; Amatus Van den Bosch, "L'intelligence de la foi chez saint Bernard," *Cîteaux* 8 (1957) 85–108; Eligius M. Buytaert, "The Anonymous Capitula Haeresum Petri Abaelardi and the Synod of Sens, 1140," *Antonianum* 43 (1968) 419–60; and Lothar Kolmar, "Abaelard und Bernhard von Clairvaux in Sens," *Zeitschrift der Savigny-Stiftung für Rechtsgeschichte* 98, *Kanonistische Abteilung* 67 (1981) 121–47. The whole history of Bernard's relations with Abelard is treated in some detail in Peter Dinzelbacher's *Bernhard von Clairvaux*, pp. 138–41, 222–31, and 236–50.

5. Innocent II, *Rescriptum contra haereses Petri Abaelardi*; PL 182: 361.

6. See the title to Ep 191 in SBOp 8:41.

7. Edward Little, "Relations Between St Bernard and Abelard Before 1139," in *Saint Bernard of Clairvaux: Studies Commemorating the Eighth Centenary of His Canonization*, p. 168. It has been traditionally supposed that Abelard's complaints in his autobiographical *Historia calamitatem*, written in the 1120s about the persecutions of two "new apostles," refer to Bernard and Norbert of Xanten. Since 1950, this supposition has been subject to intense scrutiny and sometimes rejected. Little's article summarizes the controversy and gives the sentence I have quoted as his summary. See

the whole article, pp. 155–68. Earlier, Arno Borst had demonstrated that the conflict was not a personal confrontation; see "Abälard und Bernhard," *Historische Zeitschrift* 186 (1958) 497–526. For Abelard and Bernard's exchange, sometime in the early 1130s, over the wording used in the "Lord's Prayer" at Heloise's monastery of the Paraclete, see Chrysogonus Waddell, "Peter Abelard's *Letter 10* and Cistercian Liturgical Reform," in *Studies in Medieval Cistercian History II*, pp. 75–86.

8. The letter is edited by Jean Leclercq on pp. 351–53 of "Les lettres de Guillaume de Saint-Thierry à saint Bernard," in *Recueil d'études sur saint Bernard et ses écrits* 4 (Roma: Edizioni di storia e letteratura, 1987; reprinted from *Revue Bénédictine* 79 [1969] 375–91). See also, Häring, "Saint Bernard and the *Litterati*," pp. 216–18; and Leclercq, *Bernard of Clairvaux and the Cistercian Spirit*, pp. 59–60, for good, short accounts of this and the following.

9. Ep 327; SBOp 8:263; James 314–15.

10. Henry of Sens et al., *Epistola*, 2; PL 182:541.

11. Geoffrey of Auxerre, *Vita prima* 3.5; PL 185:311.

12. Henry of Sens et al., *Epistola*, 2; PL 182:541.

13. Ep 189.4; SBOp 8:14; James 318.

14. Ep 189.4; SBOp 8:14–15; James 319.

15. Ep 189.4; SBOp 8:15; James 319. Bernard does not here mention the meeting he apparently arranged the evening before to inform the bishops of Abelard's errors. Berengar later claimed that the bishops had merely drunkenly assented to Bernard's appeals for a condemnation. See Berengar, *Apologeticus;* PL 178:1859.

16. See Ep 193; SBOp 8:44; James 321.

17. See Ep 189.3; SBOp 8:14; James 318.

18. See Ep 331; SBOp 8:269; James 324.

19. See Ep 193; SBOp 8:44; James 321.

20. Ep 332; SBOp 8:271; James 325.

21. See above, pp. 120–21.

22. See Peter the Venerable, *Epistola 98*, in Giles Constable (ed.), *The Letters of Peter the Venerable* (Cambridge, Massachusetts: Harvard University Press, 2 vols., 1967), 1:258–59.

23. Otto of Freising, *Gesta* 1.49; *Monumenta Germaniae historica, Scriptores rerum Germanicarum in usum scholarium...*, 46:68; Mierow, p. 82.

24. Joseph McCabe, *Peter Abelard* (New York: G. P. Putman's Sons, 1901), p. 298. A more extensive survey of the literature on the question, to

1960, can be found in my *Consistency of Thought in the Works of Bernard of Clairvaux,* pp. 17–24. More recent surveys can be found in Adriaan H. Bredero, "Conflicting Interpretations of the Relevance of Bernard of Clairvaux to the History of His Own Time," *Cîteaux* 31 (1980) 53–81; and in Elisabeth Gössmann, "Dialektische und rhetorische Implikationen der Auseinandersetzung zwischen Abaelard und Bernhard von Clairvaux um die Gotteserkenntnis," in Jan P. Beckmann et al. (eds.), *Sprache und Erkenntnis im Mittelalter: Akten des VI. internationalen Kongresses für mittelalterliche Philosohie der Société internationale pour l'étude de la philosophie médiévale, 29 August–3 September 1977, in Bonn* (Berlin, New York: Walter De Gruyter, 1981) 2. Halbband, pp. 890–902. It may well be that the Abelard-Bernard controversy has drawn more attention from modern scholars than it did from contemporaries. See A. Victor Murray, *Abelard and St Bernard: A Study in Twelfth Century "Modernism"* (Manchester: Manchester University Press; New York: Barnes & Noble, Inc., 1967), who observes, on p. 159: "The actual quarrel between Abelard and St Bernard does not appear to have been viewed in any very serious light by their contemporaries. John of Salisbury, the scholar, and Otto of Freising, the worldly churchman, see little more in it than a clash between two temperaments, in which there was a good deal to be said on both sides...." In addition, Nikolaus Häring, on the basis of an exhaustive study of the manuscript evidence, has demonstrated that Abelard's work was relatively unknown to his contemporaries. See "Abelard Yesterday and Today," in *Pierre Abélard, Pierre le Vénérable: Les courants philosophiques, littéraires et artistiques en Occident au milieu du XIIe siècle; Abbaye de Cluny, 2 au 9 juillet 1972,* Colloques internationaux du Centre National de la Recherche Scientifique, 546 (Paris: Éditions du Centre National de la Recherche Scientifique, 1975), pp. 341–403.

25. See Étienne Gilson, *Heloise and Abelard,* trans. L. K. Shook (Chicago: Henry Regnery, 1951), p. 106.

26. See, for example, my "Abelard and Bernard of Clairvaux," pp. 493–501; Leclercq, *Bernard of Clairvaux and the Cistercian Spirit,* p. 58; and G. R. Evans, *The Mind of St. Bernard of Clairvaux* (Oxford: Clarendon Press, 1983), pp. 162–66.

27. Hans-Georg Beck et al., *History of the Church,* 4, *From the High Middle Ages to the Eve of the Reformation,* trans. Anselm Biggs (New York: Crossroad, 1986), p. 375.

28. Stephen C. Ferruolo, *The Origins of the University: The Schools of Paris and Their Critics, 1100–1215* (Stanford, California: Stanford University Press, 1985), p. 57. Ferruolo's account and interpretation of the dispute are on pp. 54–66.

29. See SBOp 8:39–40. This letter (Ep 190 = Abael) is not included in James's translation, but the propositions are translated in Little, "Bernard and Abelard at the Council of Sens," pp. 68–69. Bernard's purported authorship of the nineteen propositions has been the subject of a hot scholarly debate, which is summarized in Little, "The Source of the *Capitula* of Sens of 1140," in *Studies in Medieval Cistercian History II,* pp. 87–91. It may be that Bernard was not the original author, but he accepted their attachment to his letter and, thus, responsibility for them. See Leclercq, SBOp 8:xii–xiii.

30. Ep 338.1; SBOp 8:277–78; James 328.

31. Ep 189.4; SBOp 8:14; James 318.

32. Ep 331; SBOp 8:269–70; James 324.

33. See above, pp. 40 and 43–45.

34. Abael 1–2; SBOp 8:17–18.

35. Abael 9; SBOp 8:24.

36. Ep 188.1; SBOp 8:11; James 316.

37. Ep 192; SBOp 8:43–44; James 321.

38. Peter Abelard, *Theologia christiana* 3; PL 178:1218.

39. Peter Abelard, *Theologia christiana* 3; PL 178:1226.

40. William of Saint Thierry, *Epistola ad Gaufrido . . . et Bernardo . . . ;* in Leclercq, "Les lettres," p. 352.

41. Actually, Abelard does not use the word *aestimatio* but, rather, *existimatio.* See Peter Abelard, *Introductio ad theologiam* 2.3; PL 178:1051. James notes, however, that, in the context of the argument, the two words are synonymous and that *existimatio* implies, if anything, still greater vagueness. See Bruno S. James, *Saint Bernard of Clairvaux: An Essay in Biography* (London: Hodder & Stoughton, 1957), p. 140, n. 1.

42. Abael 9; SBOp 8:25.

43. See above, pp. 45–50.

44. Ep 193; SBOp 8:45; James 321.

45. See above, pp. 92–93.

46. Ep 330; SBOp 8:268; James 323.

47. See Ep 331 (SBOp 8:270; James 324), Ep 332 (SBOp 8:272; James 325), Ep 336 (SBOp 8:276; James 327), and Ep 338.2 (SBOp 8:278; James 329).

48. Ep 336; SBOp 8:275–76; James 327. See Ep 333 (SBOp 8:272–73; James 325–26) and Ep 334 (SBOp 8:273–74; James 326).

49. Ep 192; SBOp 8:44; James 321.

50. Ep 188.2; SBOp 8:11; James 316.

51. Abael 2; SBOp 8:18.

52. Abael 4; SBOp 8:21.

53. Abael 5; SBOp 8:21–22.

54. Abael 5; SBOp 8:22.

55. Abael 5; SBOp 8:22.

56. Abael 6; SBOp 8:22–23.

57. See Abael 11–25; SBOp 8:26–38.

58. Abael 10; SBOp 8:26.

59. Ep 188.2; SBOp 8:11; James 316.

60. Abael 10; SBOp 8:25–26.

61. Ep 193; SBOp 8:45; James 321.

62. Ep 193; SBOp 8:45; James 321–22.

63. Apparently Bernard's distinction between error—even theological error—and heresy was a common position in the Middle Ages. See William J. Courtenay, "Inquiry and Inquisition: Academic Freedom in Medieval Universities," *Church History* 58 (1989) 168–81.

64. Although he takes a different approach than I, Thomas Renna also discusses the social dimension of the dispute in "Bernard vs. Abelard: An Ecclesiological Conflict," in *Simplicity and Ordinariness*, pp. 94–138; and in his "St Bernard and Abelard as Hagiographers," *Cîteaux* 29 (1978) 41–59. See, too, Martha G. Newman, *The Boundaries of Charity: Cistercian Culture and Ecclesiastical Reform, 1096–1180* (Stanford, California: Stanford University Press, 1996), p. 222.

65. Ep 338.1; SBOp 8:277; James 328.

66. Ep 330; SBOp 8:267; James 322.

67. See Thomas J. Renna, "Abelard versus Bernard: An Event in Monastic History," *Cîteaux* 27 (1976) 189–202.

68. Par 8; SBOp 6/2:303; CF 55:102.

69. See above, pp. 125 and 127.

70. See above, pp. 98–102.

71. Abael 8; SBOp 8:24.

72. See above, pp. 99–100.

73. SC 65.2; SBOp 2:173; CF 31:180.

74. Par 5.4; SBOp 6/2:284; CF 55:65.

75. For good, short narratives of the dispute between Bernard and Gilbert, see Häring, "Saint Bernard and the *Litterati*," pp. 219–21; and Dinzelbacher, *Bernhard von Clairvaux*, pp. 307–10. A more complete account may be found in Häring, "San Bernardo e Gilberto vescovo di Poitiers," in *Studi su s. Bernardo*, pp. 75–91. For analyses of Gilbert's thought, see Häring, "Die theologische Sprachlogik der Schule von Chartres

im zwölften Jahrhundert," in *Sprache und Erkenntniss,* 2. Halbband, pp. 930–36; and John Marenbon, "Gilbert of Poitiers," in Peter Dronke (ed.), *A History of Twelfth-Century Philosophy* (Cambridge, New York, New Rochelle, Melbourne, Sydney: Cambridge University Press, 1988), pp. 328–52. See also, Leclercq, "Textes sur saint Bernard et Gilbert de la Porée," in *Recueil* 2, pp. 341–71.

76. Otto of Freising, *Gesta* 1.61; *Monumenta Germaniae historica, Scriptores rerum Germanicarum in usum scholarium...,* 46:87; Mierow, pp. 100–101.

77. See, for example, Häring, "Saint Bernard and the *Litterati*," p. 221.

78. Csi 5.6.13–5.8.19; SBOp 3:477–83; CF 37:155–64.

79. See above, pp. 45–47.

80. Csi 5.7.16; SBOp 3:480; CF 37:159–60; see also p. 46 above.

81. See CF 37:205, n. 13.

82. SC 80.6; SBOp 2:281; CF 40:152.

83. Bernard confuses, in part, Gilbert's commentary on Boëthius with the text of Boëthius himself. See Häring, "San Bernardo e Gilberto," p. 79.

84. SC 80.6; SBOp 2:281; CF 40:152.

85. SC 80.6; SBOp 2:281; CF 40:152–53.

86. SC 80.8; SBOp 2:282; CF 40:154.

87. See above, p. 135.

88. SC 80.9; SBOp 2:283; CF 40:155.

89. See above, p. 135.

90. There were surely some ecclesiastical politics involved in Gilbert's happy survival. But whether that was result of the cardinals' opposition to Bernard himself (see Häring, "Saint Bernard and the *Litterati*," p. 220) or due to the dissatisfaction of the Roman churchmen with the independent stance of some French churchmen, including Bernard, I do not know. For the latter interpretation, see James Cotter Morison, *The Life and Times of Saint Bernard, Abbot of Clairvaux,* A.D. *1091–1153* (London: Macmillan and Co., Limited; New York: The Macmillan Company, 1901), pp. 412–13. It makes little or no difference which is (or whether both are) correct when considering Bernard's attitude toward Gilbert.

Bibliography

I. Primary Sources

A. The Works of Bernard of Clairvaux

1. *Critical Edition*

Jean Leclercq et al. (eds.). *Sancti Bernardi opera*. Roma: Editiones Cistercienses, 8 vols. in 9, 1957–1977.

2. *Individual Works and Translations*

Apologia ad Guillelmum abbatum. Opera 3:81–108.

> Trans.: *An Apology to Abbot William*. Trans. Michael Casey; intro. Jean Leclercq. The Works of Bernard of Clairvaux 1; Treatises I. Cistercian Fathers 1. Spencer, Massachusetts: Cistercian Publications, 1970, pp. 33–69.

De baptismo (Epistola 77 ad magistrum Hugonem de Sancto Victore). Opera 7:184–200.

> Trans.: Hugh Feiss, "*Bernardus Scholasticus:* The Correspondence of Bernard of Clairvaux and Hugh of Saint Victor on Baptism." In John R. Sommerfeldt (ed.), *Bernardus Magister: Papers Presented at the Nonacentenary Celebration of the Birth of Saint Bernard of Clairvaux, Kalamazoo, Michigan, Sponsored by the Institute of Cistercian Studies, Western Michigan University, 10–13 May 1990*. Cistercian Studies 135. Kalamazoo, Michigan: Cistercian Publications; Saint-Nicolas-lès-Cîteaux: Cîteaux: Commentarii Cistercienses, 1992, pp. 360–77.

De consideratione ad Eugenium papam. Opera 3:393–493.

> Trans.: *Five Books on Consideration: Advice to a Pope*. Trans. John D. Anderson and Elizabeth T. Kennan. The Works of Bernard of

176   BIBLIOGRAPHY

Clairvaux 13. Cistercian Fathers 37. Kalamazoo, Michigan: Cistercian Publications, 1976.

Epistolae. Opera 7 and 8.

Trans.: *The Letters of St. Bernard of Clairvaux.* Trans. Bruno Scott James. London: Burns Oates, 1953. Reprint: Kalamazoo, Michigan: Cistercian Publications, 1998.

Letter to Abbot Guy and the Monks of Montiéramey. Trans. Martinus Cawley. The Works of Bernard of Clairvaux 1; Treatises I. Cistercian Fathers 1. Spencer, Massachusetts: Cistercian Publications, 1970, pp. 180–82.

Epistola ad Aelredum abbatem de speculo caritatis. In A. Hoste and C. H. Talbot (eds.), *Aelredi Rievallensis opera omnia.* Corpus Christianorum Continuatio Mediaevalis 1. Turnholti: Typographi Brepols Editores Pontificii, 1971, pp. 3–4.

Trans.: *A Letter of Bernard, Abbot of Clairvaux, to Abbot Aelred.* In Aelred of Rievaulx, *The Mirror of Charity.* Trans. Elizabeth Connor. Cistercian Fathers 17. Kalamazoo, Michigan: Cistercian Publications, 1990, pp. 69–72.

Liber de diligendo Deo. Opera 3:119–54.

Trans.: *On Loving God.* Trans. and intro. Robert Walton. The Works of Bernard of Clairvaux 5; Treatises II. Cistercian Fathers 13. Washington, D.C.: Cistercian Publications, 1974, pp. 92–132. Reprinted as Cistercian Fathers 13B; Kalamazoo, Michigan: Cistercian Publications Inc., 1995.

Liber de gradibus humilitatis et superbiae. Opera 3:13–59.

Trans.: *The Steps of Humility and Pride.* Trans. M. Ambrose Conway; intro. M. Basil Pennington. The Works of Bernard of Clairvaux 5; Treatises II. Cistercian Fathers 13. Washington, D.C.: Cistercian Publications, 1974, pp. 25–82.

Liber de gratia et libero arbitrio. Opera 3:165–203.

Trans.: *On Grace and Free Choice.* Trans. Daniel O'Donovan; intro. Bernard McGinn. The Works of Bernard of Clairvaux 7; Treatises III. Cistercian Fathers 19. Kalamazoo, Michigan: Cistercian Publications Inc., 1977, pp. 51–111.

Liber ad milites Templi de laude novae militiae. Opera 3:213–39.

Trans.: *In Praise of the New Knighthood.* Trans. M. Conrad Greenia; intro. R. J. Zwi Werblowsky. The Works of Bernard of

Clairvaux 7; Treatises III. Cistercian Fathers 19. Kalamazoo, Michigan: Cistercian Publications Inc., 1977, pp. 127–67.

Liber de praecepto et dispensatione. Opera 3:254–94.
Trans.: *Monastic Obligations and Abbatial Authority: Saint Bernard's Book on Precept and Dispensation.* Trans. Conrad Greenia; intro. Jean Leclercq. The Works of Bernard of Clairvaux 1; Treatises I. Cistercian Fathers 1. Spencer, Massachusetts: Cistercian Pubications, 1970, pp. 103–50.

Parabolae. Opera 6/2:261–303.
Trans.: *The Parables.* Trans. and intro. Michael Casey. Cistercian Fathers 55. Kalamazoo, Michigan: Cistercian Publications, 2000, pp. 9–102.

Sententiae. Opera 6/2:7–255.
Trans.: *The Sentences.* Trans. Francis R. Swietek; intro. John R. Sommerfeldt. Cistercian Fathers 55. Kalamazoo, Michigan: Cistercian Publications, 2000, pp. 103–458.

Sermones per annum. Opera 4:161–492; 5; and 6/1:9–55.
Trans.: *St. Bernard's Sermons for the Seasons & Principal Festivals of the Year.* Trans. A Priest of Mount Melleray [Ailbe J. Luddy]. Reprint, Westminster, Maryland: The Carroll Press, 3 vols., 1950.

Note: a translation of some of these sermons, *Sermones in Quadragesima de psalmo "Qui habitat"* (*Opera* 4:383–492), appears as *Lenten Sermons on the Psalm "He Who Dwells"* in *Sermons on Conversion.* Trans. Marie-Bernard Saïd. Cistercian Fathers 25. Kalamazoo, Michigan: Cistercian Publications, 1981, pp. 111–261. *The Sermon on the Passing of Saint Malachy the Bishop* (*In transitu sancti Malachiae episcopi; Opera* 5:417–23) and the *Homily on the Anniversary of the Death of Saint Malachy* (*De sancto Malachia; Opera* 6/1:50–55) are translated in *The Life and Death of Saint Malachy the Irishman.* Trans. Robert T. Meyer. Cistercian Fathers 10. Kalamazoo, Michigan: Cistercian Publications, 1978, pp. 95–112. Nineteen of the liturgical sermons are translated in *Sermons for the Summer Season: Liturgical Sermons from Rogationtide and Pentecost.* Trans. Beverly Mayne Kienzle and James Jarembowski. Cistercian Fathers 53. Kalamazoo, Michigan: Cistercian Publications, 1991.

Sermones super Cantica canticorum. Opera 1 and 2.
> Trans.: Sermons 1–20: *On the Song of Songs I.* Trans. Kilian Walsh; intro. M. Corneille Halflants. The Works of Bernard of Clairvaux 2. Cistercian Fathers 4. Kalamazoo, Michigan: Cistercian Publications Inc., 1981 (first printing 1971).

> Sermons 21–46: *On the Song of Songs II.* Trans. Kilian Walsh; intro. Jean Leclercq. The Works of Bernard of Clairvaux 3. Cistercian Fathers 7. Kalamazoo, Michigan: Cistercian Publications, 1976.

> Sermons 47–66: *On the Song of Songs III.* Trans. Kilian Walsh and Irene M. Edmonds; intro. Emero Stiegman. Cistercian Fathers 31. Kalamazoo, Michigan: Cistercian Publications, 1979.

> Sermons 67–86: *On the Song of Songs IV.* Trans. Irene Edmonds; intro. Jean Leclercq. Cistercian Fathers 40. Kalamazoo, Michigan: Cistercian Publications, 1980.

Sermo ad clericos de conversione. Opera 4:69–116.
> Trans.: *On Conversion, A Sermon to Clerics.* Trans. and intro. Marie-Bernard Saïd. In *Sermons on Conversion.* Cistercian Fathers 25. Kalamazoo, Michigan: Cistercian Publications, 1981, pp. 31–79.

Sermones de diversis. Opera 6/1:73–406.
> Note: a few of these sermons, titled *Miscellaneous Sermons*, are translated in *St. Bernard's Sermons for the Seasons & Principal Festivals of the Year.* Trans. A Priest of Mount Melleray [Ailbe J. Luddy]. Reprint, Westminster, Maryland: The Carroll Press, 3 vols., 1950, 3:397–552.

Sermones in laudibus Virginis Matris [Homiliae super "Missus est" in laubibus Virginis Matris]. Opera 4:13–58.
> Trans.: *Four Homilies in Praise of the Virgin Mother.* Trans. Marie-Bernard Saïd and Grace Perigo; intro. Chrysogonus Waddell. In *Magnificat: Homilies in Praise of the Blessed Virgin Mary.* Cistercian Fathers 18. Kalamazoo, Michigan: Cistercian Publications Inc., 1979, pp. 1–58.

Vita sancti Malachiae episcopi. Opera 3:307–78.
> Trans.: *The Life of Saint Malachy.* Trans. Robert T. Meyer. In *The Life and Death of Saint Malachy the Irishman.* Cistercian Fathers 10. Kalamazoo, Michigan: Cistercian Publications, 1978, pp. 9–93.

B. Works by Other Authors

Anselm of Canterbury. *Proslogion*. Latin text and translation in M. J. Charlesworth, *St. Anselm's* Proslogion *with* A Reply on Behalf of the Fool *by Gaunilo and* The Author's Reply to Gaunilo. Oxford: At the Clarendon Press, 1965, pp. 110–55.

Benedict of Nursia. *Regula monachorum*. Ed. Cuthbertus Butler. 3rd ed. St. Louis: B. Herder Book Co., 1935.

> Trans.: *Households of God: The Rule of St Benedict with Explanations for Monks and Lay-people Today*. Trans. David Parry. Cistercian Studies 39. Kalamazoo, Michigan: Cistercian Publications, 1980.

Geoffrey of Auxerre. *Fragmenta de vita et miraculis s. Bernardi*. Ed. Robert Lechat. In *Analecta Bollandiana* 50 (1932) 83–122.

> Trans. (in part): *Bernard of Clairvaux: Early Biographies*, 2, *By Geoffrey and Others*. Trans. Martinus Cawley. Lafayette, Oregon: Guadalupe Translations, 1990.

———. *Sancti Bernardi abbatis Clarae-Vallensis vita et res gestae [Vita prima]* libri 3–5. In J.-P. Migne (ed.), *Patrologia latina*. Paris: apud J.-P. Migne editorem, 1841. Vol. 185, cols. 301–410.

Henry of Sens et al. *Epistola ad Innocentium pontificum*. In J.-P. Migne (ed.), *Patrologia latina*. Paris: apud J.-P. Migne editorem, 1841. Vol. 185, cols. 540–42.

Innocent II. *Rescriptum contra haereses Petri Abaelardi*. In J.-P. Migne (ed.), *Patrologia latina*. Paris: apud J.-P. Migne editorem, 1841. Vol. 182, cols. 359–61.

Otto of Freising. *Gesta Friderici I. imperatoris*. In G. Waitz and B. de Simpson (eds.), *Monumenta Germaniae historica, Scriptores rerum Germanicarum in usum scholarium . . .*, 46. 3rd ed. Hannover, Leipzig: Impensis Bibliopolii Hahniani, 1912, reprint 1978, pp. 9–161.

> Trans.: Otto of Freising and His Continuator Rahewin. *The Deeds of Frederick Barbarossa*. Trans. Charles Christopher Mierow. Records of Civilization, Sources and Studies. Reprint, New York: W. W. Norton & Company, Inc., 1966, pp. 21–169.

Peter Abelard. *Historia calamitatem*. Ed. J. T. Muckle. *Mediaeval Studies* 12 (1950) 163–213.

———. *Introductio ad theologiam*. In J.-P. Migne (ed.), *Patrologia latina*. Paris: apud J.-P. Migne editorem, 1841. Vol. 178, cols. 979–1114.

———. *Theologia christiana*. In J.-P. Migne (ed.), *Patrologia latina*. Paris: apud J.-P. Migne editorem, 1841. Vol. 178, cols. 1123–1330.

Peter Berengar of Poitiers. *Apologeticus contra Bernardum, Claraevallensem abbatem, et alios qui condemnaverunt Petrum Abaelardum.* In J.-P. Migne (ed.), *Patrologia latina.* Paris: apud J.-P. Migne editorem, 1841. Vol. 178, cols. 301–410.

Peter the Venerable. *Epistola 98.* In Giles Constable (ed.), *The Letters of Peter the Venerable.* Cambridge, Massachusetts: Harvard University Press, 2 vols., 1967, 1:258–59.

Samson of Reims et al. *Epistola ad Innocentium.* In Jean Leclercq et al. (eds.), *Sancti Bernardi opera.* Roma: Editiones Cistercienses, 8 vols. in 9, 1957–1977, 8:41–43.

William of Saint Thierry. *Epistola ad Gaufrido, Carnotensium episcopo, et Bernardo, Claraevallis abbati.* In Jean Leclercq (ed.), "Les lettres de Guillaume de Saint-Thierry à saint Bernard." In Jean Leclercq, *Recueil d'études sur saint Bernard et ses écrits* 4. Roma: Edizioni di storia e letteratura, 1987, pp. 351–53. Reprinted from *Revue Bénédictine* 79 (1969) 375–91.

———. *Vita prima, Liber primus.* In. J.-P. Migne (ed.), *Patrologia latina.* Paris: apud J.-P. Migne editorem, 1841. Vol. 185, cols. 225–66.

        Trans: *Bernard of Clairvaux: Early Biographies,* 1, *By William of St. Thierry.* Trans. Martinus Cawley. Lafayette, Oregon: Guadalupe Translations, 1989.

II. SECONDARY SOURCES

Altisent, Agustín M. "Inteligencia y cultura en la vida espiritual, segun los 'Sermones Super Cantica' de S. Bernardo." In *Los monjes y los estudios: IV semana de estudios monasticos, Poblet 1961.* Poblet: Abadía de Poblet, 1963, pp. 147–62.

Anderson, Luke. "The Appeal to Reason in St Bernard's *De diligendo Deo.*" In E. Rozanne Elder and John R. Sommerfeldt (eds.), *The Chimaera of His Age: Studies in Medieval Cistercian History V.* Cistercian Studies 63. Kalamazoo, Michigan: Cistercian Publications Inc., 1980, pp. 132–39.

———. "The Postlapsarian Influence on Bernard's Doctrine of *Imago Dei* in his *Super Cantica.*" Unpublished paper read at the 1991 Cistercian Conference, held in conjunction with the Twenty-sixth International Medieval Congress at Kalamazoo, Michigan.

———. "Wisdom and Eloquence in St Bernard's *In dedicatione ecclesiae sermo primus.*" In John R. Sommerfeldt (ed.), *Erudition at God's Service:*

Studies in Medieval Cistercian History XI. Cistercian Studies 98. Kalamazoo, Michigan: Cistercian Publications Inc., 1987, pp. 117–31.

Baldwin, John W. *The Scholastic Culture of the Middle Ages, 1000–1300.* Lexington, Massachusetts: D. C. Heath and Company, 1971.

Beck, Hans-Georg, et al. *History of the Church, 4, From the High Middle
Ages to the Eve of the Reformation.* Trans. Anselm Biggs. New York:
Crossroad, 1986.

Bell, David N. "Plato Monasticus: Plato and the Platonic Tradition Among
the Cistercians." In Mark Joyal (ed.), *Studies in Plato and the Platonic
Tradition: Essays Presented to John Whitaker.* Aldershot, Brookfield, Singapore, Sydney: Ashgate, 1997, pp. 83–96.

Bernhart, Joseph. *Die philosophische Mystik des Mittelalters von ihren antiken
Ursprung bis zur Renaissance.* Geschichte der Philosophie in Einzel-
darstellungen 3, Die christliche Philosophie 14. München: Verlag Ernst
Reinhardt, 1922.

Borst, Arno. "Abälard und Bernhard." *Historische Zeitschrift* 186 (1958)
497–526.

Bouyer, Louis. *The Cistercian Heritage.* Trans. Elizabeth A. Livingstone.
London: A. R. Mowbray & Co. Limited, 1958.

Brauneck, Ingeborg. *Bernhard von Clairvaux als Mystiker.* Hamburg: G. H.
Nolte, 1935.

Bredero, Adriaan H. "Conflicting Interpretations of the Relevance of
Bernard of Clairvaux to the History of His Own Time." *Cîteaux: Commentarii cistercienses* 31 (1980) 1:53–81.

Burch, George Boswell. "Introduction" to *The Steps of Humility by Bernard,
Abbot of Clairvaux.* Cambridge, Massachusetts: Harvard University
Press, 1942, pp. 3–112.

Butler, Cuthbert. *Western Mysticism: The Teaching of SS. Augustine, Gregory
and Bernard on Contemplation and the Contemplative Life, with Afterthoughts.* 2nd ed. London: Arrow Books, 1960.

Buytaert, Eligius M. "The Anonymous Capitula Haeresum Petri Abaelardi
and the Synod of Sens, 1140." *Antonianum* 43 (1968) 419–60.

Casey, Michael. *Athirst for God: Spiritual Desire in Bernard's Sermons on the
Song of Songs.* Cistercian Studies 77. Kalamazoo, Michigan: Cistercian
Publications, 1988.

———. "The Last Two Sermons by Bernard of Clairvaux." *Cistercian Studies*
22 (1987) 37–54.

Chenu, M.-D. *Nature, Man, and Society in the Twelfth Century: Essays on New
Theological Perspectives in the Latin West.* Trans. Jerome Taylor and Lester
K. Little. Chicago, London: The University of Chicago Press, 1968.

Congar, Yves. "Die Ekklesiologie des hl. Bernhard." In Joseph Lortz (ed.), *Bernhard von Clairvaux, Mönch und Mystiker: Internationaler Bernhardkongress, Mainz 1953.* Veröffentlichungen des Instituts für euopäische Geschichte Mainz, 6. Wiesbaden: Franz Steiner Verlag GmbH, 1955, pp. 76–119.

Courtenay, William J. "Inquiry and Inquisition: Academic Freedom in Medieval Universities." *Church History* 58 (1989) 168–81.

De Warren, Henry-Bernard. "Bernard, les princes et la société féodale." In *Bernard de Clairvaux.* Commission d'histoire de l'Ordre de Cîteaux, 3. Paris: Alsatia, 1953, pp. 649–57.

DiLorenzo, Raymond D. "Dante's Saint Bernard and the Theology of Liberty in the *Commedia.*" In John R. Sommerfeldt (ed.), *Bernardus Magister: Papers Presented at the Nonacentenary Celebration of the Birth of Saint Bernard of Clairvaux, Kalamazoo, Michigan, Sponsored by the Institute of Cistercian Studies, Western Michigan University, 10–13 May 1990.* Cistercian Studies 135. Kalamazoo, Michigan: Cistercian Pubications; Saint-Nicolas-lès-Cîteaux: Cîteaux: Commentarii Cistercienses, 1992, pp. 497–514.

Dimier, Anselme. "Les premiers Cisterciens: Etaient-ils ennemis des études?" In *Los monjes y los estudios: IV semana de estudios monasticos, Poblet 1961.* Poblet: Abadía de Poblet, 1963, pp. 119–46.

Dinzelbacher, Peter. *Bernhard von Clairvaux: Leben und Werk des berühmten Zisterziensers.* Gestalten des Mittelalters und der Renaissance. Darmstadt: Wissenschaftliche Buchgesellschaft, 1998.

Dumont, Charles. "Aelred of Rievaulx: His Life and Works." The introduction to Aelred of Rievaulx, *The Mirror of Charity.* Trans. Elizabeth Connor. Cistercian Studies 17. Kalamazoo, Michigan: Cistercian Publications, 1990, pp. 11–67.

Evans, Gillian R. "The Classical Education of Bernard of Clairvaux." *Cîteaux: Commentarii cistercienses* 33 (1982) 121–34.

———. *The Mind of St. Bernard of Clairvaux.* Oxford: Clarendon Press, 1983.

Feiss, Hugh. "Bernardus Scholasticus: The Correspondence of Bernard of Clairvaux and Hugh of Saint Victor on Baptism." In John R. Sommerfeldt (ed.), *Bernardus Magister: Papers Presented at the Nonacentenary Celebration of the Birth of Saint Bernard of Clairvaux, Kalamazoo, Michigan, Sponsored by the Institute of Cistercian Studies, Western Michigan University, 10–13 May 1990.* Cistercian Studies 135. Kalamazoo, Michigan: Cistercian Publications; Saint-Nicolas-lès-Cîteaux: Cîteaux: Commentarii Cistercienses, 1992, pp. 349–78.

Ferguson, Wallace K. *The Renaissance in Historical Thought: Five Centuries of Interpretation.* Cambridge: The Riverside Press, 1948.

Ferruolo, Stephen C. *The Origins of the University: The Schools of Paris and Their Critics, 1100–1215.* Stanford, California: Stanford University Press, 1985.

Frank, William. "*Sine proprio*: On Liberty and Grace, A Juxtaposition of Bernard of Clairvaux and John Duns Scotus." In John R. Sommerfeldt (ed.), *Bernardus Magister: Papers Presented at the Nonacentenary Celebration of the Birth of Saint Bernard of Clairvaux, Kalamazoo, Michigan, Sponsored by the Institute of Cistercian Studies, Western Michigan University, 10–13 May 1990.* Cistercian Studies 135. Kalamazoo, Michigan: Cistercian Publications; Saint-Nicolas-lès-Cîteaux: Cîteaux: Commentarii Cistercienses, 1992, pp. 461–78.

Fritegotto, Raphael. *De vocatione christiana S. Bernardi doctrina.* Studia Antoniana 15. Roma: Pontificum Athenaeum Antonianum, 1961.

Gilson, Étienne. *Heloise and Abelard.* Trans. L. K. Shook. Chicago: Henry Regnery, 1951.

———. *The Mystical Theology of Saint Bernard.* Trans. A. H. C. Downes. London, New York: Sheed & Ward, 1940. Reprinted in the Cistercian Studies series, 120. Kalamazoo, Michigan: Cistercian Publications, 1990.

Gössmann, Elisabeth. "Dialektische und rhetorische Implikationen der Auseinandersetzung zwischen Abaelard und Bernhard von Clairvaux um die Gotteserkenntnis." In Jan P. Beckmann et al. (eds.), *Sprache und Erkenntnis im Mittelalter: Akten des VI. internationalen Kongresses für mittelalterliche Philosophie der Société internationale pour l'étude de la philosophie médiévale, 29 August–3 September 1977, in Bonn.* Berlin, New York: Walter De Gruyter, 1981, 2. Halbband, pp. 890–902.

Häring, Nikolaus M. "Abelard Yesterday and Today." In *Pierre Abélard, Pierre le Vénérable: Les courants philosophiques, littéraires et artistiques en Occident au milieu du XIIe siècle; Abbaye de Cluny, 2 au 9 juillet 1972.* Colloques internationaux du Centre National de la Recherche Scientifique 546. Paris: Éditions du Centre National de la Recherche Scientifique, 1975, pp. 341–403.

———. "Saint Bernard and the *Litterati* of His Day." *Cîteaux: Commentarii cistercienses* 25 (1974) 199–222.

———. "San Bernardo e Gilberto vescovo di Poitiers." In *Studi su s. Bernardo di Chiaravalle nell'octavo centenario della canonizzazione, Convegno internazionale Certosa di Firenze: (6–9 novembre 1974).* Bibliotheca cisterciensis 6. Roma: Editiones Cistercienses, 1975, pp. 75–91.

———. "Die theologische Sprachlogik der Schule von Chartres im zwölften Jahrhundert." In Jan P. Beckmann et al. (eds.), *Sprache und Erkenntnis im Mittelalter: Akten des VI. internationalen Kongresses für mittelalterliche Philosophie der Société internationale pour l'étude de la philosophie médiévale, 29. August–3. September 1977, in Bonn.* Berlin, New York: Walter De Gruyter, 1981, 2. Halbband, pp. 930–36.

Jacqueline, Bernard. "Répertoire des citations d'auteurs profanes dans les oeuvres de saint Bernard." In *Bernard de Clairvaux.* Commission d'histoire de l'Ordre de Cîteaux 3. Paris: Alsatia, 1953, pp. 549–54.

———. "Saint Grégoire le Grand et l'ecclésiologie de saint Bernard." *Collectanea Cisterciensia* 36 (1974) 69–73.

James, Bruno S. *Saint Bernard of Clairvaux: An Essay in Biography.* London: Hodder & Stoughton, 1957.

Jordan, Mark D. "Thomas [Aquinas] on Bernard and the Life of Contemplation." In John R. Sommerfeldt (ed.), *Bernardus Magister: Papers Presented at the Nonacentenary Celebration of the Birth of Saint Bernard of Clairvaux, Kalamazoo, Michigan, Sponsored by the Institute of Cistercian Studies, Western Michigan University, 10–13 May 1990.* Cistercian Studies 135. Kalamazoo, Michigan: Cistercian Publications; Saint-Nicolas-lès-Cîteaux: Cîteaux: Commentarii Cistercienses, 1992, pp. 449–60.

Elizabeth T. Kennan. "Antithesis and Argument in the *De consideratione.*" In M. Basil Pennington (ed.), *Bernard of Clairvaux: Studies Presented to Dom Jean Leclercq.* Cistercian Studies 23. Washington, D.C.: Cistercian Publications, 1973, pp. 91–109.

———. "The 'De consideratione' of St. Bernard of Clairvaux and the Papacy in the Mid-twelfth Century: A Review of Scholarship." *Traditio* 23 (1967) 73–115.

———. "Rhetoric and Style in the *De consideratione.*" In John R. Sommerfeldt (ed.), *Studies in Medieval Cistercian History II.* Cistercian Studies 24. Kalamazoo, Michigan: Cistercian Publications, 1976, pp. 40–48.

Kleineidam, Erich. "Wissen, Wissenschaft, Theologie bei Bernhard von Clairvaux." In Joseph Lortz (ed.), *Bernhard von Clairvaux, Mönch und Mystiker: Internationaler Bernhardkongress Mainz 1953.* Veröffentlichungen des Instituts für europäische Geschichte Mainz 6. Wiesbaden: Franz Steiner GmbH, 1955, pp. 128–67.

Kolmar, Lothar. "Abaelard und Bernhard von Clairvaux in Sens." *Zeitschrift der Savigny-Stiftung für Rechtsgeschichte* 98, *Kanonistische Abteilung* 67 (1981) 121–47.

Lackner, Bede K. "The Monastic Life According to Saint Bernard." In John R. Sommerfeldt (ed.), *Studies in Medieval Cistercian History II.* Cistercian Studies 24. Kalamazoo, Michigan: Cistercian Publications, 1976, pp. 49–62.

———. "Saint Bernard: On Bishops and Rome." *The American Benedictine Review* 40 (1989) 380–82.

Landgraf, Arthur Michael. "Probleme um den hl. Bernhard von Clairvaux." *Cistercienser-Chronik* 61 (1959) 1–16.

Lane, A. N. S. "Bernard of Clairvaux: A Forerunner of Jean Calvin?" In John R. Sommerfeldt (ed.), *Bernardus Magister: Papers Presented at the Nonacentenary Celebration of the Birth of Saint Bernard of Clairvaux, Kalamazoo, Michigan, Sponsored by the Institute of Cistercian Studies, Western Michigan University, 10–13 May 1990.* Cistercian Studies 135. Kalamazoo, Michigan: Cistercian Publications; Saint-Nicolas-lès-Cîteaux: Cîteaux: Commentarii Cistercienses, 1992, pp. 531–43.

Leclercq, Jean. "L'art de la composition dans les sermons de s. Bernard." In Jean Leclercq, *Recueil d'études sur saint Bernard et ses écrits* 3. Roma: Edizioni di stori e letteratura, 1969, pp. 105–62. Reprinted from *Revue Bénédictine* 76 (1966) 87–115.

———. *Bernard of Clairvaux and the Cistercian Spirit.* Trans. Claire Lavoie. Cistercian Studies 16. Kalamazoo, Michigan: Cistercian Publications, 1976.

———. "Sur le caractère littéraire des sermons de s. Bernard." In Jean Leclercq, *Recueil d'études sur saint Bernard et ses écrits* 3. Roma: Edizioni di storia e letteratura, 1969, pp. 163–210. Reprinted from *Studi medievali* 7 (1966) 701–44.

———. "*Curiositas* and the Return to God in St Bernard of Clairvaux." *Cistercian Studies* 25 (1990) 92–100.

———. *Études sur saint Bernard et le texte de ses écrits.* In *Analecta Sacri Ordinis Cisterciensis* 9 (1953) fasc. 1–2. Roma: Apud Curiam Generalem Sacri Ordinis Cisterciensis, 1953.

———. "Introduction" to *Bernard of Clairvaux: Selected Works.* The Classics of Western Spirituality. New York, Mahwah, N.J.: Paulist Press, 1987, pp. 13–57.

———. "Introduction" to *St Bernard's Apology to Abbot William.* In Bernard of Clairvaux, *Treatises I.* The Works of Bernard of Clairvaux 1. Cistercian Fathers 1. Spencer, Massachusetts: Cistercian Publications, 1970, pp. 3–30.

———. "The Love of Beauty as a Means and an Expression of the Love of Truth." *Mittellateinisches Jahrbuch* 16 (1981) 62–72.

———. *The Love of Learning and the Desire for God: A Study of Monastic Culture.* Trans. Catherine Misrahi. New York: A Mentor Omega Book Published by the New American Library, 1962.

————. "The Making of a Masterpiece." The introduction to Bernard of Clairvaux, *On the Song of Songs IV*. Cistercian Fathers 40. Kalamazoo, Michigan: Cistercian Publications, 1980, pp. ix–xxiv.

————. *Monks and Love in Twelfth-Century France: Psycho-Historical Essays*. Oxford:
at the Clarendon Press, 1979.

————. "Saint Bernard on the Church." *Downside Review* 85 (1967) 274–94.

————. "Saint Bernard écrivain." In Jean Leclercq, *Recueil d'études sur saint
Bernard et ses écrits* 1. Roma: Edizioni di storia e letteratura, 1962, pp.
321–51. Reprinted from *Revue Bénédictine* 70 (1960) 562–90.

————. "St. Bernard and the Formative Community." *Cistercian Studies* 14
(1979) 99–119.

————. *Saint Bernard mystique*. N.p.: Desclée De Brouwer, 1948.

————. "Saint Bernard in Our Times." Trans. Garth L. Fowden. Published as
a pamphlet by the Stubbs Society. Oxford: Impensis Roberti Lyle &
prostant venales apud G.L.J.S.; Printed for the Society at The Holywell
Press in Alfred Street, 1973. Also in M. Basil Pennington (ed.), *Saint
Bernard of Clairvaux: Studies Commemorating the Eighth Centenary of
His Canonization*. Cistercian Studies 28. Kalamazoo, Michigan: Cistercian Publications, 1977, pp. 1–26.

————. "Spiritual Guidance and Counseling According to St Bernard." In John
R. Sommerfeldt (ed.), *Abba: Guides to Wholeness and Holiness East and
West*. Cistercian Studies 38. Kalamazoo, Michigan: Cistercian Publica-
tions, 1982, pp. 64–87.

————. "Textes sur saint Bernard et Gilbert de la Porée." In Jean Leclercq,
Recueil d'études sur saint Bernard et ses écrits 2. Roma: Edizioni di storia
e letteratura, 1966, pp. 341–71. Reprinted from *Mediaval Studies* 14
(1952) 107–28.

————. "The Theme of Jesting in St Bernard and His Contemporaries." *Cistercian Studies* 9 (1974) 7–21.

————. *Women and Saint Bernard of Clairvaux*. Trans. Marie-Bernard Saïd. Cistercian Studies 104. Kalamazoo, Michigan: Cistercian Publications, 1989.

Lekai, Louis J. *The Cistercians: Ideals and Reality*. Kent, Ohio: The Kent
State University Press, 1977.

Linhardt, Robert. *Die Mystik des heiligen Bernhard von Clairvaux*. München:
Verlag Natur u. Kultur, 1923.

Little, Edward. "Bernard and Abelard at the Council of Sens." In M. Basil
Pennington (ed.), *Bernard of Clairvaux: Studies Presented to Dom Jean
Leclercq*. Cistercian Studies 23. Washington, D.C.: Cistercian Publica-
tions, 1973, pp. 55–71.

————. "Relations Between St Bernard and Abelard Before 1139." In M. Basil Pennington (ed.), *Saint Bernard of Clairvaux: Studies Commemorating the Eighth Centenary of His Canonization.* Cistercian Studies 28. Kalamazoo, Michigan: Cistercian Publications, 1977, pp. 155–68.

————. "The Source of the *Capitula* of Sens of 1140." In John R. Sommerfeldt (ed.), *Studies in Medieval Cistercian History II.* Cistercian Studies 24. Kalamazoo, Michigan: Cistercian Publications, 1976, pp. 87–91.

Mann, Horace K. *The Lives of the Popes in the Middle Ages.* 2nd ed. London: Kegan Paul, Trench, Trubner & Co., Ltd.; St. Louis, Mo.: B. Herder Book Co., 18 vols., 1914–1932.

Marebon, John. "Gilbert of Poitiers." In Peter Dronke (ed.), *A History of Twelfth-Century Philosophy.* Cambridge, New York, New Rochelle, Melbourne, Sydney: Cambridge University Press, 1988, pp. 328–52.

Marilier, Jean. "Les prèmieres années; Les études à Châtillon." In *Bernard de Clairvaux.* Commission d'histoire de l'Ordre de Cîteaux, 3. Paris: Editions Alsatia, 1953, pp. 17–27.

McCabe, Joseph. *Peter Abélard.* New York: G. P. Putnam's Sons, 1901.

McGinn, Bernard. "*Alter Moyses:* The Role of Bernard of Clairvaux in the Thought of Joachim of Fiore." In John R. Sommerfeldt (ed.), *Bernardus Magister: Papers Presented at the Nonacentenary Celebration of the Birth of Bernard of Clairvaux, Kalamazoo, Michigan, Sponsored by the Institute of Cistercian Studies, Western Michigan University, 10–13 May 1990.* Cistercian Studies 135. Kalamazoo, Michigan: Cistercian Publications; Saint-Nicolas-lès-Cîteaux: Cîteaux: Commentarii Cistercienses, 1992, pp. 429–48.

————. *The Growth of Mysticism.* The Presence of God: A History of Western Christian Mysticism 2. New York: Crossroad, 1994.

————. "Introduction" to *On Grace and Free Choice.* The Works of Bernard of Clairvaux 7; Treatises III. Cistercian Fathers 19. Kalamazoo, Michigan: Cistercian Publications Inc., 1977, pp. 3–50.

Mews, Constant J. "The Council of Sens (1141): Abelard, Bernard, and the Fear of Social Upheaval." *Speculum* 77 (2002) 342–82.

Mills, Barton R. V. "Introduction" to *Saint Bernard: The Twelve Degrees of Humility and Pride.* London: Society for Promoting Christian Knowledge; New York, Toronto: The Macmillan Co., 1929, pp. vii–xxxv.

Mohrmann, Christine. "Le style de saint Bernard." In *S. Bernardo: Pubblicazione commemorativa nell'VIII centenario della sua morte.* Pubblicazioni dell'Università Cattolica del S. Cuore, nuova scric 46. Milano: Società Editrice "Vita e Pensiero," 1954, pp. 166–84.

Morison, James Cotter. *The Life and Times of Saint Bernard, Abbot of Clair-vaux*, A.D. *1091–1153*. London: Macmillan and Co., Limited; New York: The Macmillan Company, 1901.

Murray, A. Victor. *Abelard and St Bernard: A Study in Twelfth Century "Modernism."* Manchester: Manchester University Press; New York: Barnes & Noble, Inc., 1967.

Newhauser, Richard. "The Sin of Curiosity and the Cistercians." In John R. Sommerfeldt (ed.), *Erudition at God's Service: Studies in Medieval Cistercian History XI*. Cistercian Studies 98. Kalamazoo, Michigan: Cistercian Publications Inc., 1987, pp. 71–95.

Newman, Martha G. *The Boundaries of Charity: Cistercian Culture and Ecclesiastical Reform, 1098–1180*. Figurae: Reading Medieval Culture. Stanford, California: Stanford University Press, 1996.

Ott, Ludwig. *Untersuchungen zur theologischen Briefliteratur der Frühscholastik unter besondere Berücksichtigung des Viktorinerkreises*. Beiträge zur Geschichte der Philosophie und Theologie des Mittelalters 34. Münster i. W.: Aschendorff, 1937.

Ozment, Steven. *The Age of Reform, 1250–1550: An Intellectual and Religious History of Late Medieval and Reformation Europe*. New Haven: Yale University Press, 1980.

Paré, G., et al. *La renaissance du XIIe siècle: Les écoles et l'enseignement*. Publications de l'Institut d'Études Médiévales d'Ottawa 3. Paris: J. Vrin, 1933.

Paulsell, William O. "Ethical Theory in the Sermons on the Song of Songs." In E. Rozanne Elder and John R. Sommerfeldt (eds.), *The Chimaera of His Age: Studies on Bernard of Clairvaux; Studies in Medieval Cistercian History V*. Cistercian Studies 63. Kalamazoo, Michigan: Cistercian Publications Inc., 1980, pp. 12–22.

Posset, Franz. "*Divus Bernhardus:* Saint Bernard as Spiritual and Theological Mentor of the Reformer Martin Luther." In John R. Sommerfeldt (ed.), *Bernardus Magister: Papers Presented at the Nonacentenary Celebration of the Birth of Saint Bernard of Clairvaux, Kalamazoo, Michigan, Sponsored by the Insitutute of Cistercian Studies, Western Michigan University, 10–13 May 1990*. Cistercian Studies 135. Kalamazoo, Michigan: Cistercian Publications; Saint-Nicolas-lès-Cîteaux: Cîteaux: Commentarii Cistercienses, 1992, pp. 515–30.

Pourrat, Pierre. *Christian Spirituality in the Middle Ages*. Trans. S. P. Jacques. Westminster, Maryland: The Newman Press, 1953.

Reiter, Josef. "Bernard de Clairvaux, philosophe malgré lui entre coeur et raison?" In Rémi Brague (ed.), *Saint Bernard et la philosophie*. Paris: Presses Universitaires de France, 1993, pp. 11–25.

Renna, Thomas J. "Abelard versus Bernard: An Event in Monastic History." *Cîteaux: Commentarii cistercienses* 27 (1976) 189–202.

———. "Bernard vs. Abelard: An Ecclesiological Conflict." In John R. Sommerfeldt (ed.), *Simplicity and Ordinariness: Studies in Medieval Cistercian History IV*. Cistercian Studies 61. Kalamazoo, Michigan: Cistercian Publications, 1980, pp. 94–138.

———. "The City in Early Cistercian Thought." *Cîteaux: Commentarii cistercienses* 34 (1983) 5–19.

———. "St Bernard and Abelard as Hagiographers." *Cîteaux: Commentarii cistercienses* 29 (1978) 41–59.

———. "St Bernard and the Pagan Classics: An Historical View." In E. Rozanne Elder and John R. Sommerfeldt (eds.), *The Chimaera of His Age: Studies on Bernard of Clairvaux; Studies in Medieval Cistercian History V*. Cistercian Studies 63. Kalamazoo, Michigan: Cistercian Publications Inc., 1980, pp. 122–31.

Ries, Joseph. *Das geistliche Leben in seinen Entwicklungsstufen nach der Lehre des hl. Bernhard*. Freiburg i. Br.: Herder, 1906.

Rissetto, Marion. "The Recruitment Letters of Bernard of Clairvaux." *Word and Spirit: A Monastic Review* 12 (1990) 148–61.

Rovighi, Sofia Vanni. "San Bernardo e la filosofia." In *S. Bernardo: Pubblicazione commemorativa nell'VIII centenario della sua morte*. Pubblicazioni dell'Università Cattolica del S. Cuore, nuova serie 46. Milano: Società Editrice "Vita e Pensiero," 1954, pp. 132–50.

Russel, Edith. "Bernard et les dames de son temps." In *Bernard de Clairvaux*. Commission d'histoire de l'Ordre de Cîteaux 3. Paris: Alsatia, 1953, pp. 411–25.

Sabersky, Dorette. "The Compositional Structure of Bernard's Eighty-fifth Sermon on the Song of Songs." In E. Rozanne Elder, *Goad and Nail: Studies in Medieval Cistercian History X*. Cistercian Studies 84. Kalamazoo, Michigan: Cistercian Publications, 1985, pp. 86–108.

———. "*Nam iteratio, affectionis expressio est*: Zum Stil Bernhards von Clairvaux." *Cîteaux: Commentarii cistercienses* 36 (1985) 5–20.

Smalley, Beatrice. "Gilbertus Universalis, Bishop of London (1128–34) and the Problem of the 'Glossa Ordinaria.'" *Revue de Théologie ancienne et médiévale* 7 (1935) 235–62.

Sommerfeldt, John R. "Abelard and Bernard of Clairvaux." *Papers of the Michigan Academy of Science, Arts, and Letters* 46 (1961) 493–501.

———. "Bernard on Charismatic Knowledge: The Truth as Gift." *Cistercian Studies Quarterly* 32 (1997) 295–301.

———. "Bernard of Clairvaux as Sermon Writer and Sentence Speaker." The introduction to Bernard of Clairvaux, *The Sentences*. Trans. Francis R.

Swietek. Cistercian Fathers 55. Kalamazoo, Michigan: Cistercian Publications, 2000, pp. 105–14.

———. "Bernard as Contemplative." In John R. Sommerfeldt (ed.), *Bernardus Magister: Papers Presented at the Nonacentenary Celebration of the Birth of Saint Bernard of Clairvaux, Kalamazoo, Michigan, Sponsored by the Institute of Cistercian Studies, Western Michigan University, 10–13 May 1990*. Cistercian Studies 135. Kalamazoo, Michigan: Cistercian Publications; Saint-Nicolas-lès-Cîteaux: Cîteaux: Commentarii Cistercienses, 1992, pp. 73–84.

———. "Bernard of Clairvaux: The Mystic and Society." In E. Rozanne Elder (ed.), *The Spirituality of Western Christendom*. Cistercian Studies 30. Kalamazoo, Michigan: Cistercian Publications Inc., 1976, pp. 72–84 and 194–96.

———. "Bernard of Clairvaux and Scholasticism." *Papers of the Michigan Academy of Science, Arts, and Letters* 48 (1963) 265–77.

———. "Bernard of Clairvaux's Abbot: Both Daniel and Noah." In Francis R. Swietek and John R. Sommerfeldt (eds.), Studiosorum Speculum: *Studies in Honor of Louis J. Lekai, O.Cist.* Cistercian Studies 141. Kalamazoo, Michigan: Cistercian Publications, 1993, pp. 355–62.

———. "Bernard and the Trivial Arts: A Contemplative's Thoughts on Literature and Philosophy." In E. Rozanne Elder (ed.), *Praise No Less Than Charity: Studies in Honor of M. Chrysogonus Waddell, Monk of Gethsemani Abbey*. Cistercian Studies 193. Kalamazoo, Michigan: Cistercian Publications, 2002, pp. 141–59.

———. "Bernard of Clairvaux on the Truth Accessible Through Faith." In E. Rozanne Elder (ed.), *The Joy of Learning and the Love of God: Studies in Honor of Jean Leclercq*. Cistercian Studies 160. Kalamazoo, Michigan; Spencer, Massachusetts: Cistercian Publications, 1995, pp. 239–51.

———. "Charismatic and Gregorian Leadership in the Thought of Bernard of Clairvaux." In M. Basil Pennington (ed.), *Bernard of Clairvaux: Studies Presented to Dom Jean Leclercq*. Cistercian Studies 23. Washington, D.C.: Cistercian Publications, 1973, pp. 73–90.

———. "The Chimaera Revisited." *Cîteaux: Commentarii cisterciensis* 38 (1987) 5–13.

———. *Consistency of Thought in the Works of Bernard of Clairvaux: A Study of Mystical Leadership in the Twelfth Century*. Unpublished doctoral dissertation, The University of Michigan, 1960. Available from University Microfilms, Inc., Ann Arbor, Michigan (Mic 60-2571).

———. "Epistemological and Social Hierarchies: A Potential Reconciliation of Some Inconsistencies in Bernard's Thought." *Cîteaux: Commentarii cis-*

tercienses 31 (1980) 1:83–92. Reprinted in Marion Leathers Kuntz and Paul Grimley Kuntz (eds.), *Jacob's Ladder and the Tree of Life: Concepts of Hierarchy and the Great Chain of Being*. American University Studies, Series 5. Philosophy 14. New York, Bern, Frankfurt am Main, Paris: Peter Lang, 1987, pp. 141–51.

———. "The Epistemological Value of Mysticism in the Thought of Bernard of Clairvaux." In John R. Sommerfeldt (ed.), *Studies in Medieval Culture [I]*. Kalamazoo, Michigan: Western Michigan University, 1964, pp. 48–58.

———. "Epistemology, Education, and Social Theory in the Thought of Bernard of Clairvaux." In M. Basil Pennington (ed.), *Saint Bernard of Clairvaux: Studies Commemorating the Eighth Centenary of His Canonization*. Cistercian Studies 28. Kalamazoo, Michigan: Cistercian Publications, 1977, pp. 169–79.

———. "Images of Visitation: The Vocabulary of Contemplation in Aelred of Rievaulx' *Mirror of Love*, Book II." In John R. Sommerfeldt (ed.), *Erudition at God's Service: Studies in Medieval Cistercian History XI*. Cistercian Studies 98. Kalamazoo, Michigan: Cistercian Publications Inc., 1987, pp. 161–68.

———. "The Intellectual Life According to Saint Bernard." *Cîteaux: Commentarii cistercienses* 25 (1974) 249–56.

———. "The Social Teachings of Bernard of Clairvaux." In Joseph F. O'Callaghan (ed.), *Studies in Medieval Cistercian History Presented to Jeremiah F. O'Sullivan*. Cistercian Studies 13. Spencer, Massachusetts: Cistercian Publications, 1971, pp. 35–48.

———. *The Spiritual Teachings of Bernard of Clairvaux*. An Intellectual History of the Early Cistercian Order [1]. Cistercian Studies 125. Kalamazoo, Michigan: Cistercian Publications, 1991.

———. "The Vocabulary of Contemplation in Aelred of Rievaulx' *On Jesus at the Age of Twelve, A Rule of Life for a Recluse*, and *On Spiritual Friendship*." In E. Rozanne Elder (ed.), *Heaven on Earth: Studies in Medieval Cistercian History IX*. Cistercian Studies 68. Kalamazoo, Michigan: Cistercian Publications, 1983, pp. 72–89.

Southern, R. W. "The Schools of Paris and the School of Chartres." In Robert L. Benson and Giles Constable (eds.), *Renaissance and Renewal in the Twelfth Century*. Cambridge, Massachusetts: Harvard University Press, 1982, pp. 113–37.

Stiegman, Emero. "The Literary Genre of Bernard of Clairvaux's *Sermones super Cantica canticorum*." In John R. Sommerfeldt (ed.), *Simplicity and Ordinariness: Studies in Medieval Cistercian History IV*. Cistercian Studies 61. Kalamazoo, Michigan: Cistercian Publications, 1980, pp. 68–93.

————. "Saint Bernard: The Aesthetics of Authenticity." In Meredith Parsons Lillich (ed.), *Studies in Cistercian Art and Architecture 2*. Cistercian Studies 69. Kalamazoo, Michigan: Cistercian Publications Inc., 1984, pp. 1–13.

Vancandard, E. *Vie de saint Bernard*. 4th ed. Paris: Victor Lecoffre, 2 vols., 1927.

Van den Bosch, Amatus. "L'intelligence de la foi chez saint Bernard." *Cîteaux in de Nederlanden* 8 (1957) 85–108.

Verschelden, Goswinus. "Het Kennisaspect van Bernardus' Godservaring." In *Sint Bernardus van Clairvaux: Gedenkboek door monniken van de noord- en zuidnederlandse Cisterciënserabdijen samengesteld bij het achtste eeuwfeest van sint Bernardus' dood, 20 Augustus 1153–1953*. Rotterdam: N.V. Uitgeverij De Forel, 1953, pp. 65–88.

Waddell, Chrysogonus. "Peter Abelard's *Letter 10* and Cistercian Liturgical Reform." In John R. Sommerfeldt (ed.), *Studies in Medieval Cistercian History II*. Cistercian Studies 24. Kalamazoo, Michigan: Cistercian Publications, 1976, pp. 75–86.

Walsh, James J. *The Thirteenth, Greatest of Centuries*. 4th ed. New York: Catholic Summer School Press, 1912.

White, Hayden V. *The Conflict of Papal Leadership Ideals from Gregory VII to Bernard of Clarivaux with Special Reference to the Schism of 1130*. Unpublished Ph.D. dissertation, The University of Michigan, 1955.

————. "The Gregorian Ideal and St. Bernard of Clairvaux." *Journal of the History of Ideas* 21 (1960) 321–48.

Wilmart, André. "L'instigateur du *Speculum caritatis* d'Aelred, abbé de Rievaulx." *Revue d'ascétique et de mystique* 14 (1933) 369–95.

Zerbi, Piero. "San Bernardo di Chiaravalle e il Concilio di Sens." In *Studi su s. Bernardo di Chiaravalle nell'octavo centenario della canonizzazione, Convegno internazionale Certosa di Firenze: (6–9 novembre 1974)*. Bibliotheca cisterciensis 6. Roma: Editiones Cistercienses, 1975, pp. 49–73.

Index

Abbots. *See* Monasticism

Abelard, Peter, 30, 110, 120–35, 137, 138; method, 123–29; theology, 129–35

Aelred of Rievaulx, 82–83, 85, 115, 131

Alberich, 34

Anderson, Luke, 4

Angels, 76

Anselm, St., 45, 46

Anti-intellectualism, 124–25

Apology to Abbot William (Bernard of Clairvaux), 108

Ardutius, bishop of Geneva, 60

Aristotle, 97, 98, 101, 103

Artes litterarum. See Literary arts

Baptism, 16

Beauty, 17; of expression, 5, 6, 37–38

Benedict, St., 57, 70, 94

Bernard of Clairvaux, St., 4; writings, 107–19; *see also* specific topics and writings, e.g.: Epistemology; Faith; *On Conversion* (Bernard of Clairvaux)

Bernard of Portes, 110

Bishops. *See* Clergy

Bruno of Cologne, archbishop, 61

Canon law, 4, 6, 51–54, 106

Charismatic knowledge, 5, 17–22, 55, 69

Christ. *See* Jesus Christ

Christian Theology (Abelard), 127–28

Church, 30–31; as bride, 7–8, 26; orders of, 9; and society, 7–11, 120–21; *see also* specific headings, e.g.: Clergy

Cistercians, 4–5, 86–87

Clergy, 9, 72; and learning, 31–35, 106, 138; as peacemakers, 32

Common sense, 6, 55–56; *see also* Consideration; Counsel

Consideration: practical consideration, 56–59; scientific consideration, 55, 56; speculative consideration, 56; *see also* Meditation

Contemplation, 5, 22–29, 55, 56, 69–70, 71, 72–73; and experience, 23–24; as mysticism, 5; versus intellectual activity, 115–16; *see also* Meditation

Counsel, 6, 59–65, 69, 70; of laity, 67–68

Crusades, 20, 113

Curiosity, 94–97

Stephen of Palestrina, 125, 130
*Steps of Humility and Pride. See
On the Steps of Humility and
Pride* (Bernard of Clairvaux)
Suger, abbot of Saint Denis, 63,
64, 114

Teaching. *See* Preaching
Theobald of Canterbury, arch-
bishop, 34
Theobald of Champagne, 65
Thomas of Saint Omar, 83–84,
85–86
Thurstan, archbishop of York,
88
Trinity, 14, 74, 130, 136
Trivium, 6, 30, 36
Truth, 5, 13; *see also* specific

topics, e.g.: Contemplation;
Faith

Understanding, 75, 78–79, 97;
faith contrasted with, 44
Unity, 9–10; and Trinity, 14

"Vain studies," 84–85, 88–90
Verschelen, Goswinus, 82
Voltaire, 3

Waddell, Chrysogonus, 5
Walter of Chaumont, 84, 89–90
William of Champeaux, 34
William of Nevers, count, 86
William of Saint Thierry, 36, 37,
82, 96, 109, 110, 113, 115;
and Abelard, 121, 128

Other books in The Newman Press series:

ANCIENT CHRISTIAN WRITERS (59-volume series)
FROM APOSTLES TO BISHOPS by Francis A. Sullivan
THE DIDACHE by Aaron Milavec
THE RULE OF SAINT BENEDICT by Mayeul de Dreuille, O.S.B.